Poses for Artists Series, Volume 11 by Justin R. Martin
www.PoseMuse.com for details and links

PoseMuse
PO Box 2105
Edwards, CO 81632 USA
www.PoseMuse.com
justin@posemuse.com

Ordering Information:
Available on Amazon.com in paperback or Kindle formats, and Gumroad.com in pdf format via PoseMuse.com. All ebook formats available on SmashWords.com. Special discounts are available on quantity purchases by businesses, corporations, associations, and others. For details, contact PoseMuse above.

Publisher's Cataloging-in-Publication Data:
Martin, Justin R.
Poses for Artists Volume 11: An essential reference for figure drawing and the human form. Inspiring Art and Artists
Series/ Justin R. Martin
1. Nonfiction - Art - Techniques - Drawing
2. Nonfiction - Art - Reference
3. Nonfiction - Art - Illustration

First Edition, First Printing 2025
ISBN: 978-1-7377937-5-5
Imprint: POSEmuse
14 13 12 11 10 9 8 7 6 5 4 3 2 1
Printed in the United States of America

TABLE OF CONTENTS

Khrystyana

Poses for Artists Volume 11 includes art references in collaboration with international model Khrystyana, a prominent voice in the body positivity and self-love movements. She has gained a broad visibility of her values through working with major modeling agencies, worldwide brands, as a featured Playboy Playmate, and as a runner-up on the show America's Next Top Model.

Through her Real Catwalk project, she actively challenges conventional beauty standards and promotes diversity. Khrystyana fosters a community that celebrates self-acceptance, ethnicities, and diverse body types. Her work demonstrates a commitment to using her influence to empower individuals and advocate for a more inclusive and representative fashion industry.
www.khrystyana.com
@khrystyana

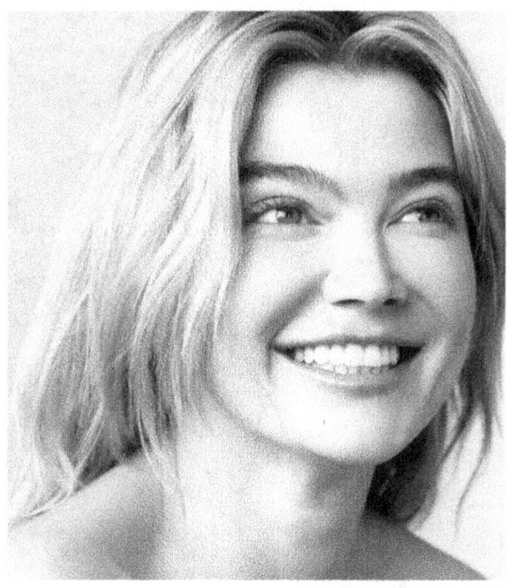

Ricky Tompkins @trickyrickyt

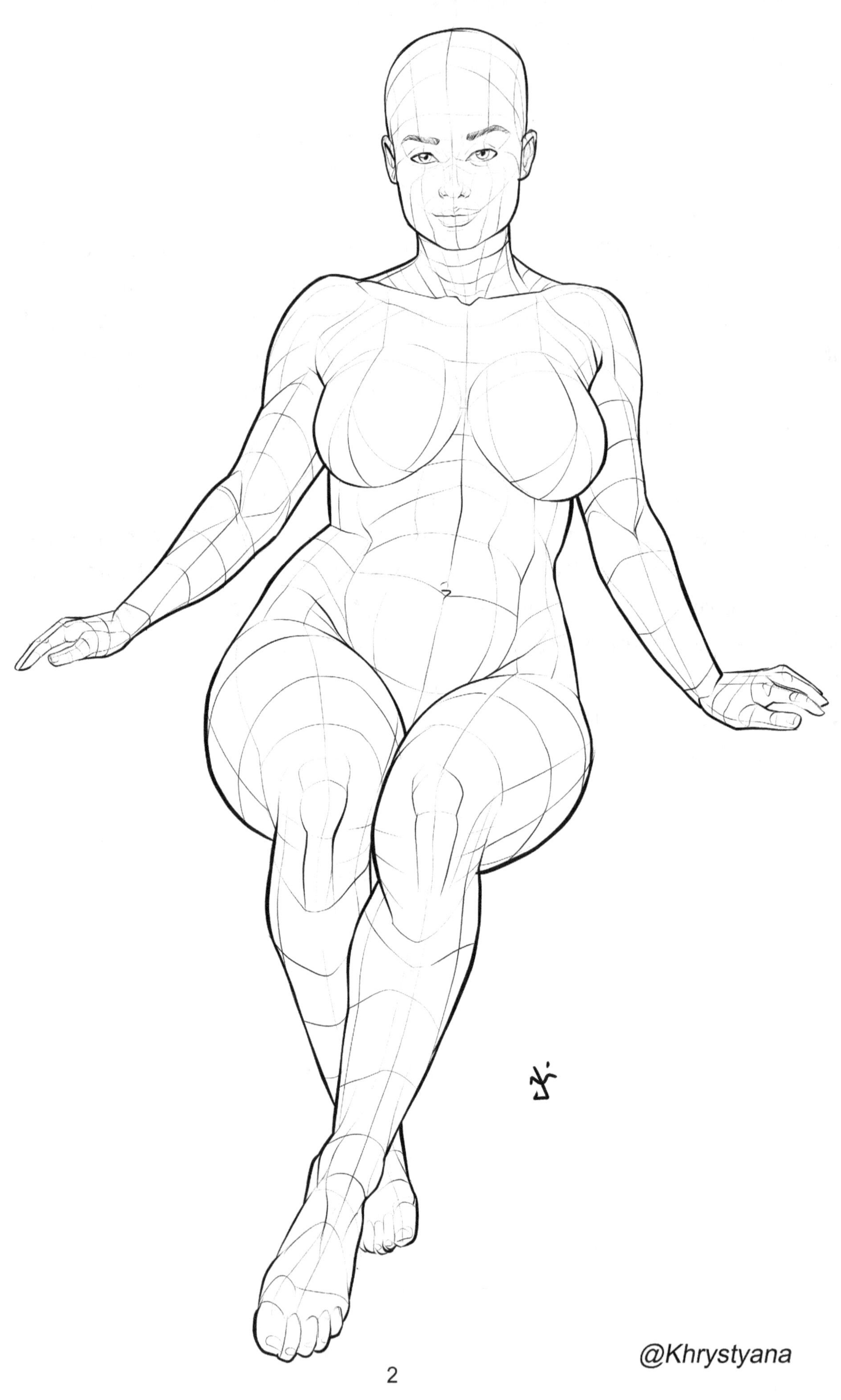

@Khrystyana
2

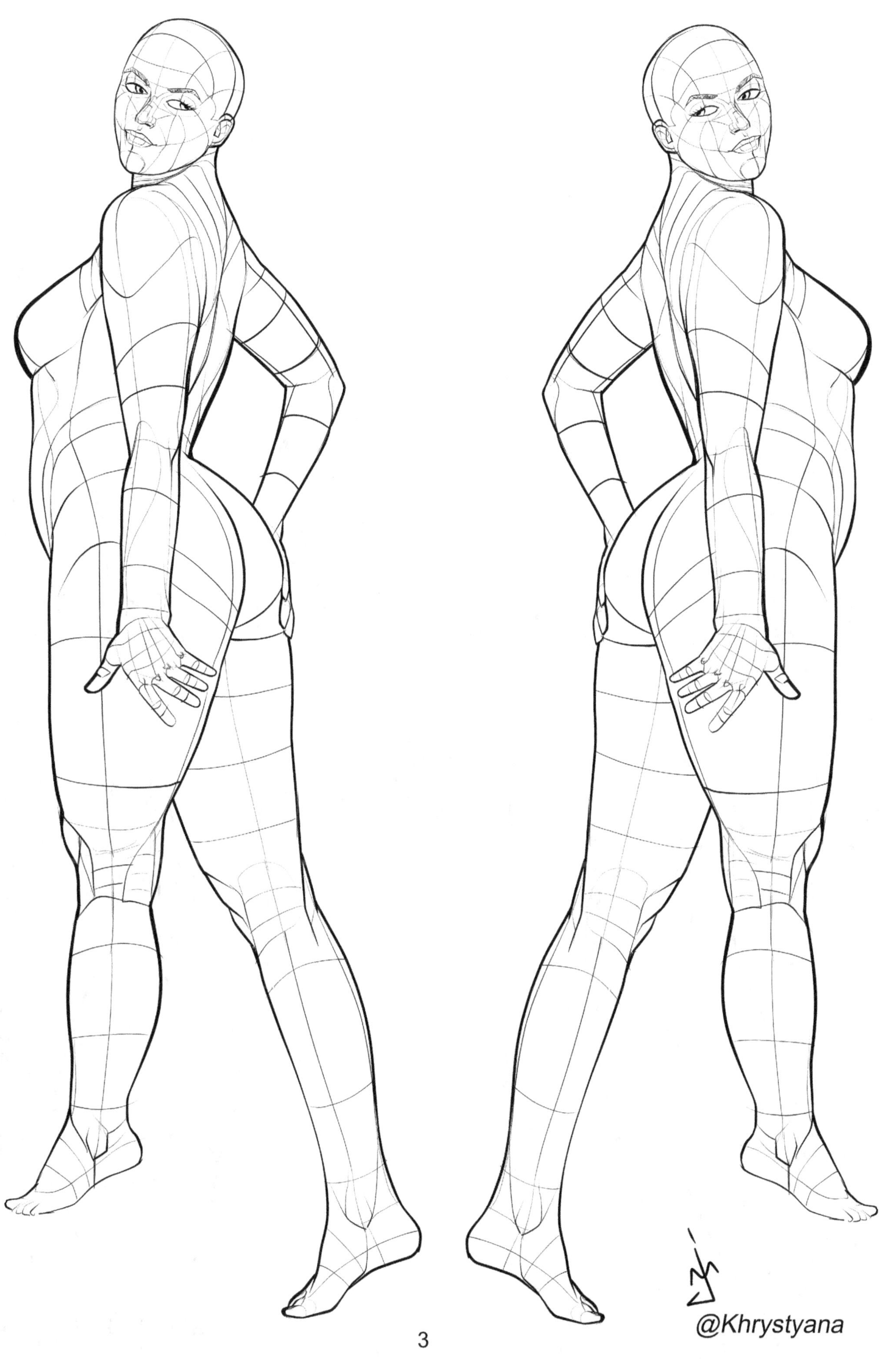

@Khrystyana

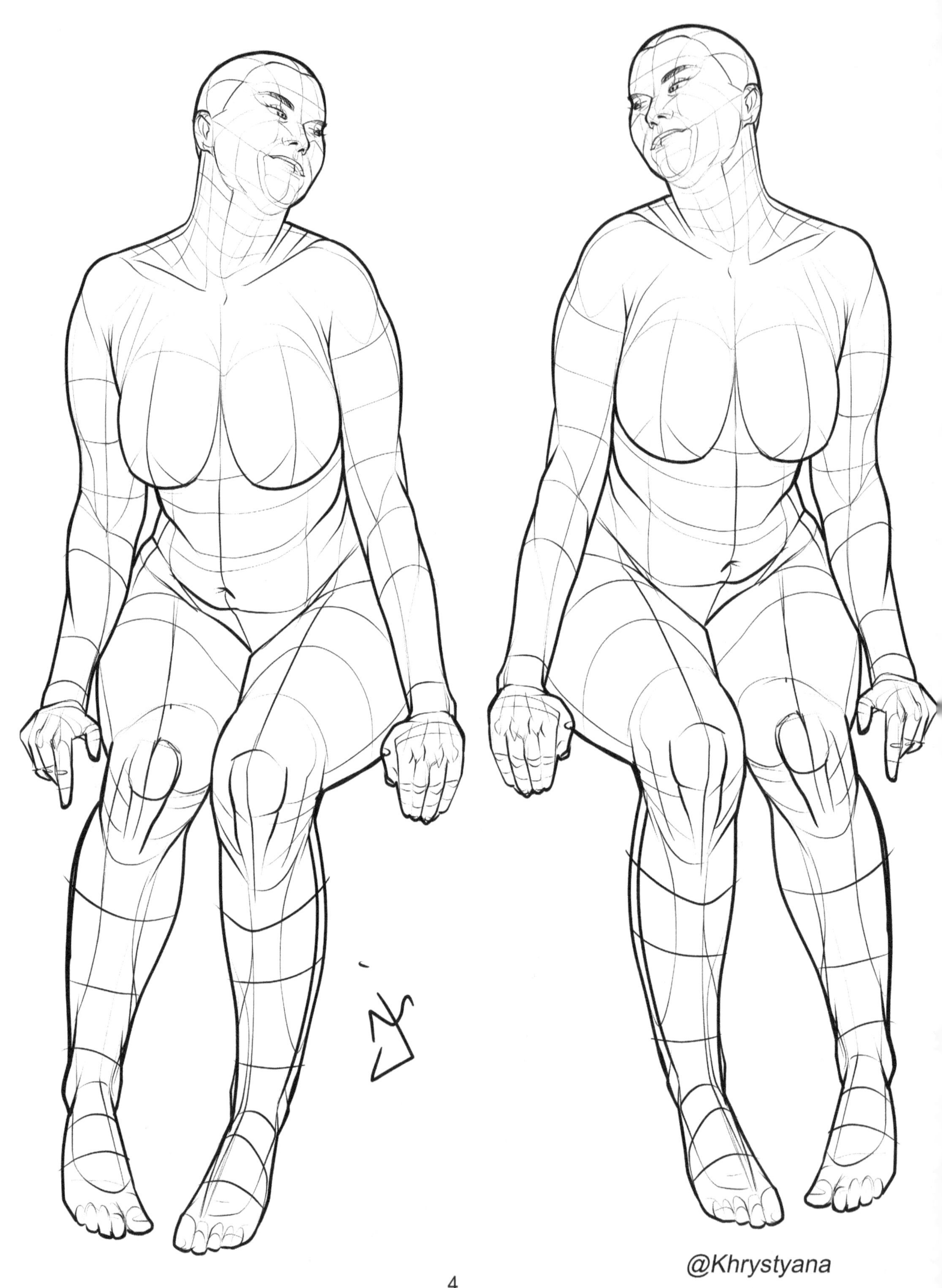

@Khrystyana

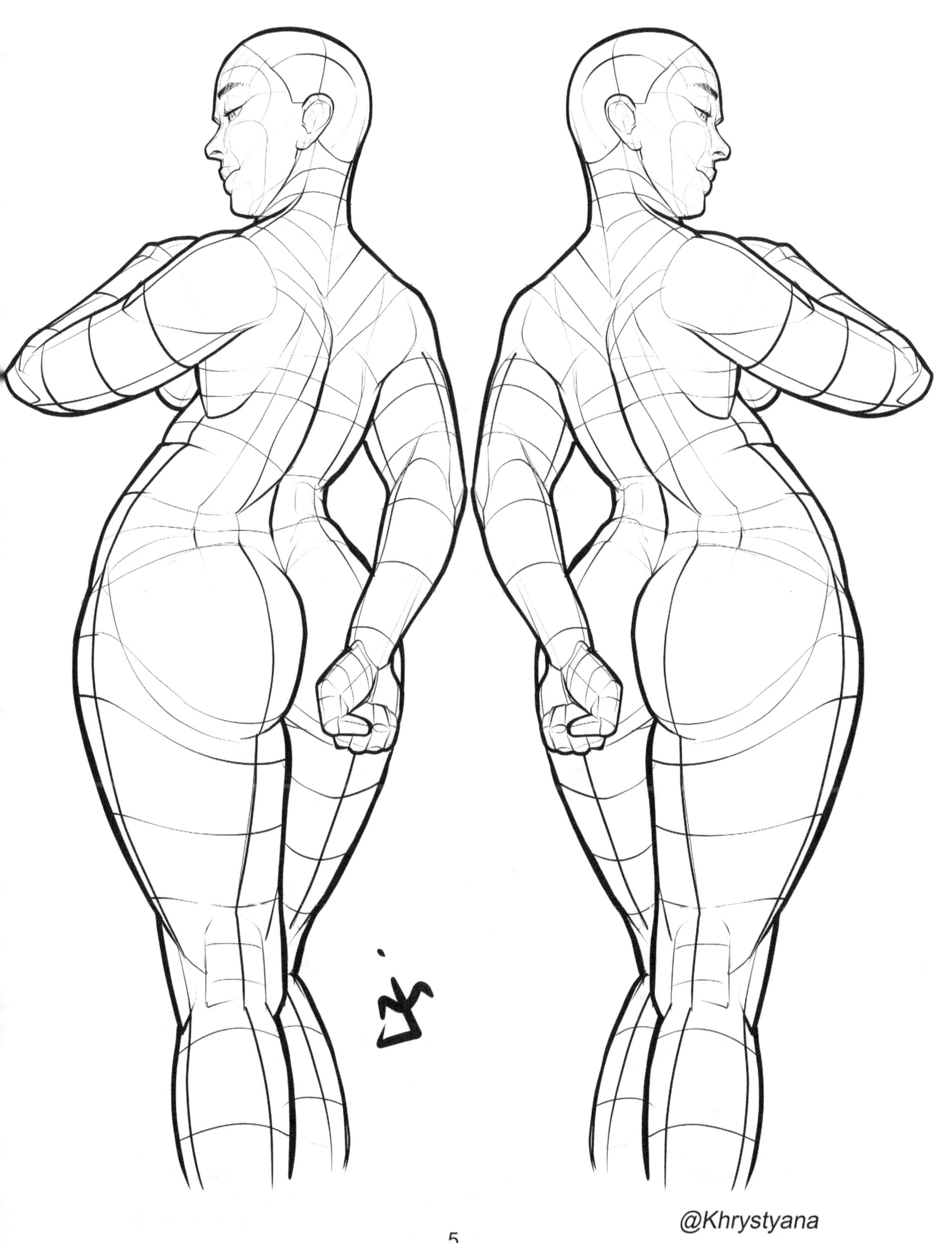

@Khrystyana

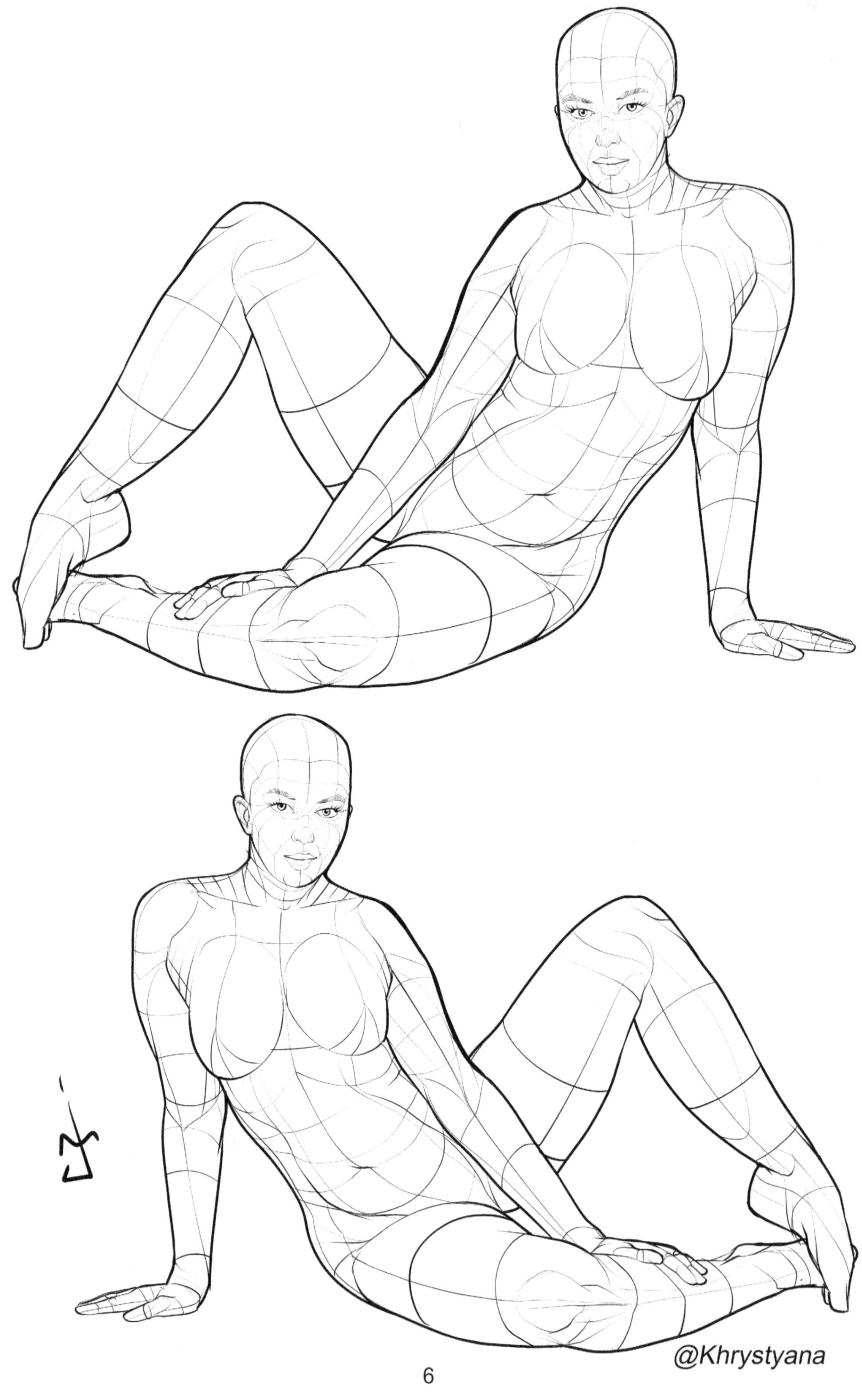

@Khrystyana

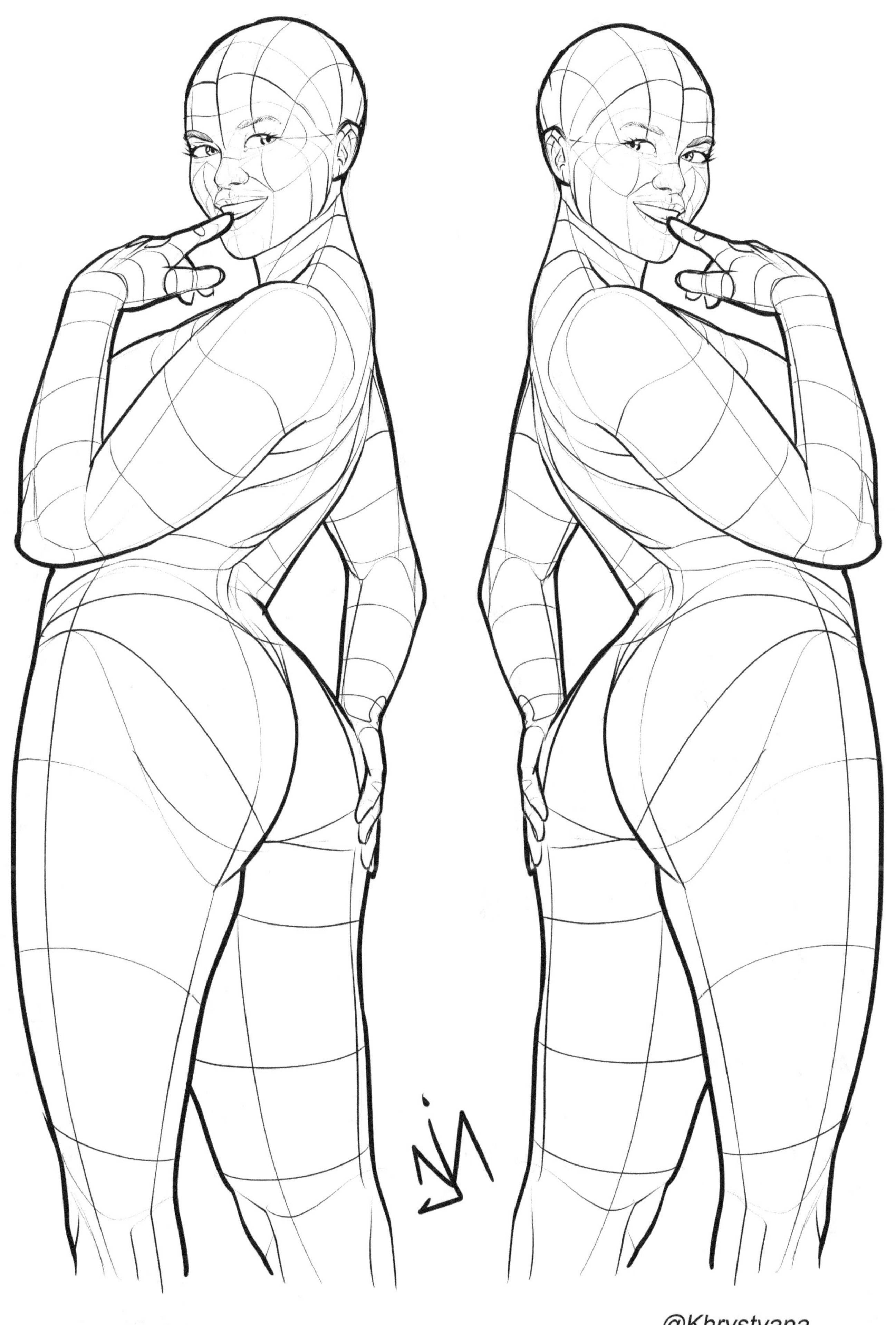

@Khrystyana

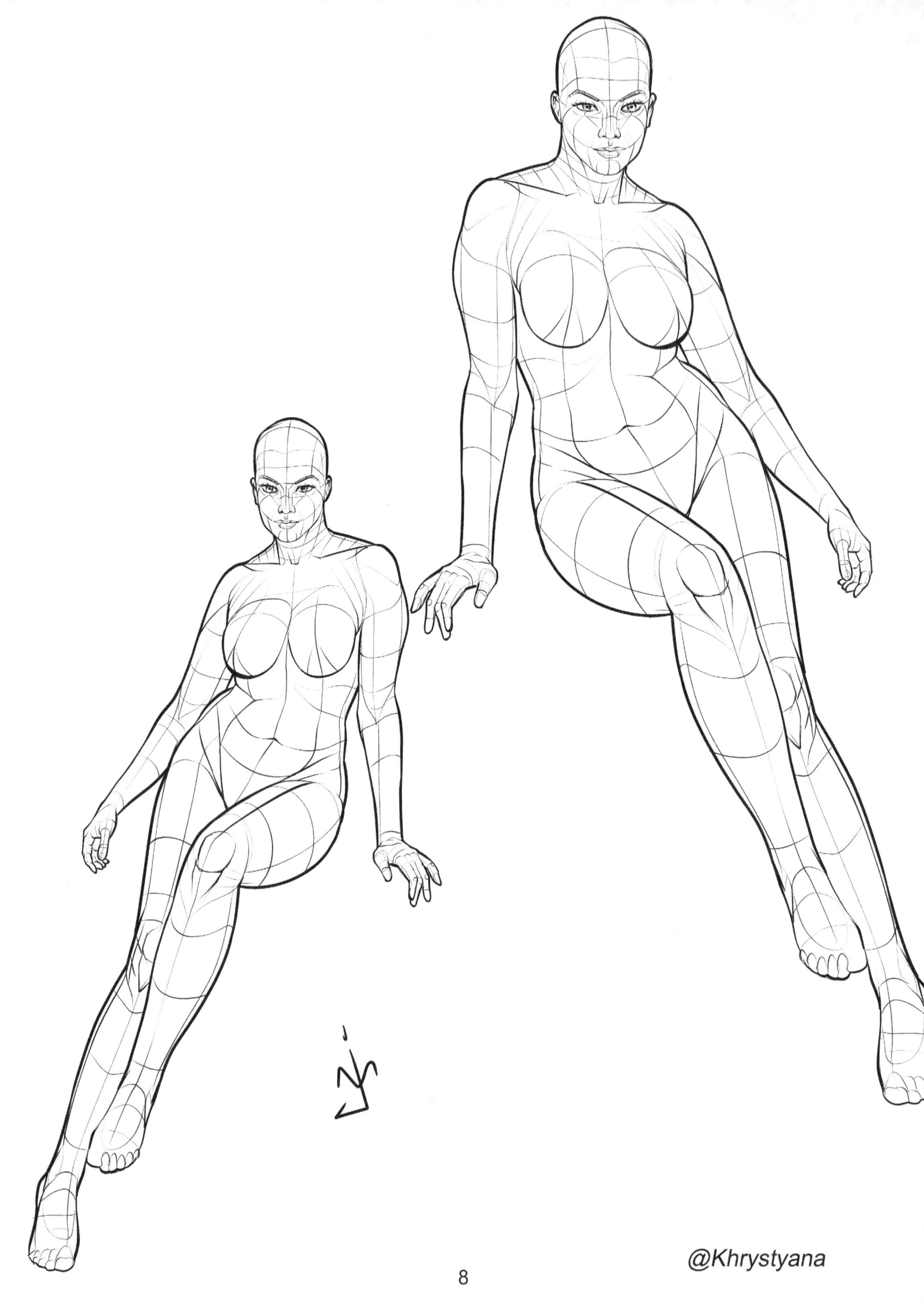

@Khrystyana

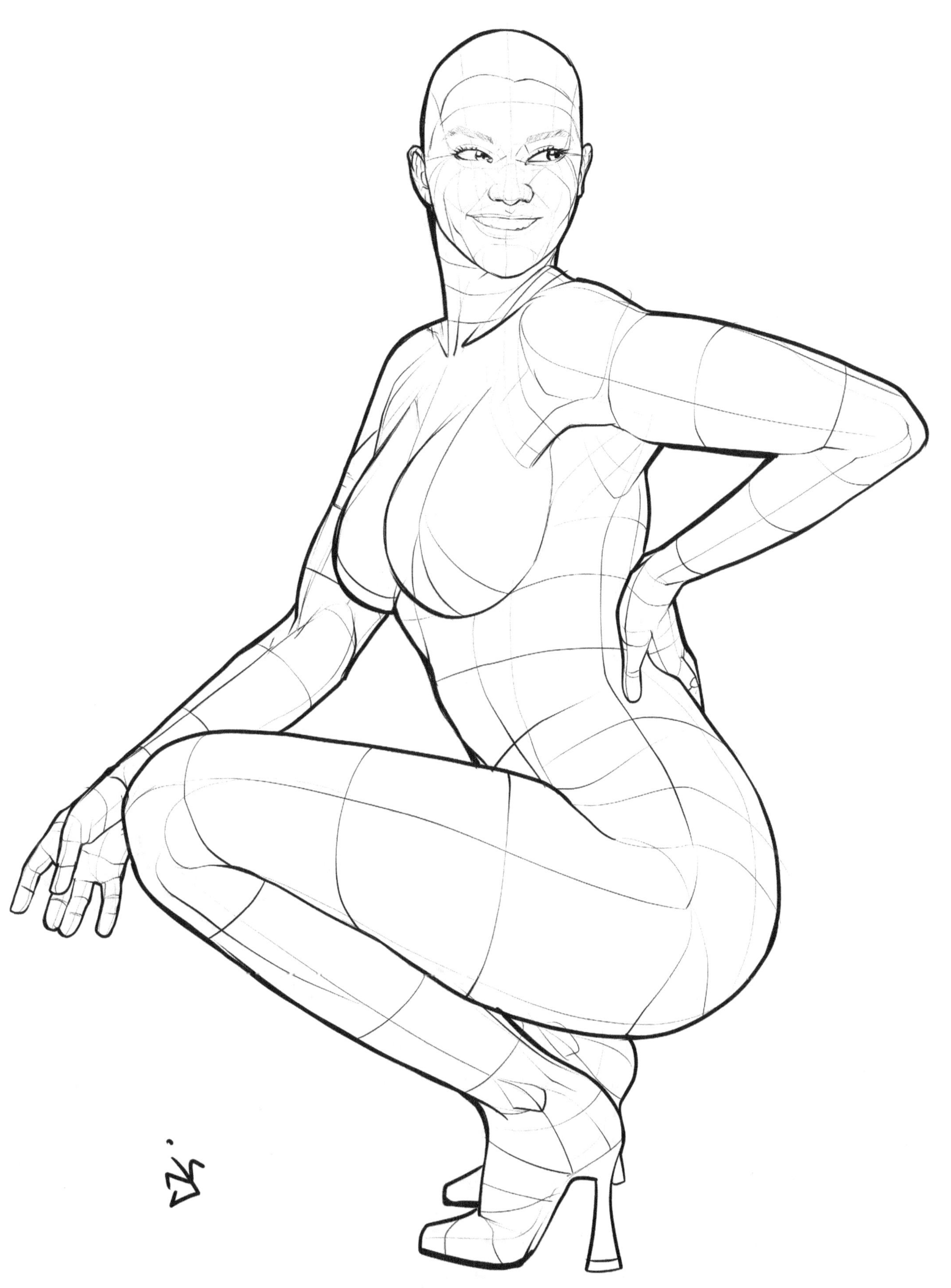

@Khrystyana

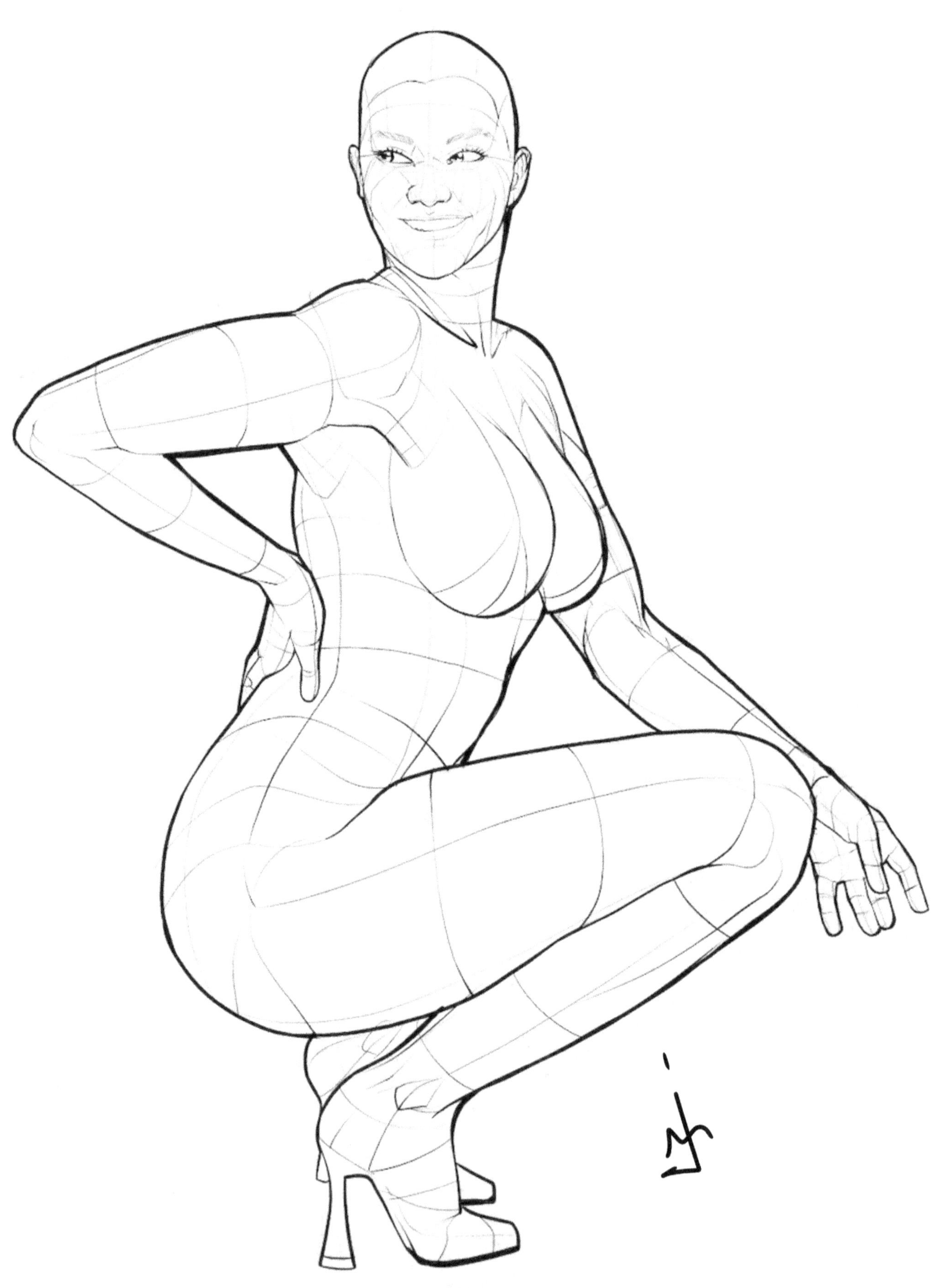

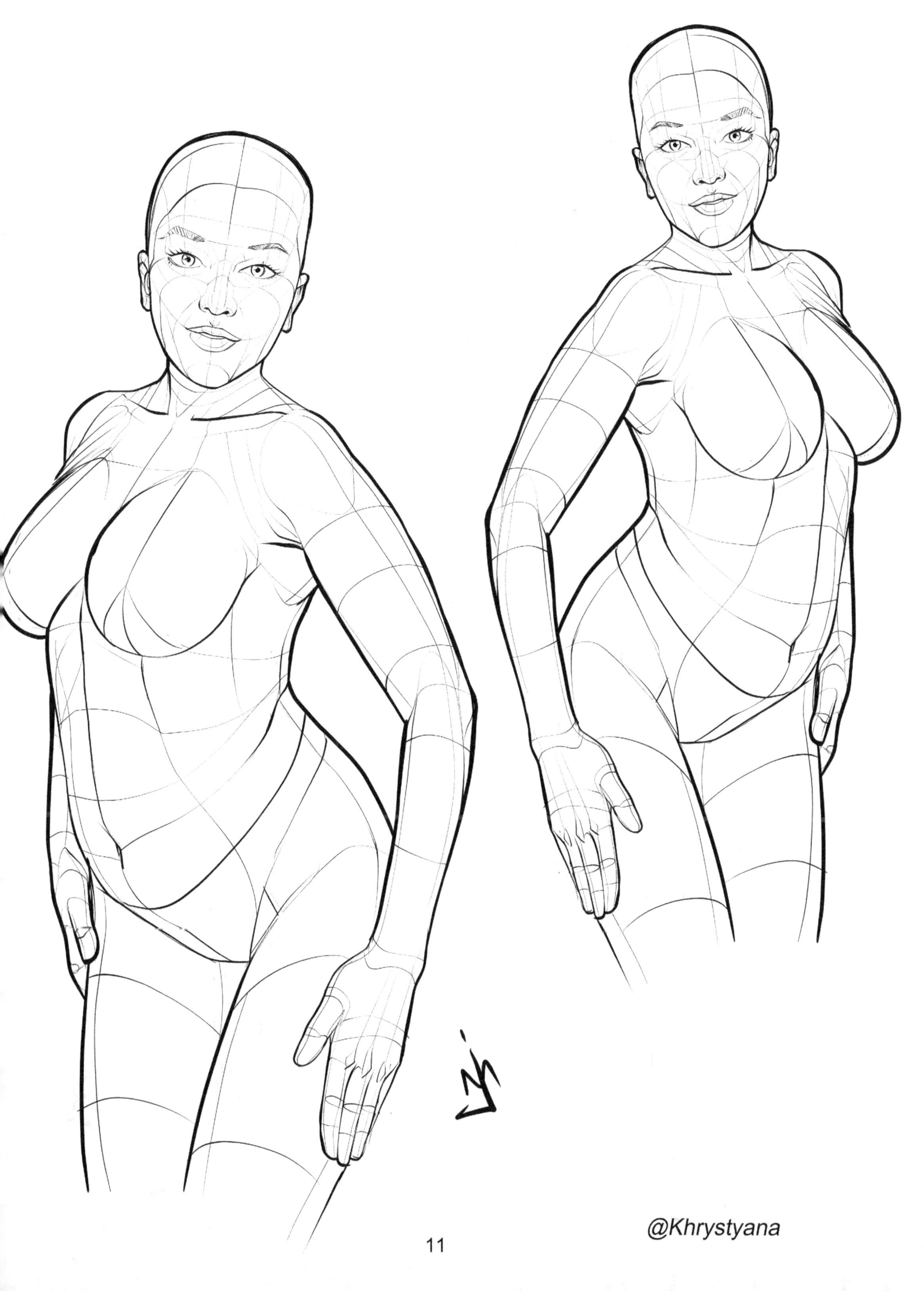
@Khrystyana

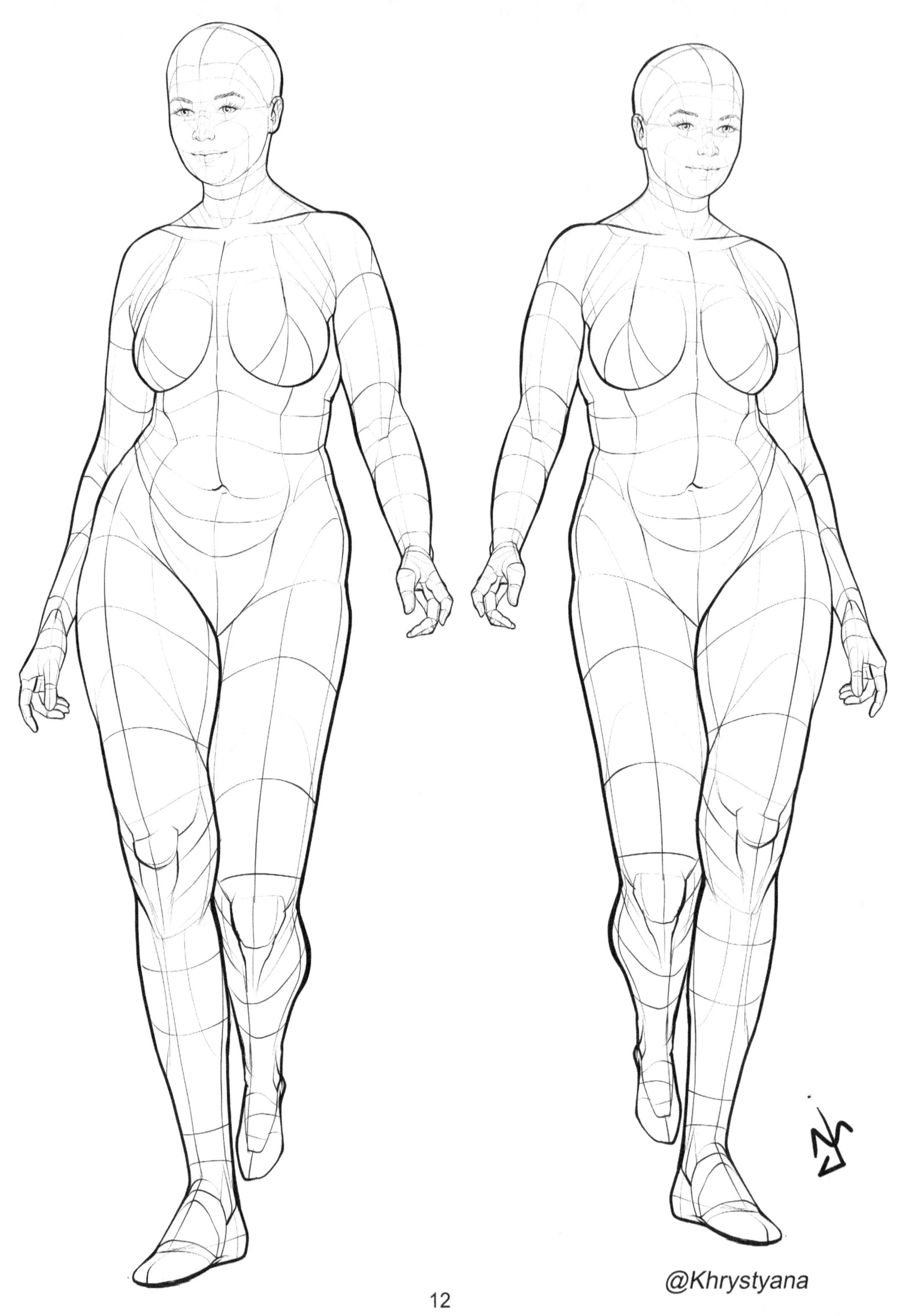

@Khrystyana

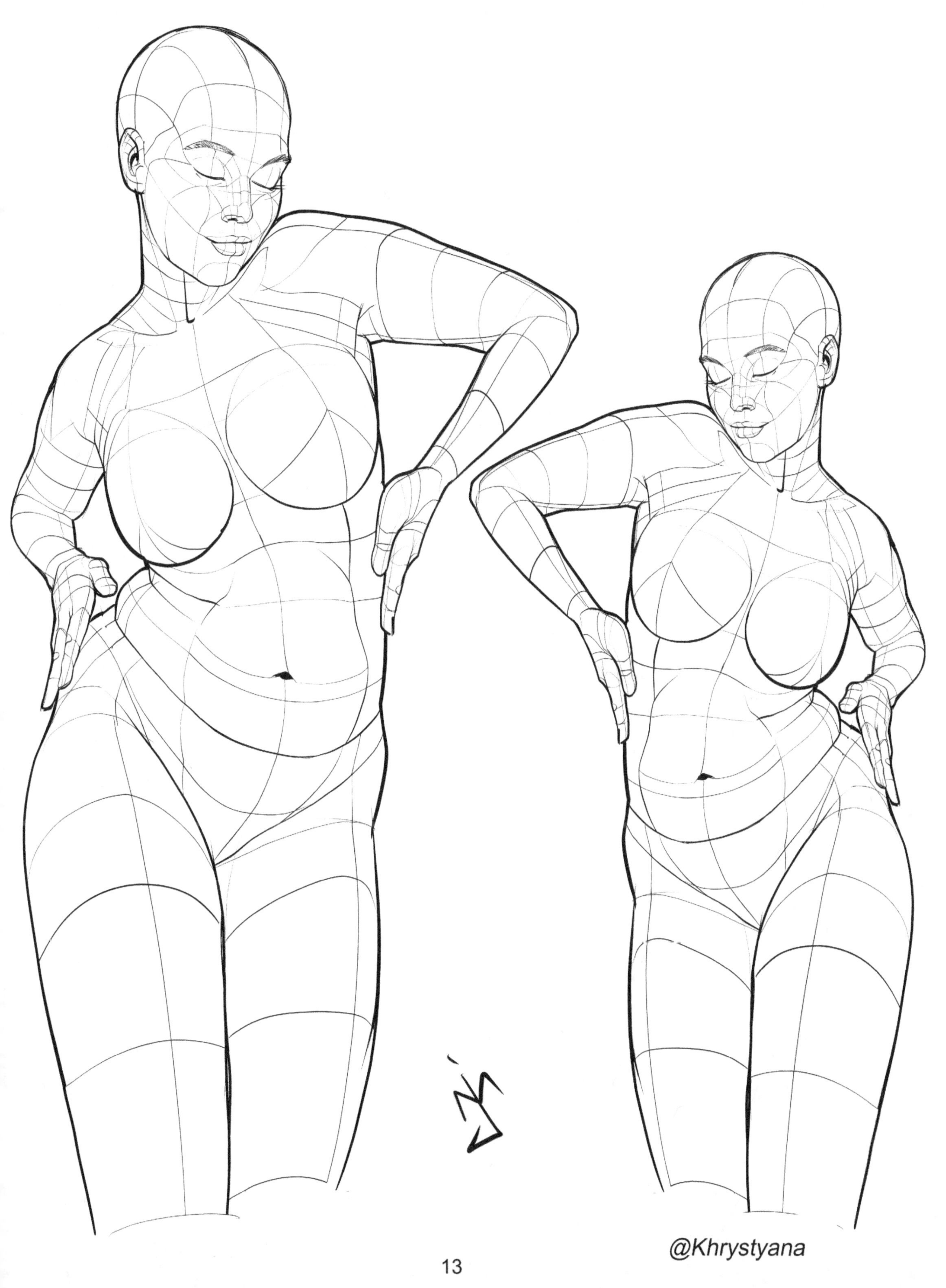

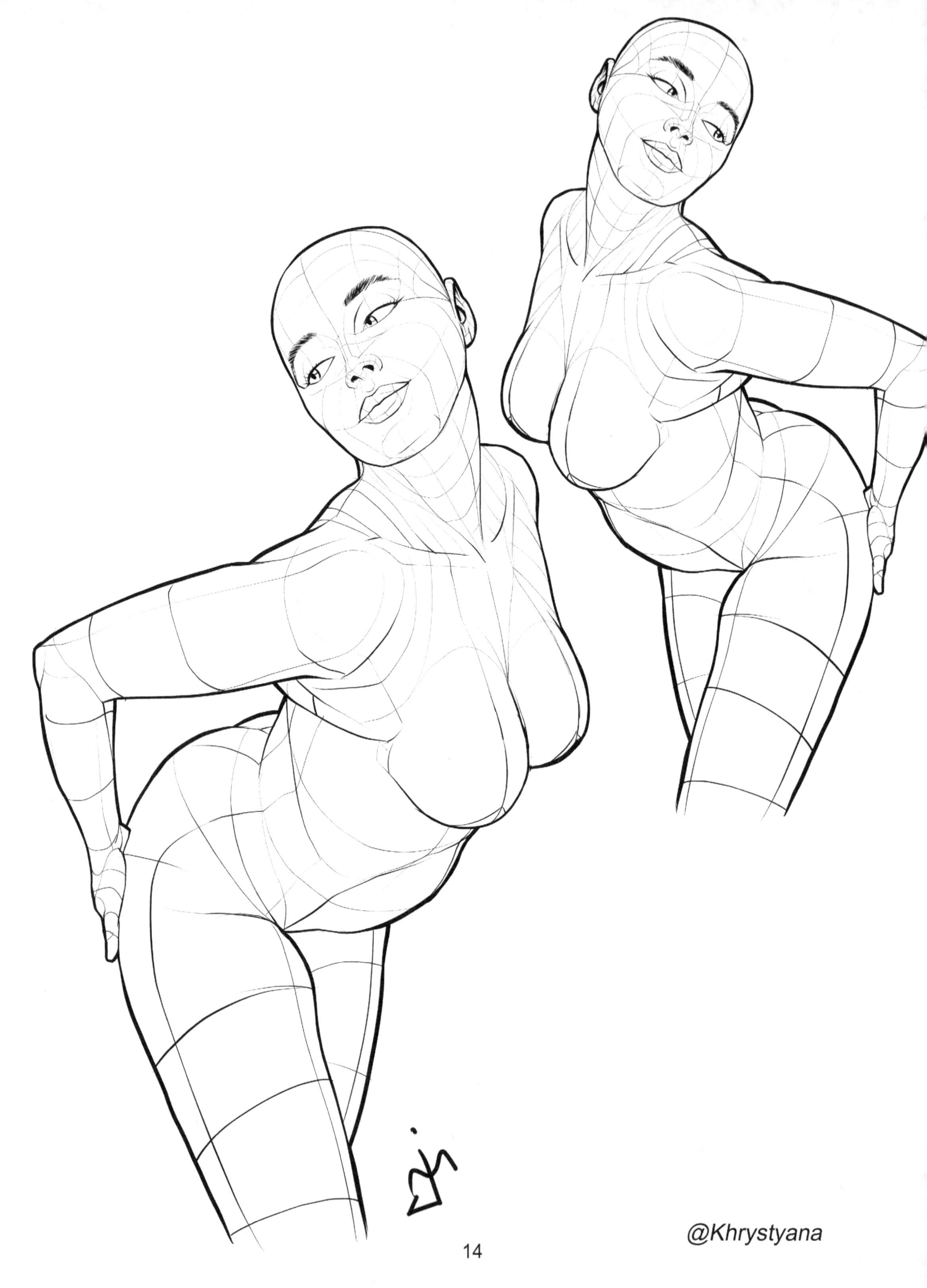

@Khrystyana

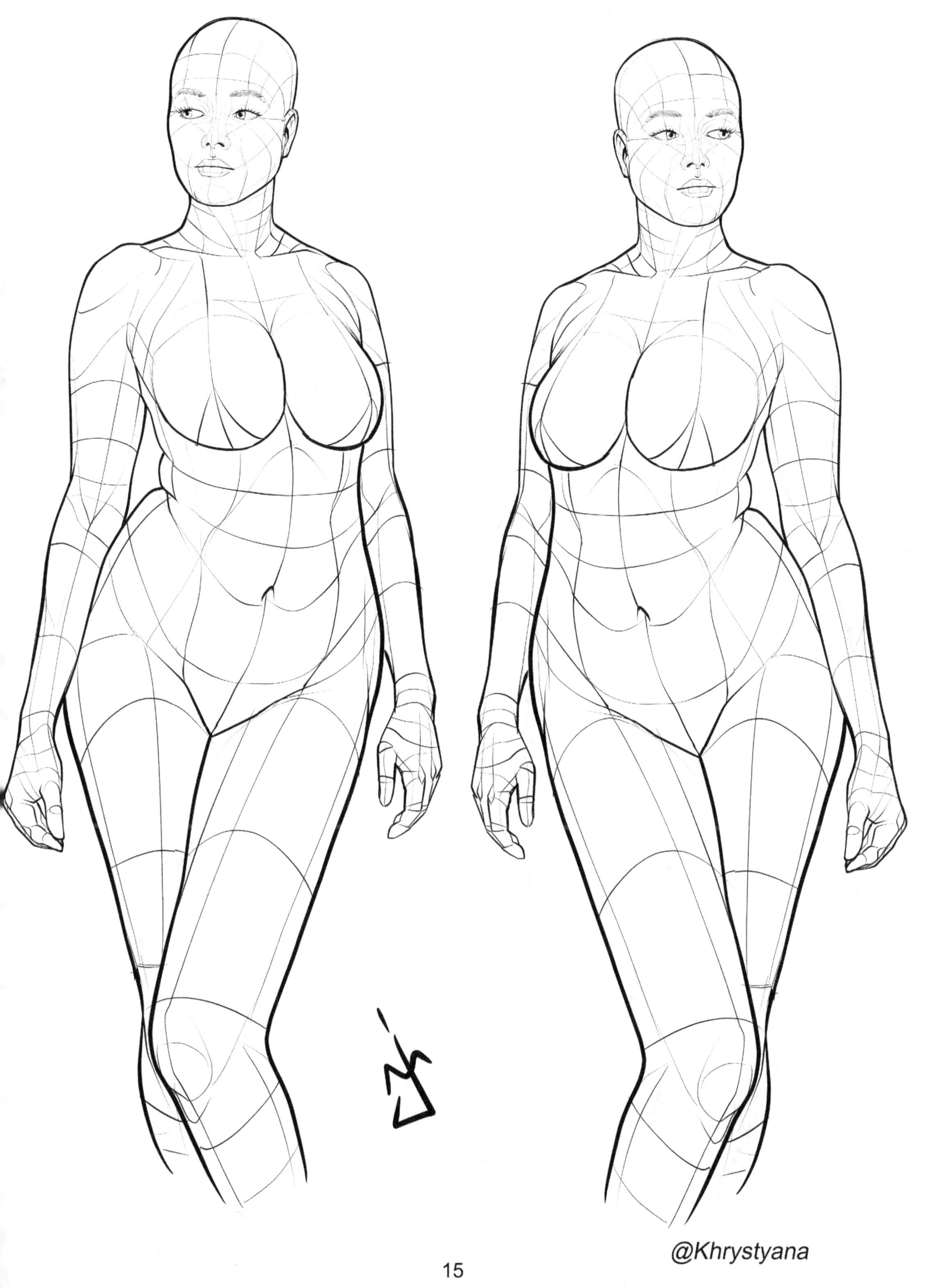

@Khrystyana

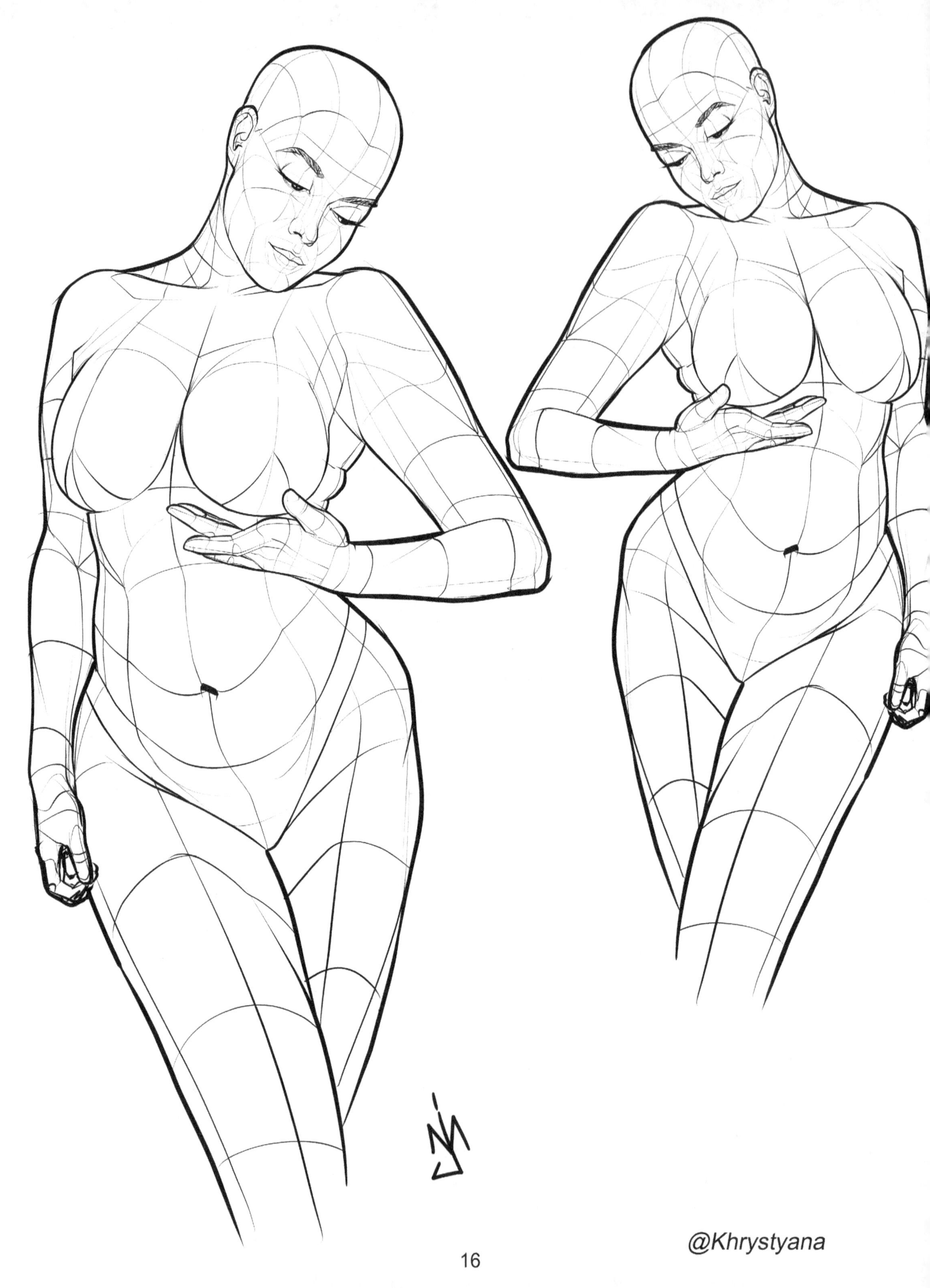
@Khrystyana

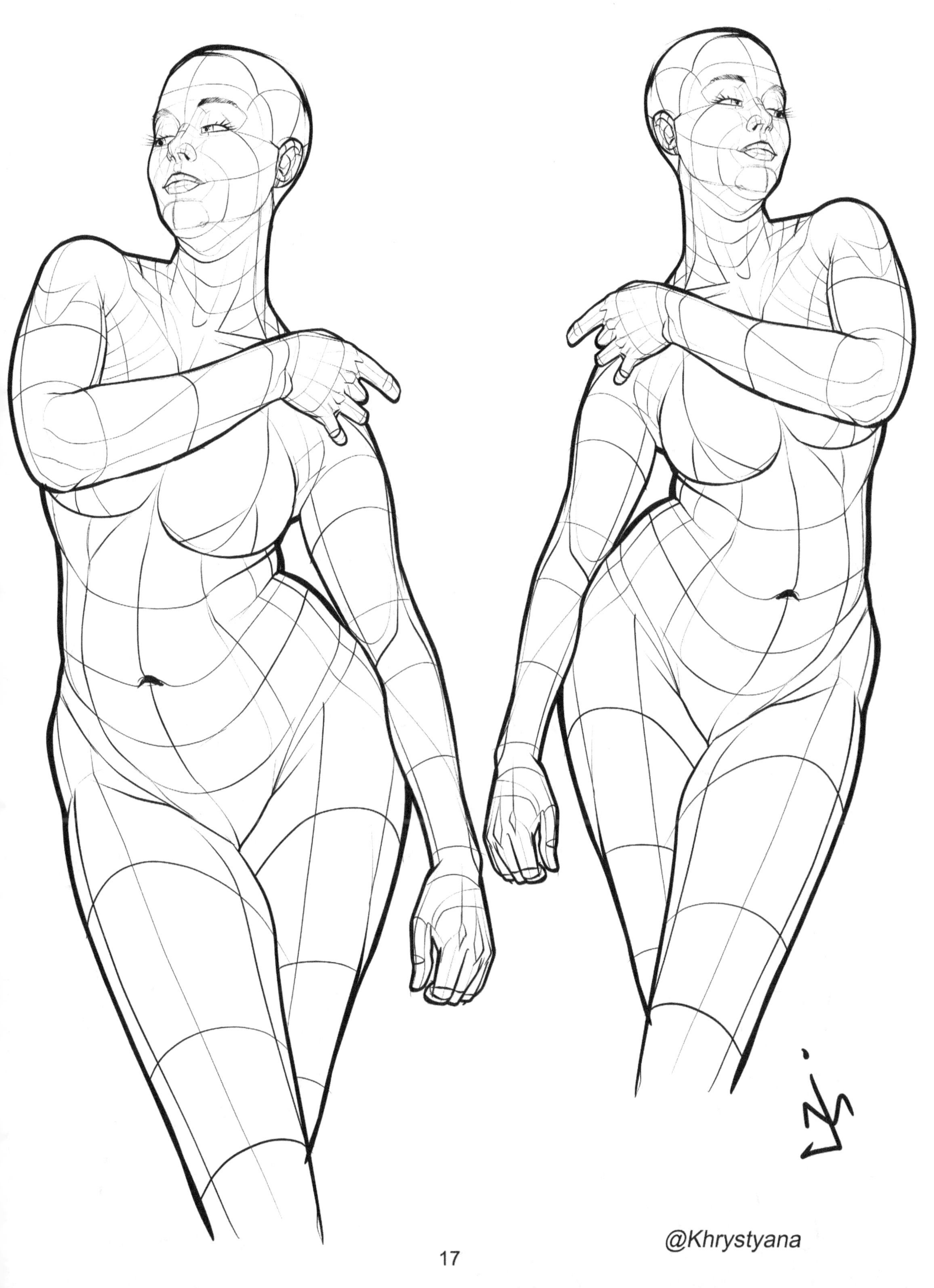

@Khrystyana

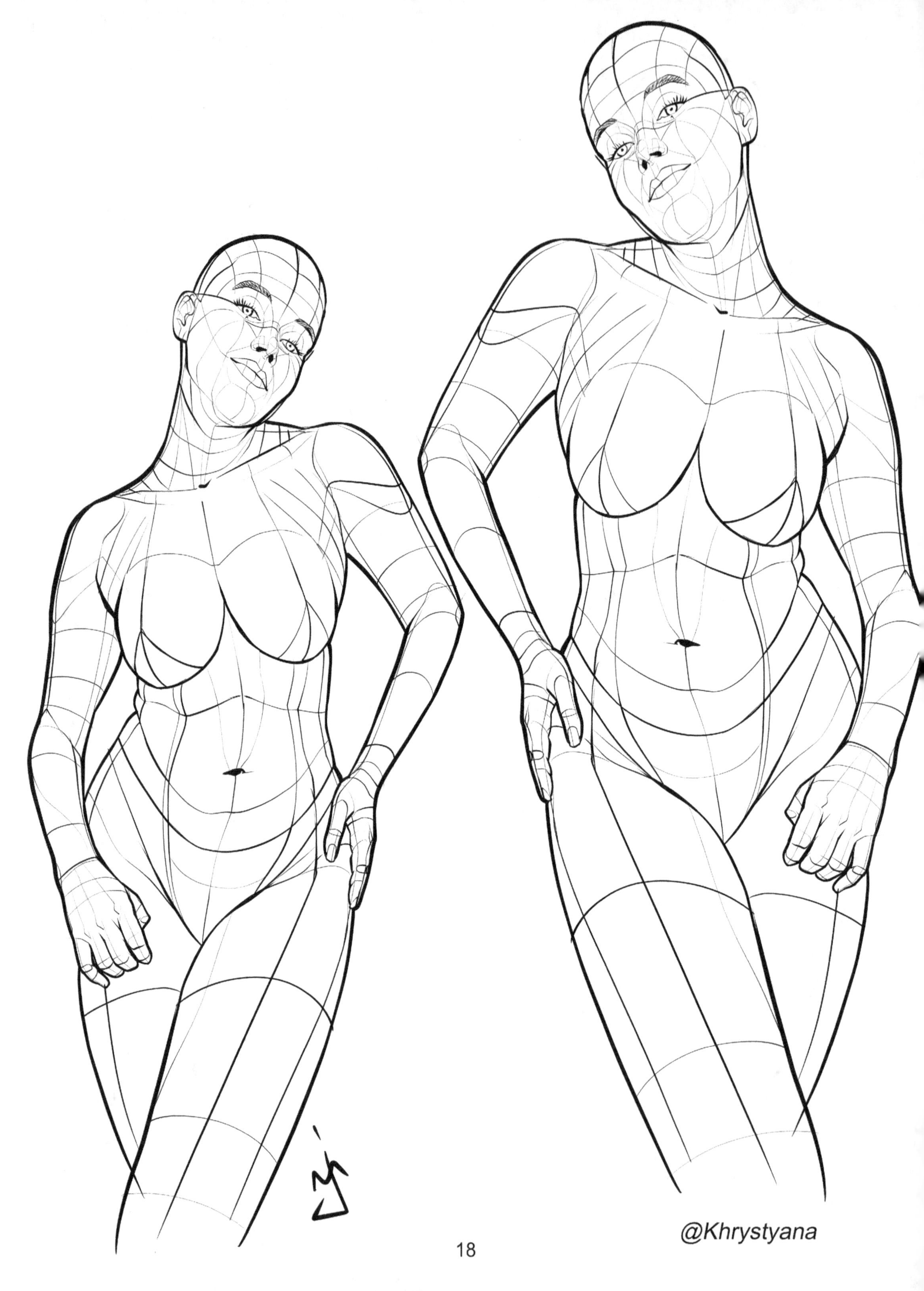

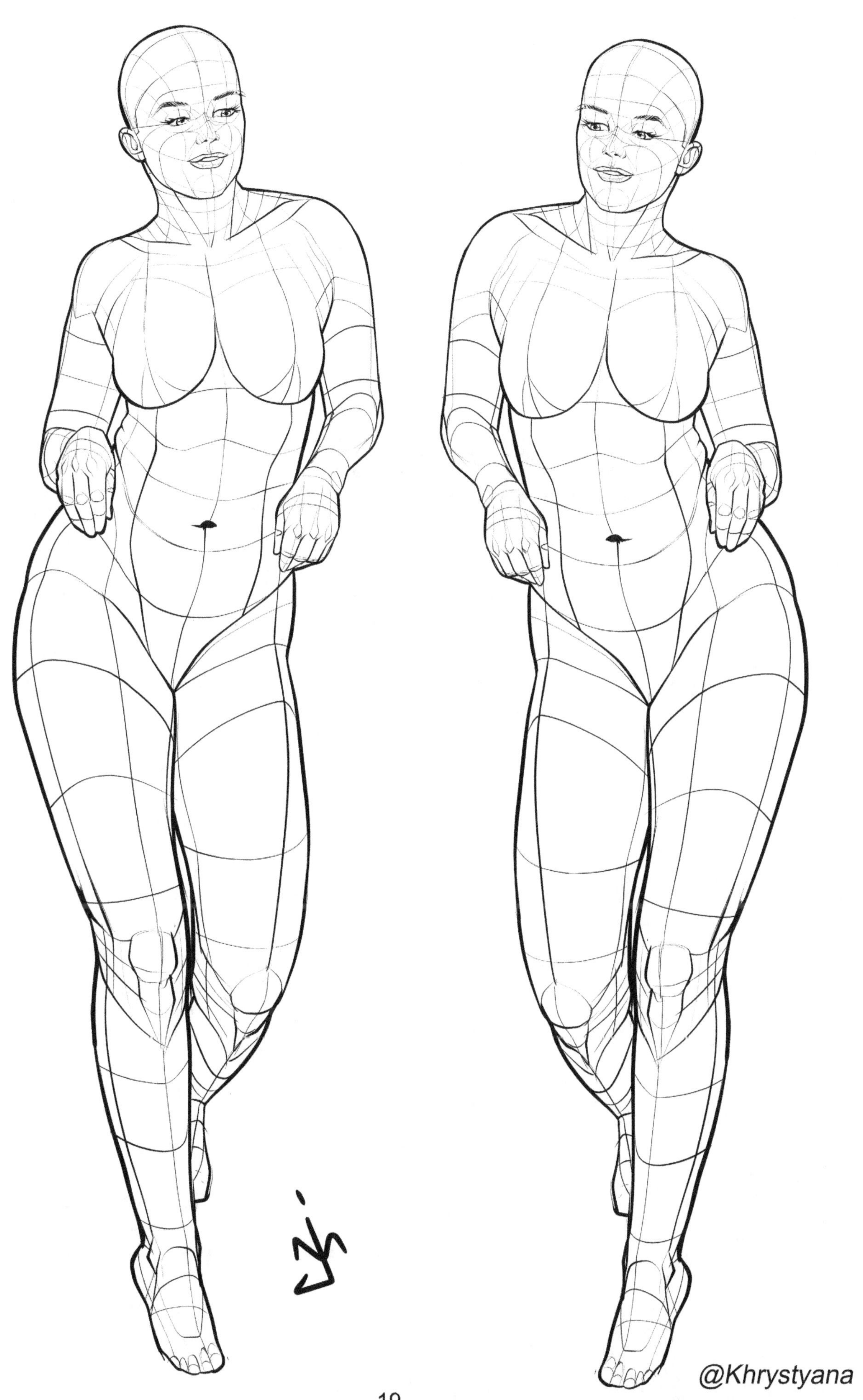

@Khrystyana

Sitting Poses

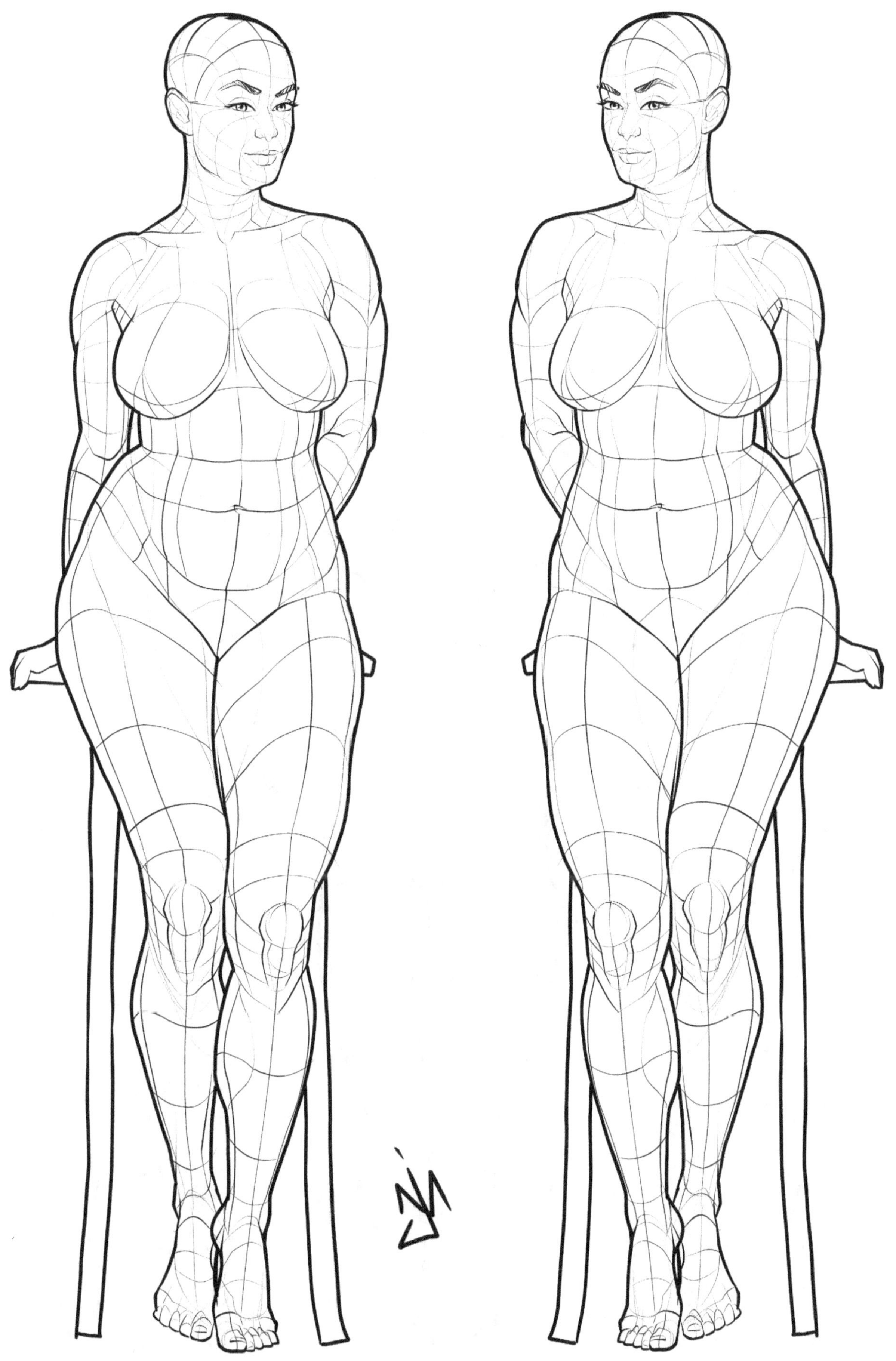

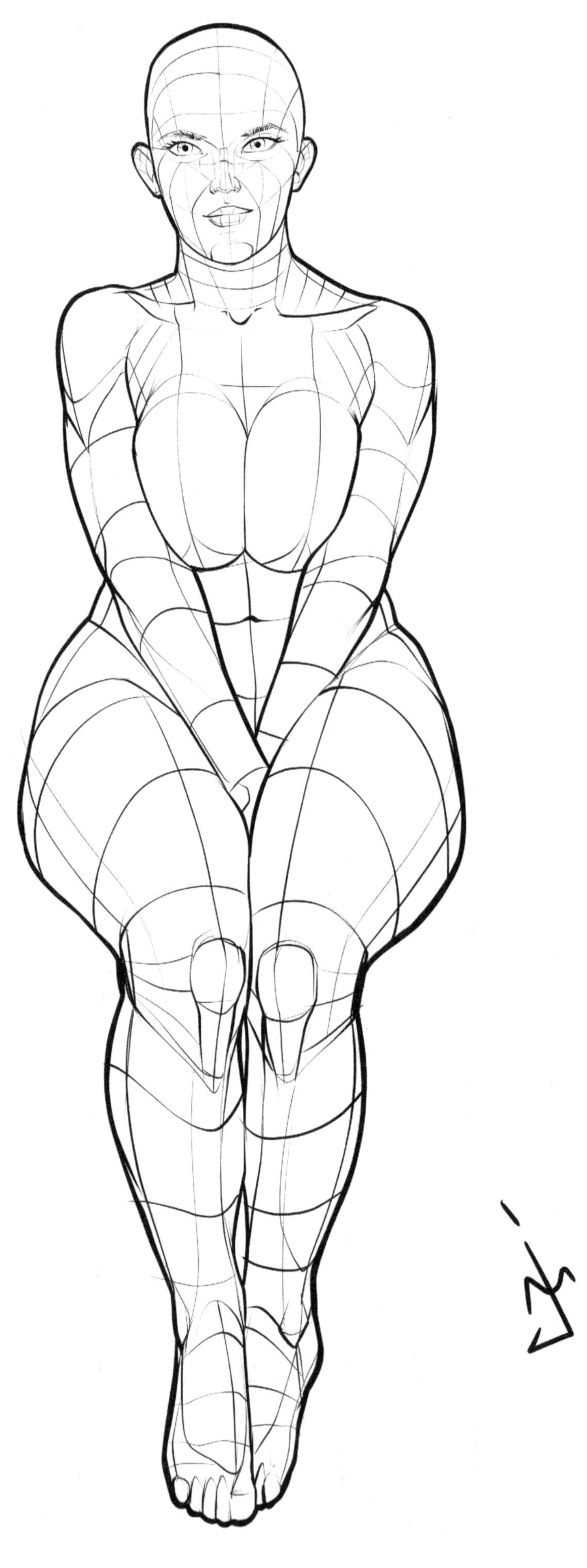

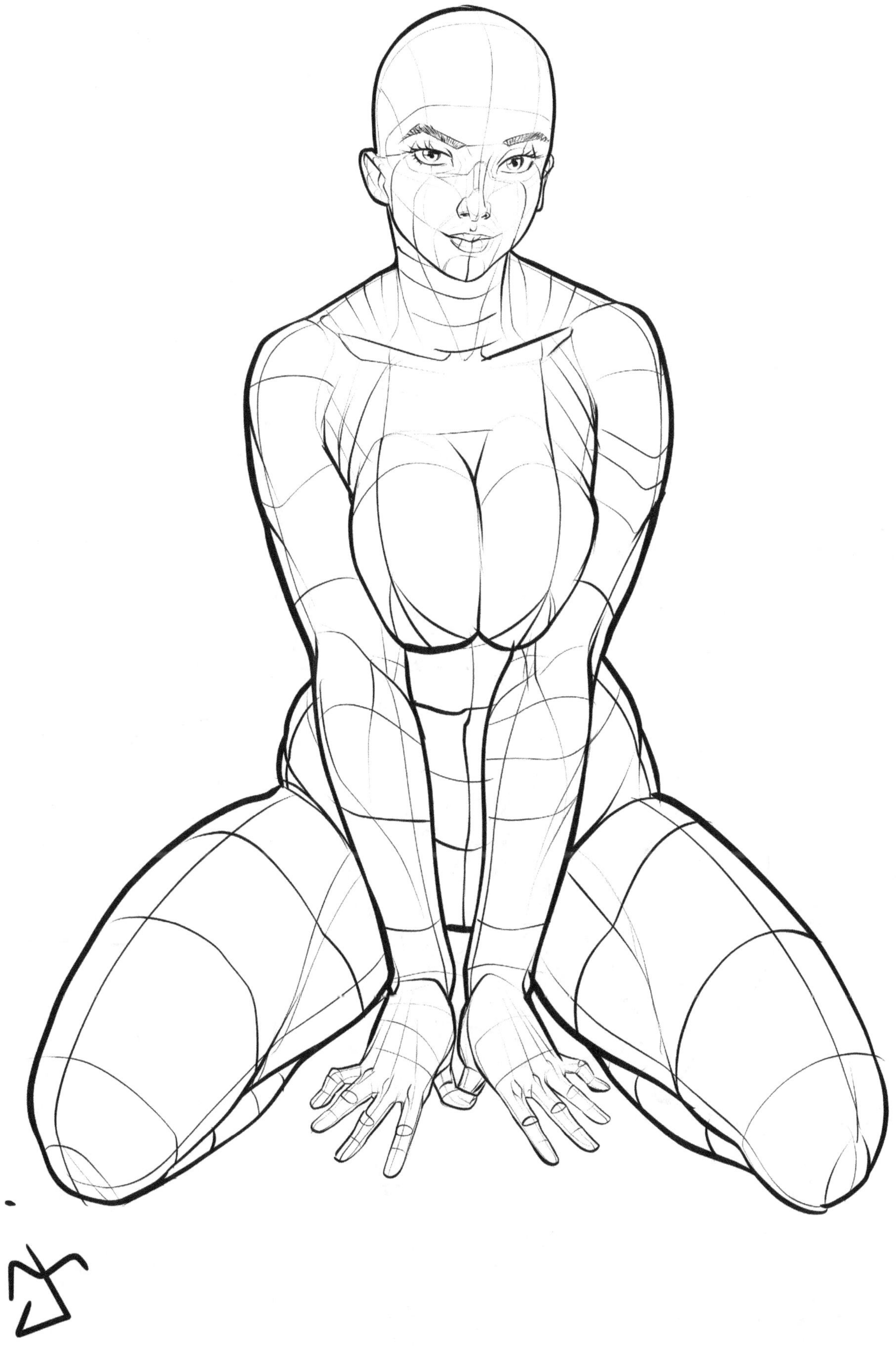

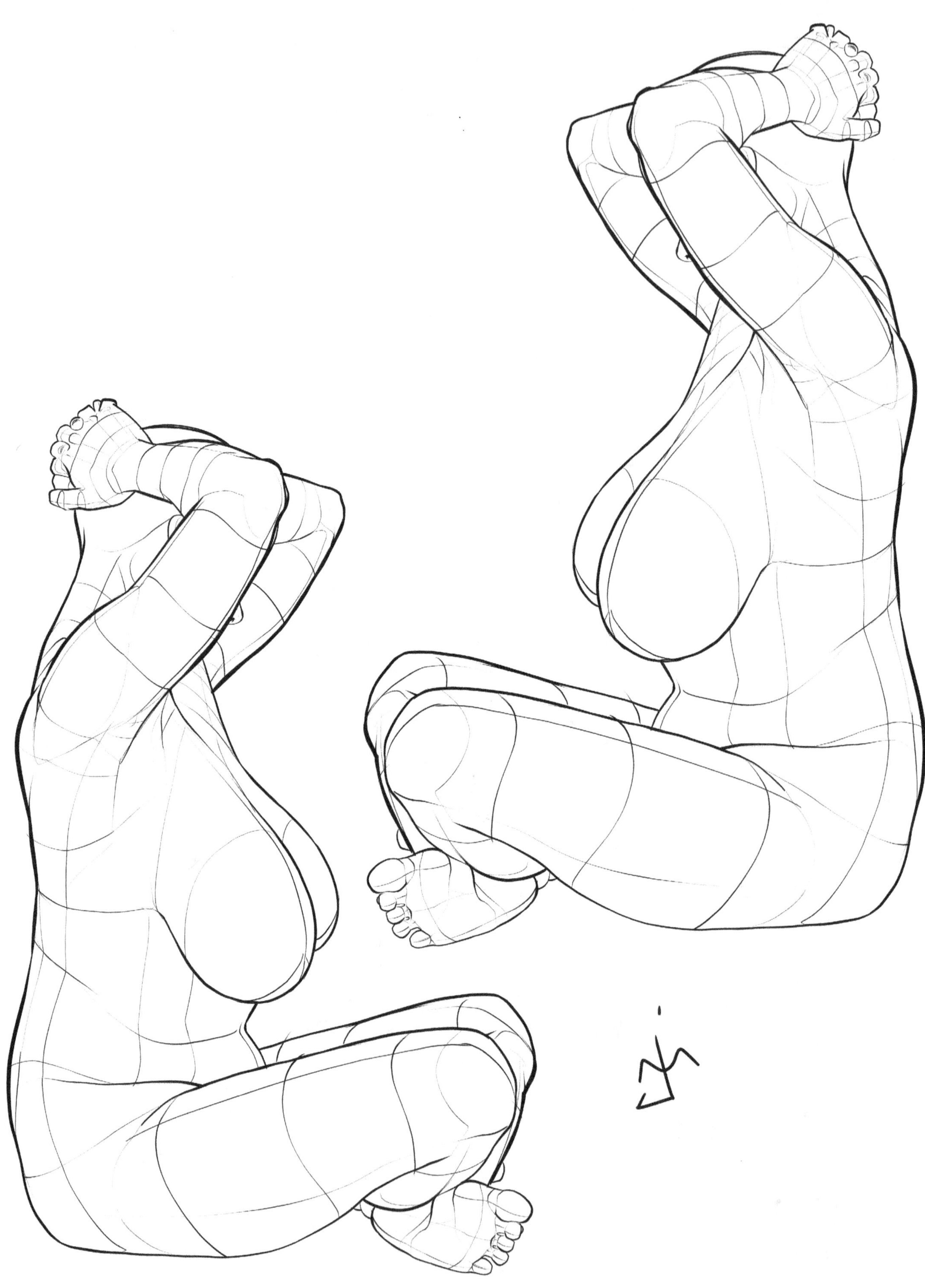

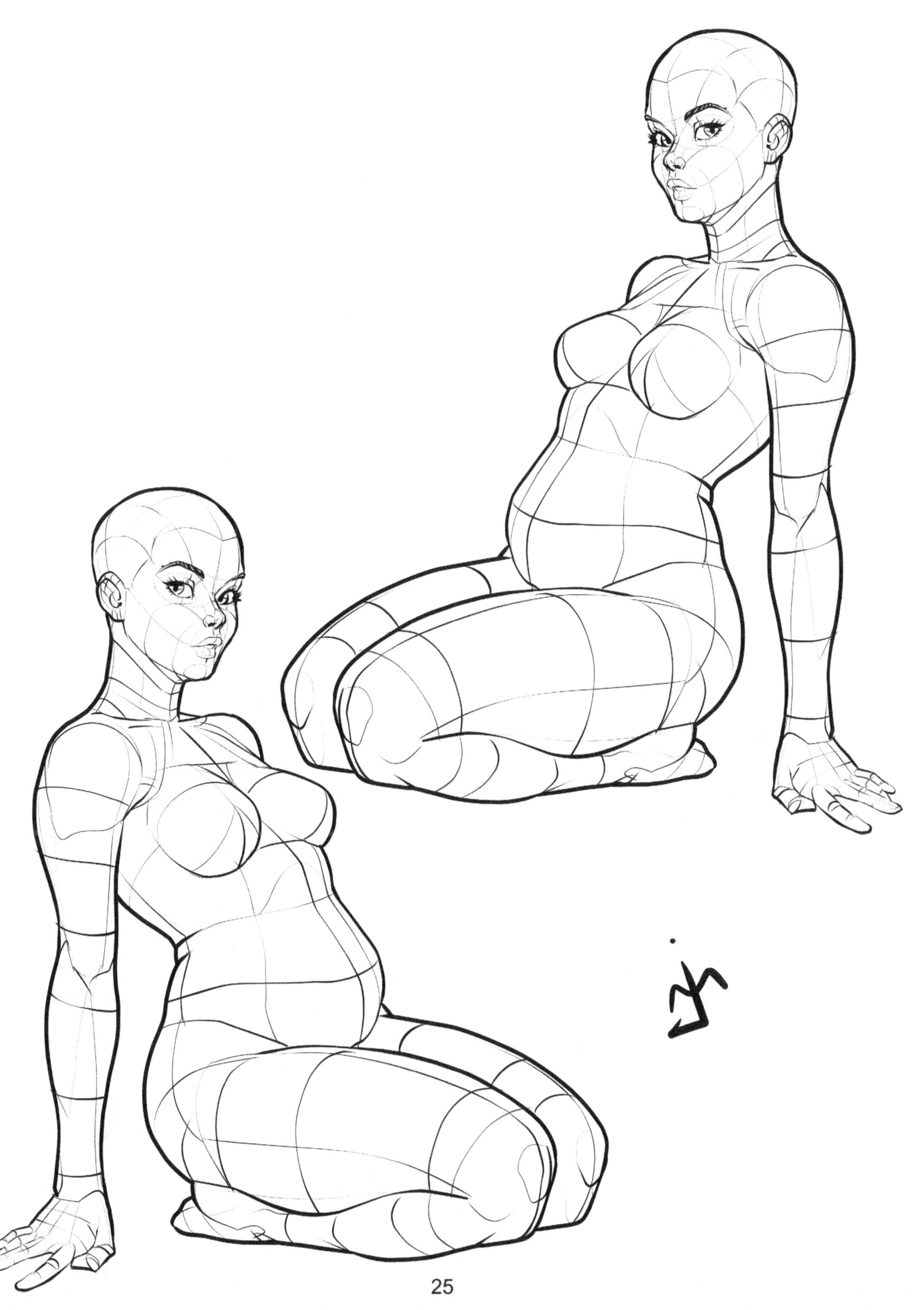

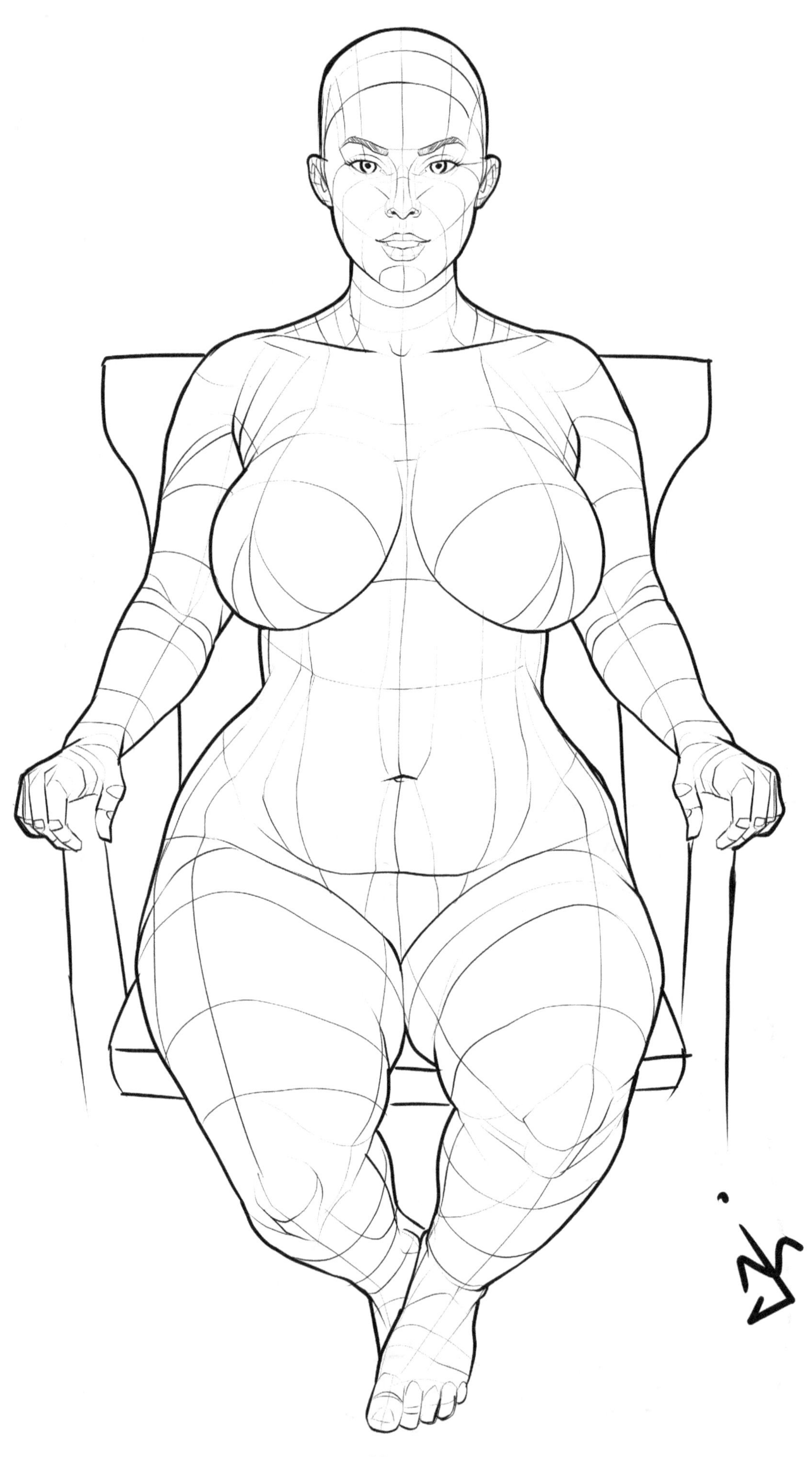

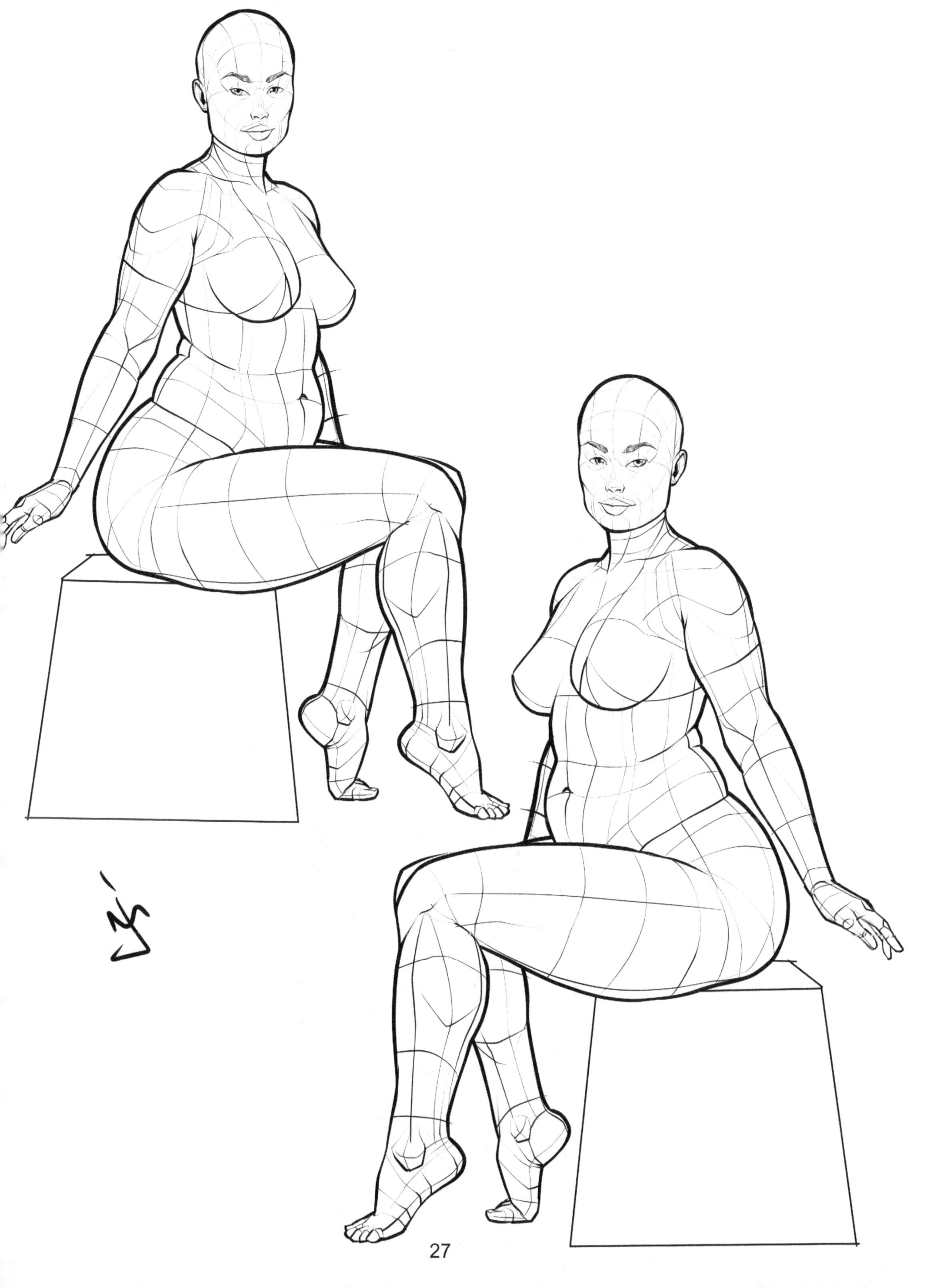

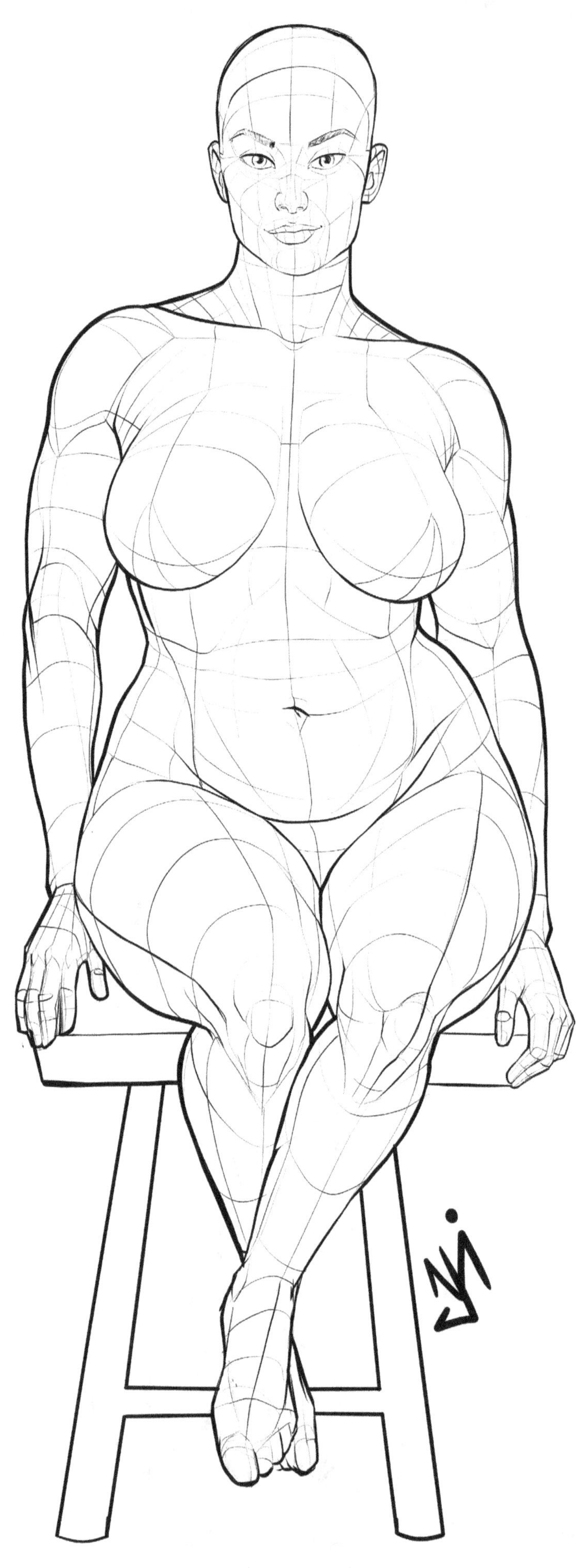

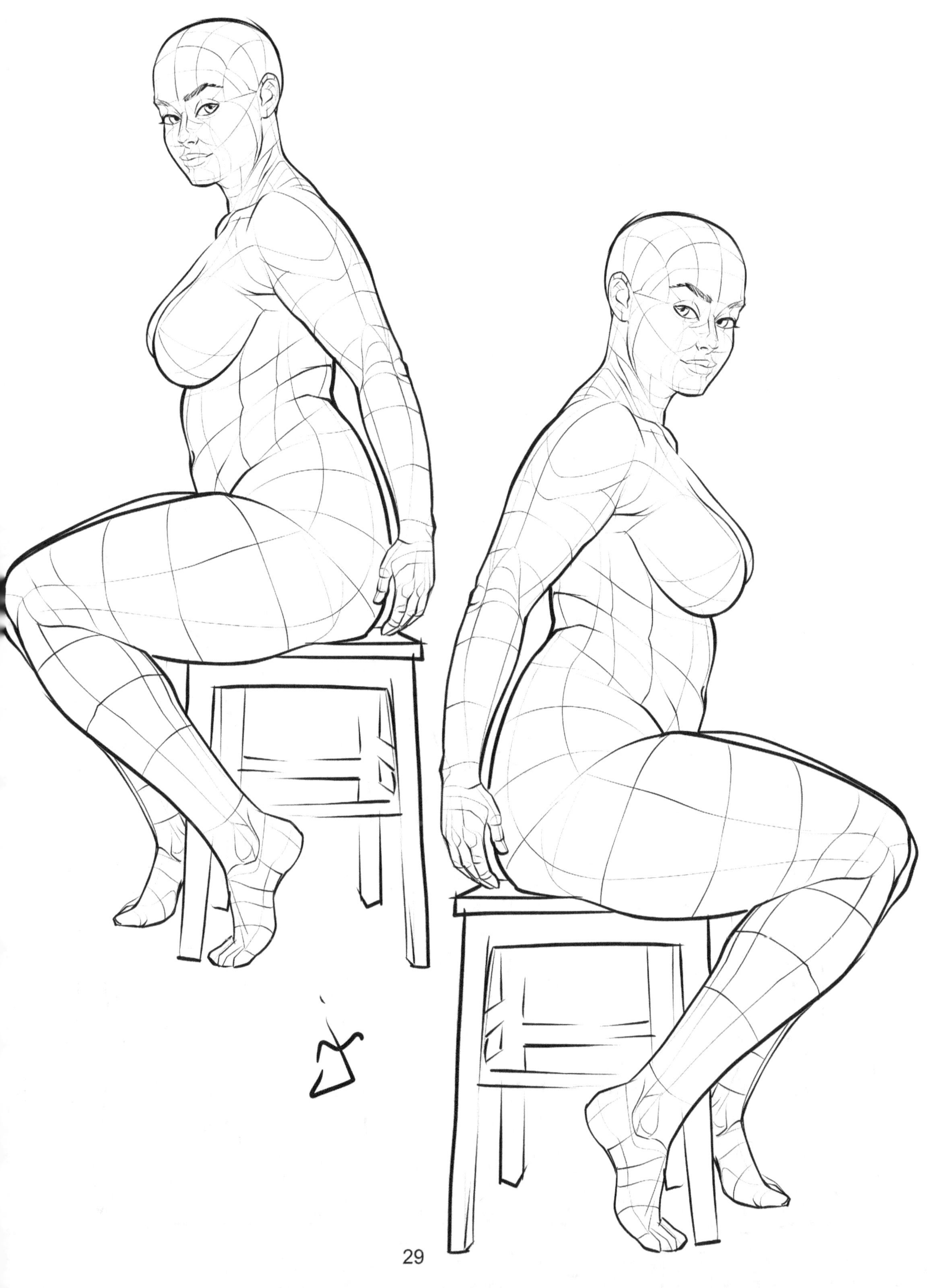

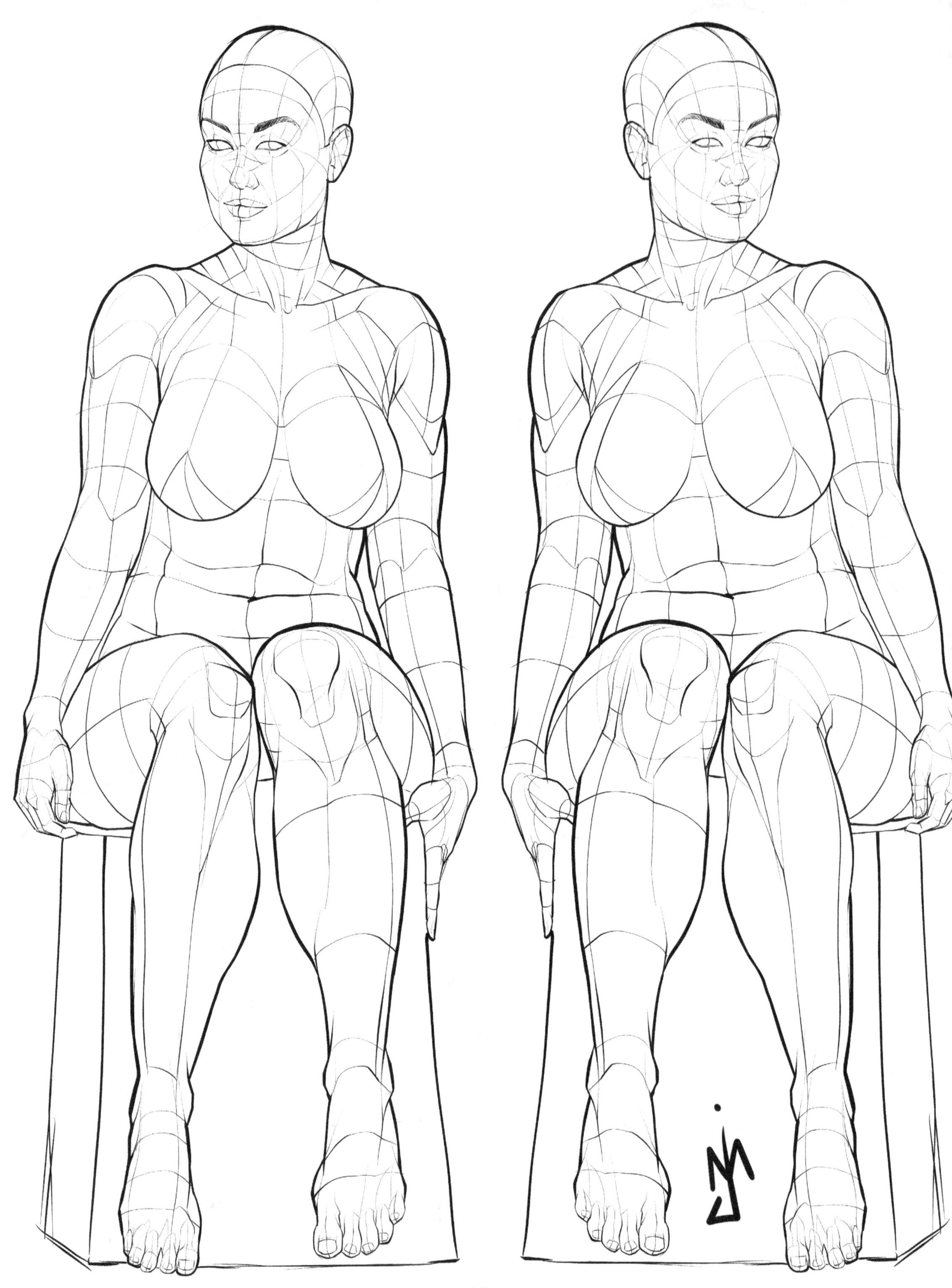

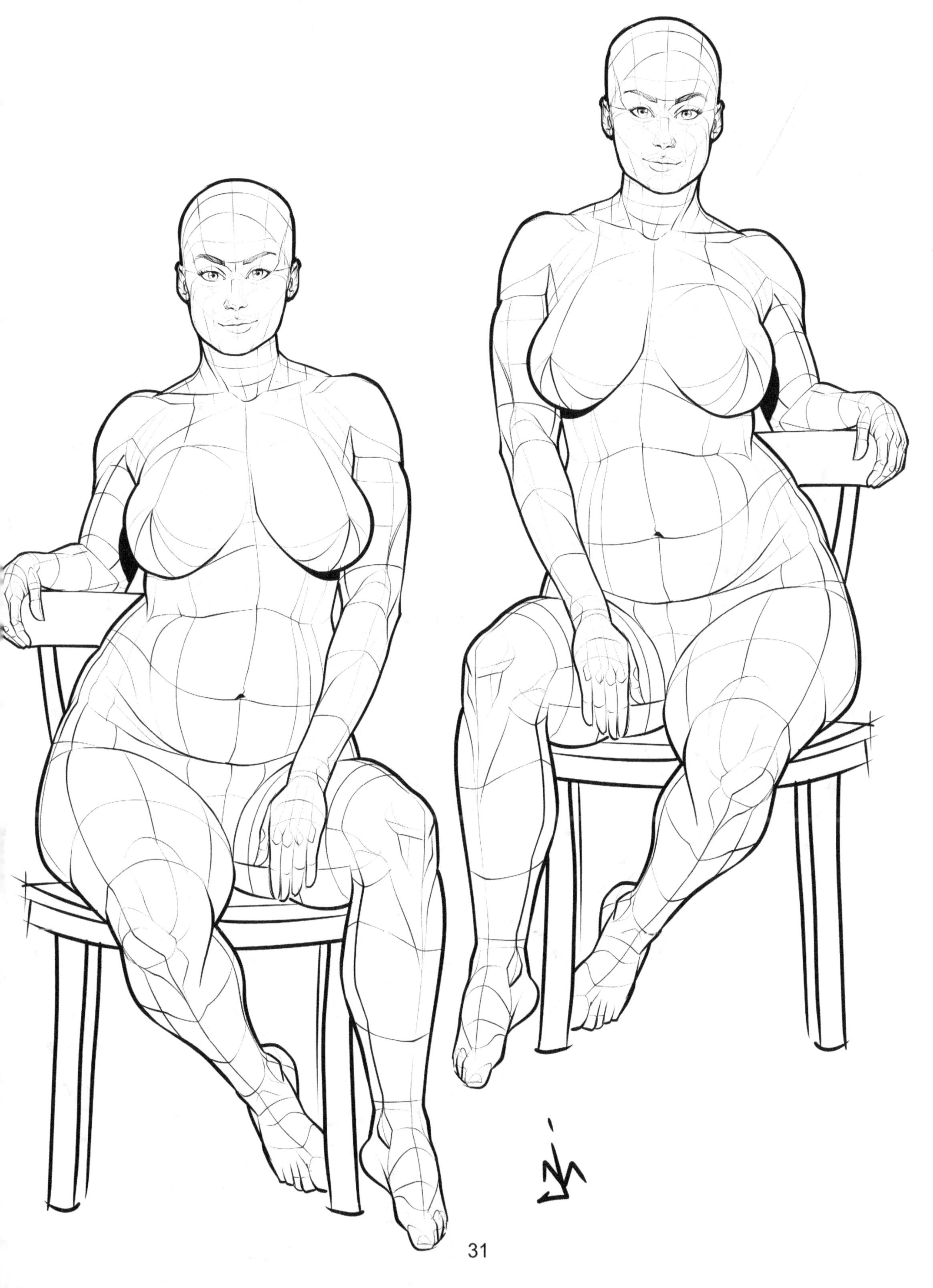

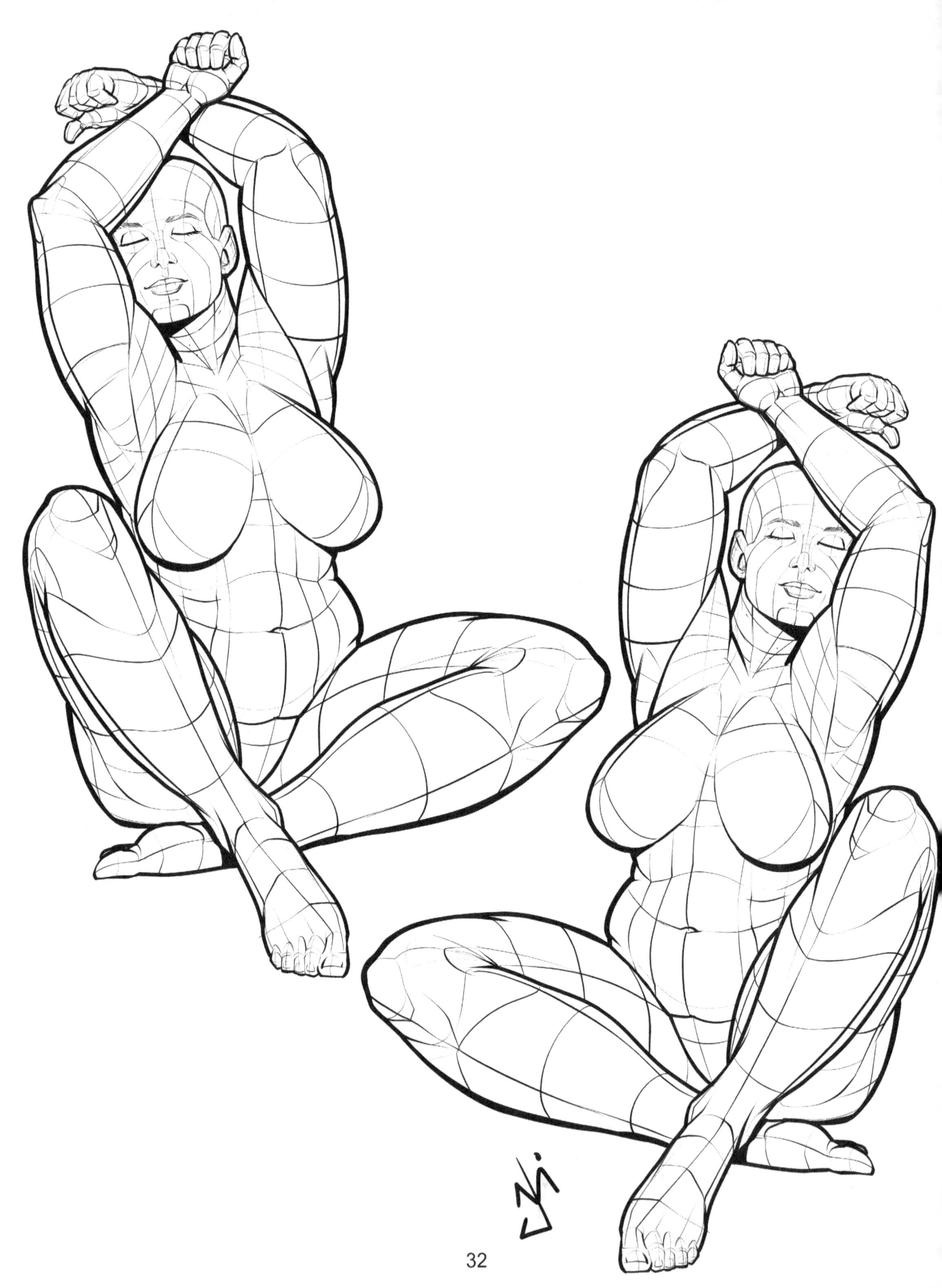

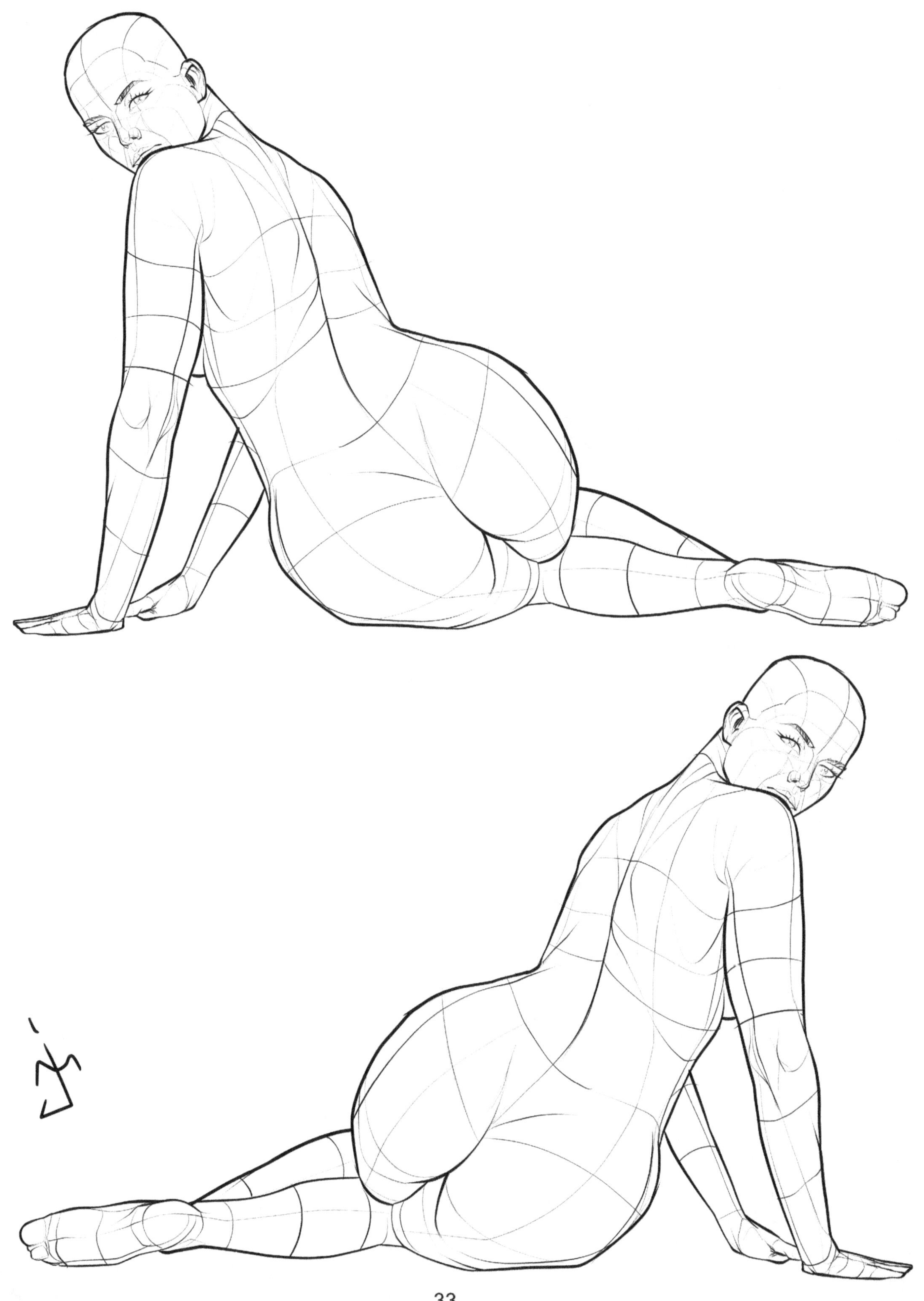

Standing Poses

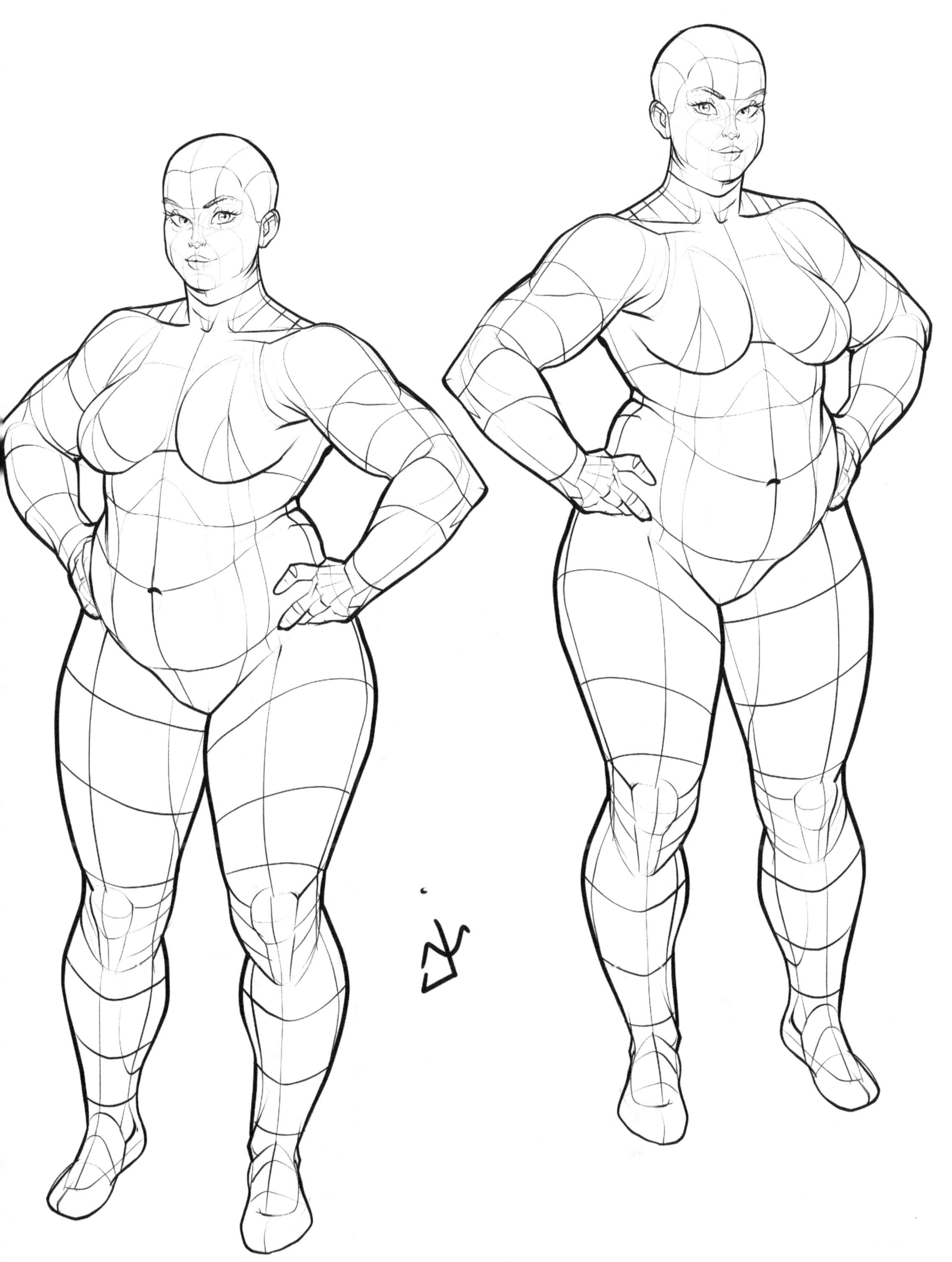

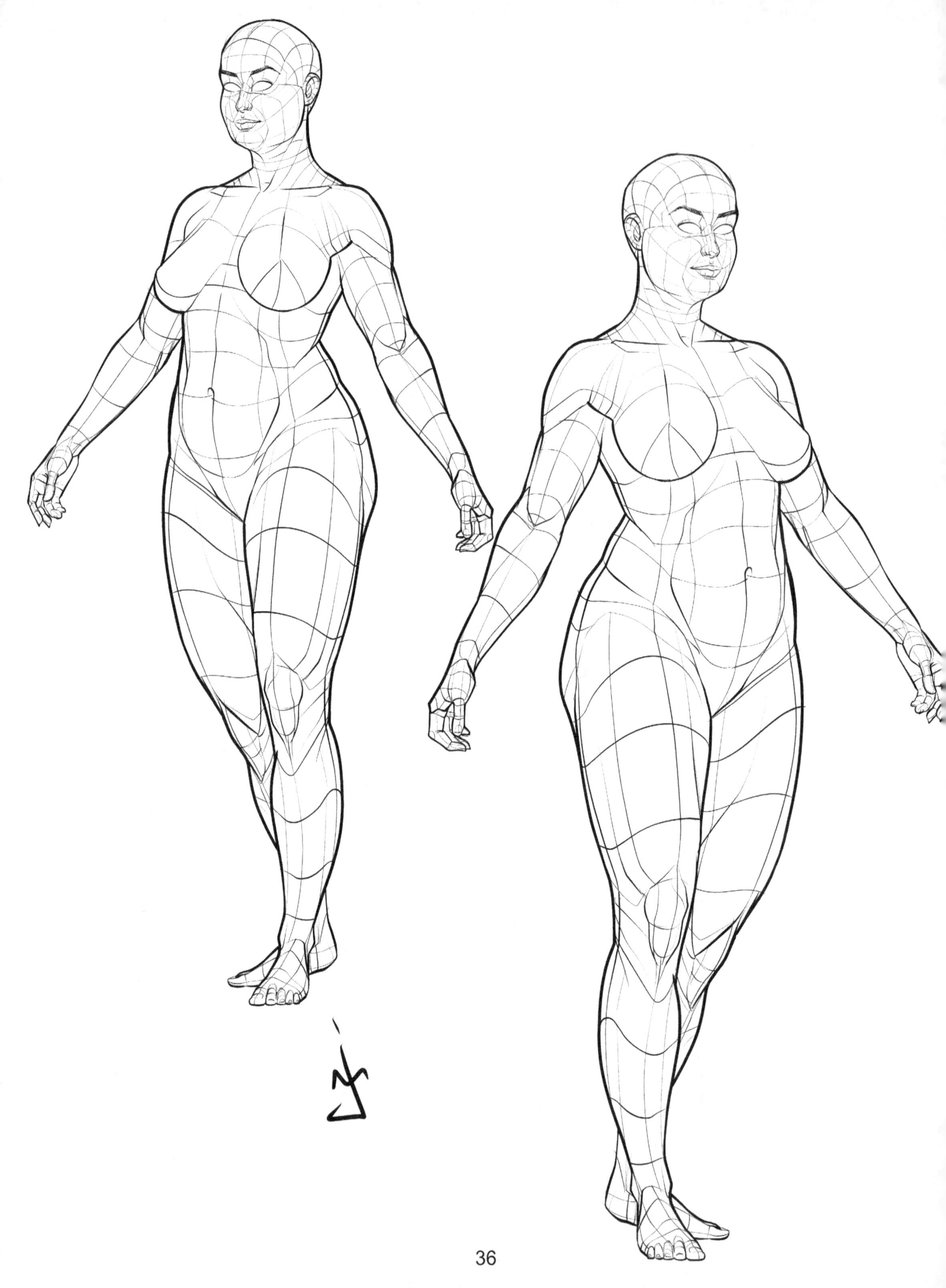

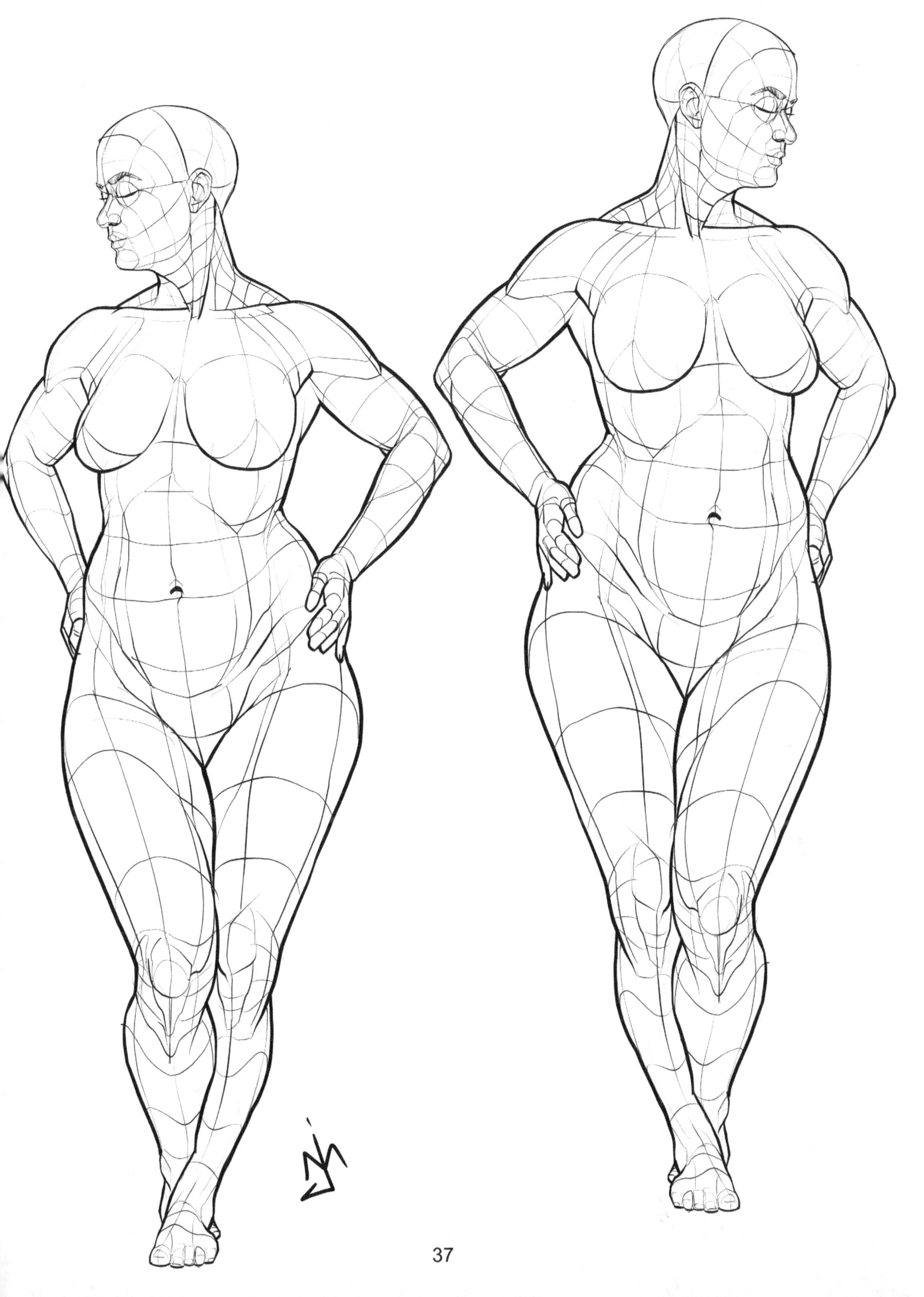

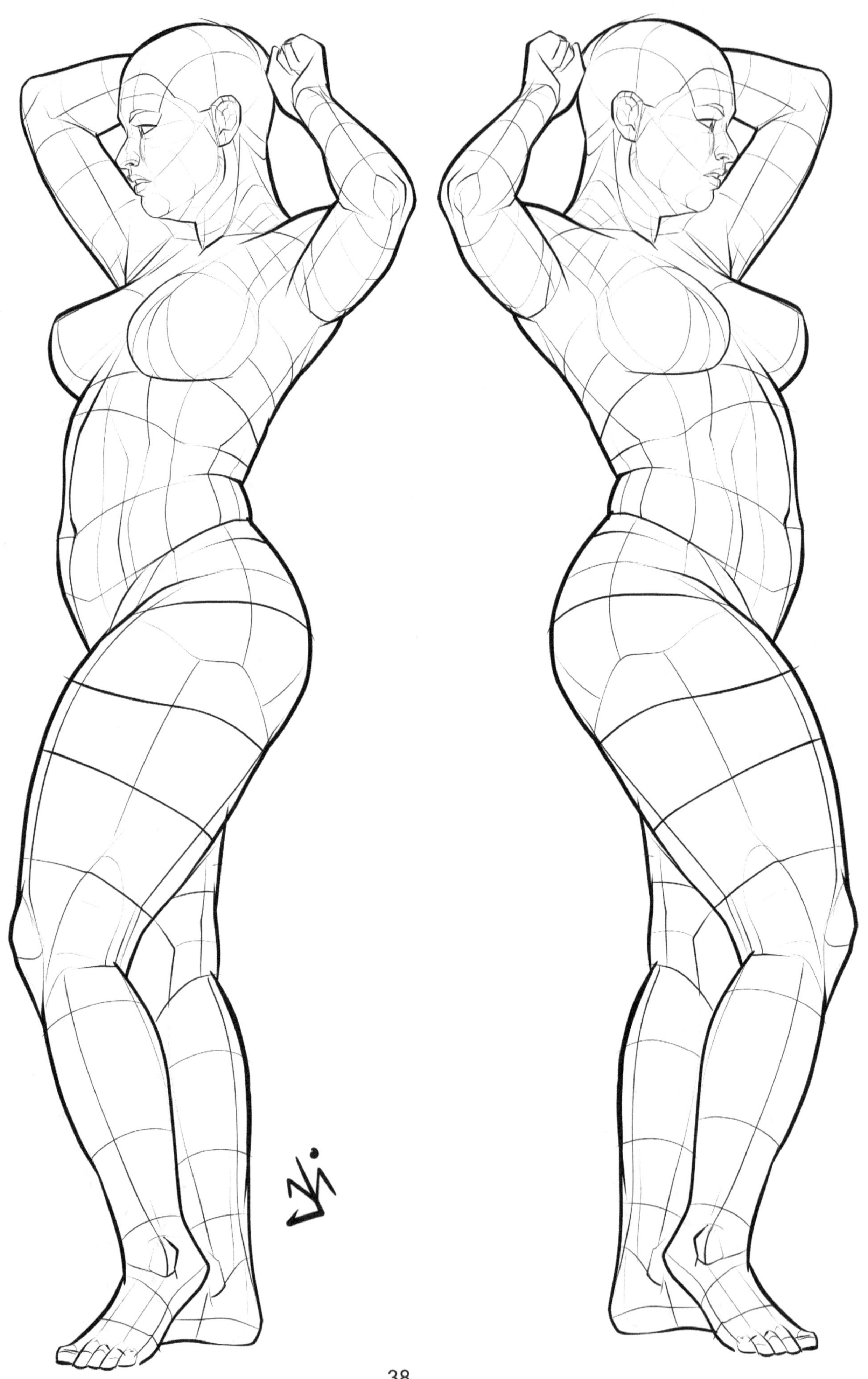

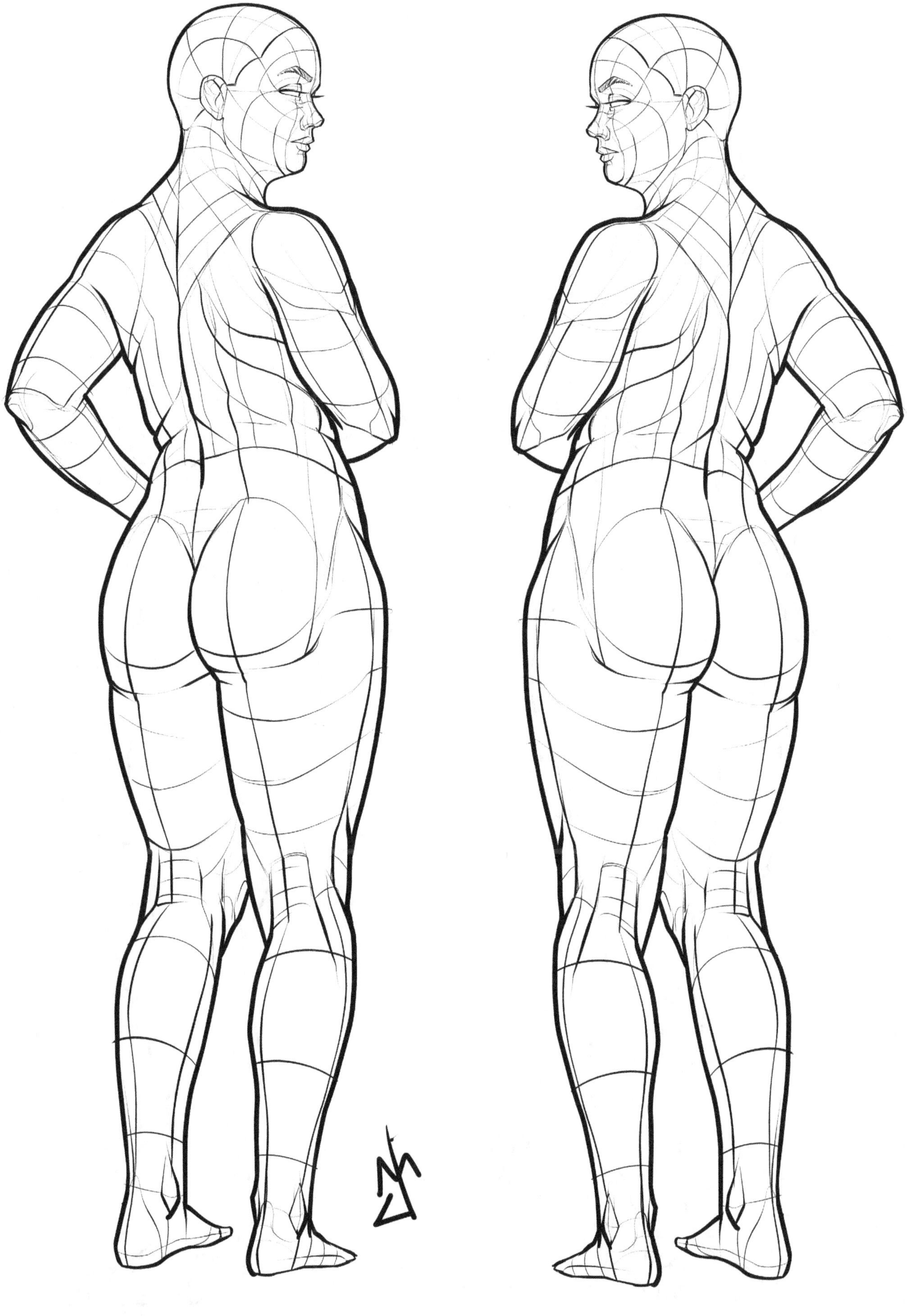

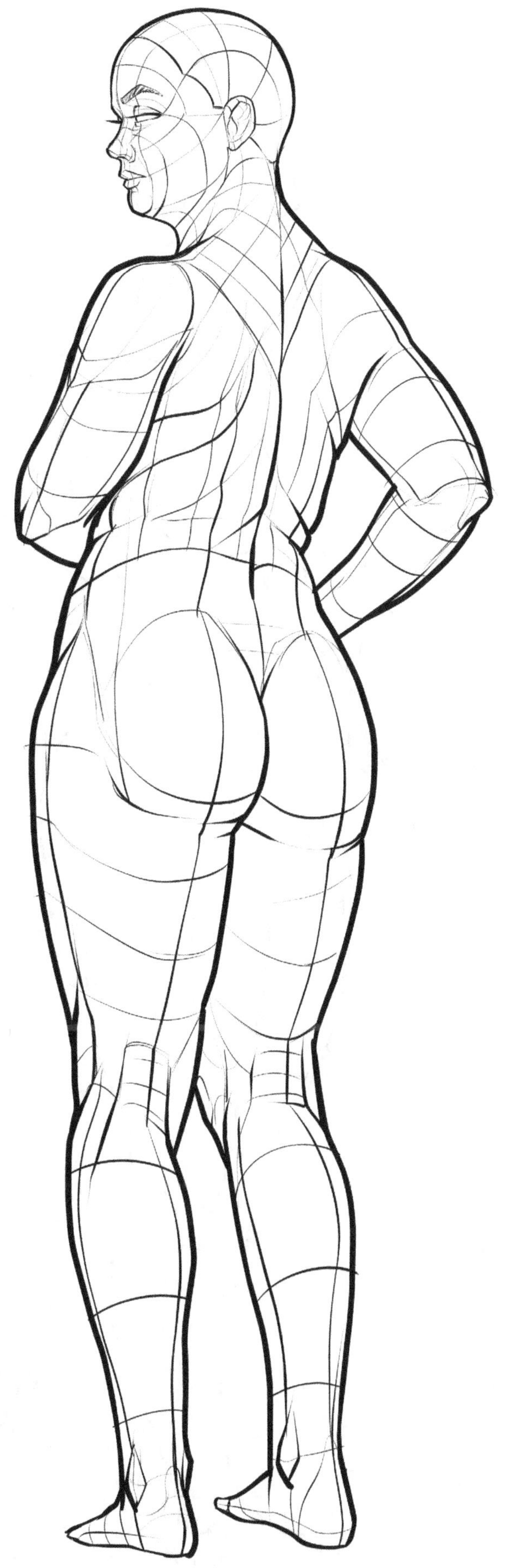

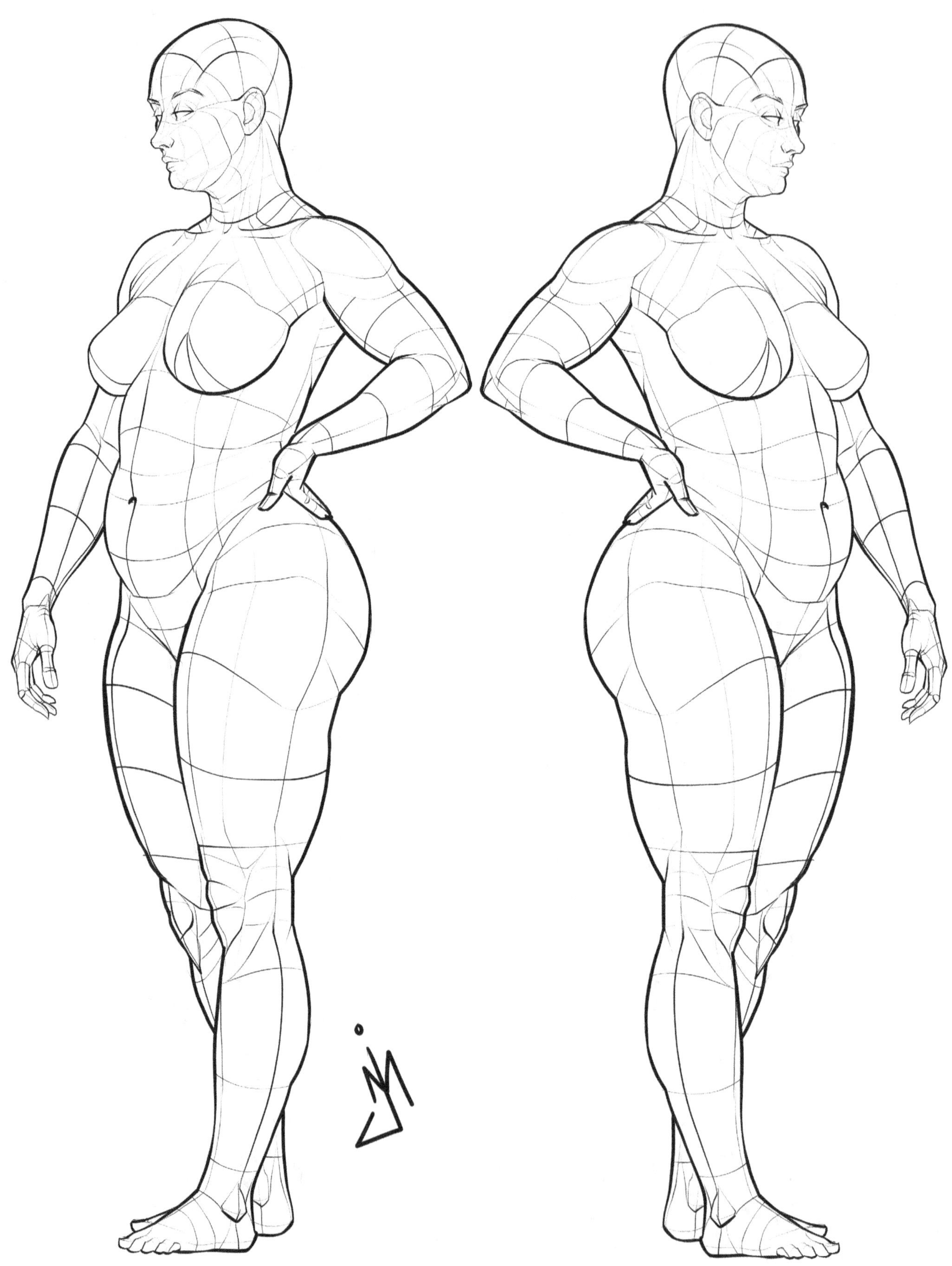

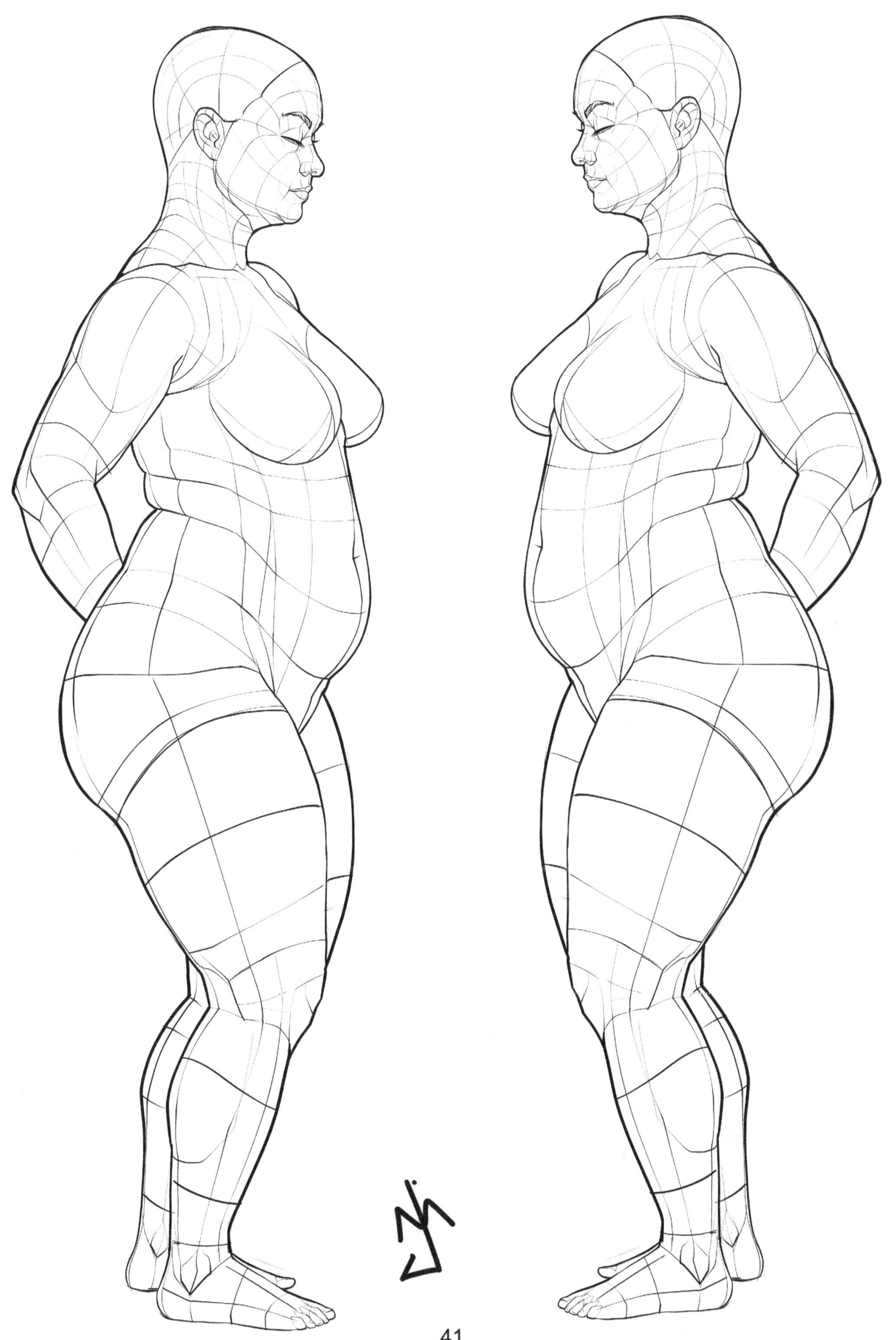

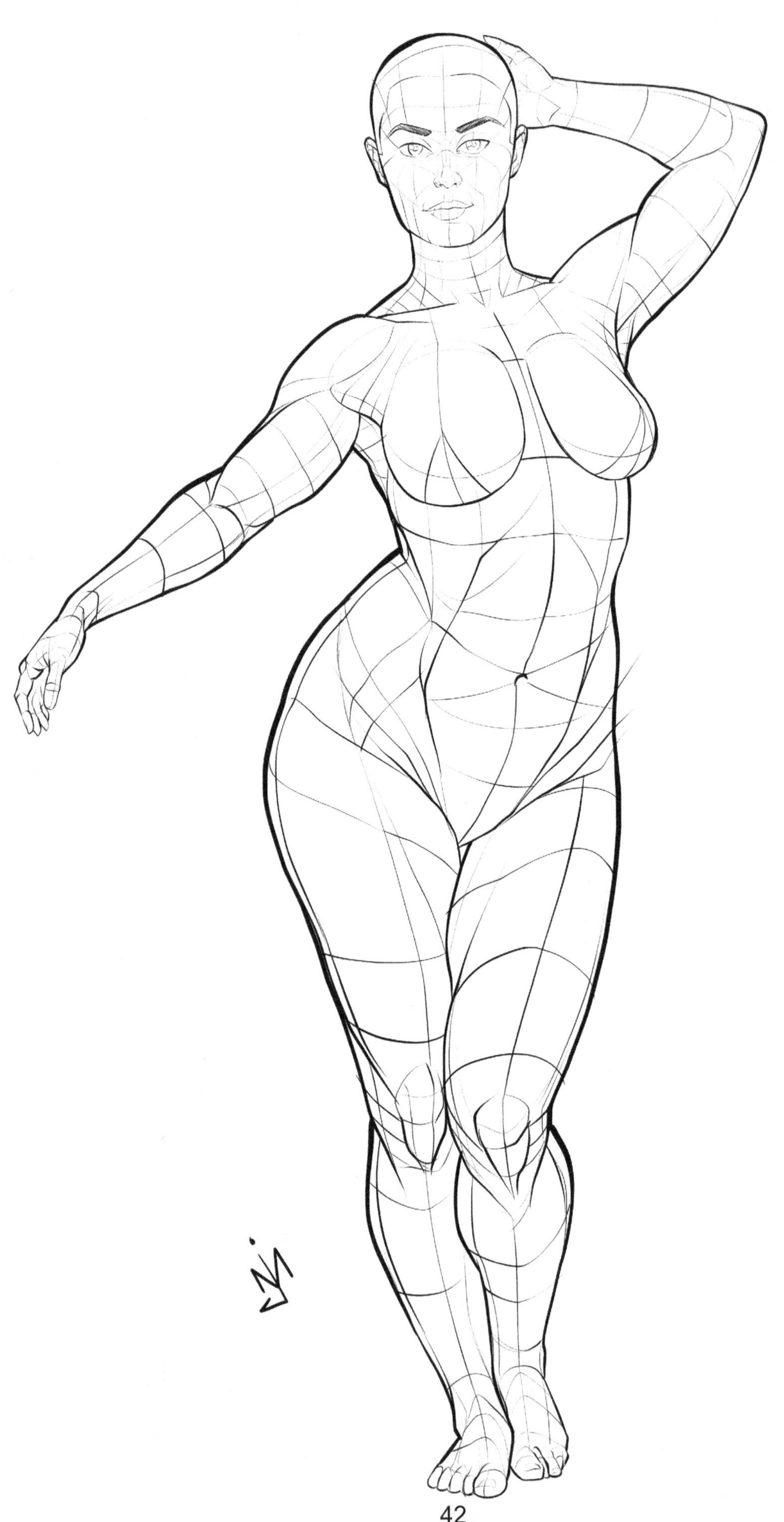

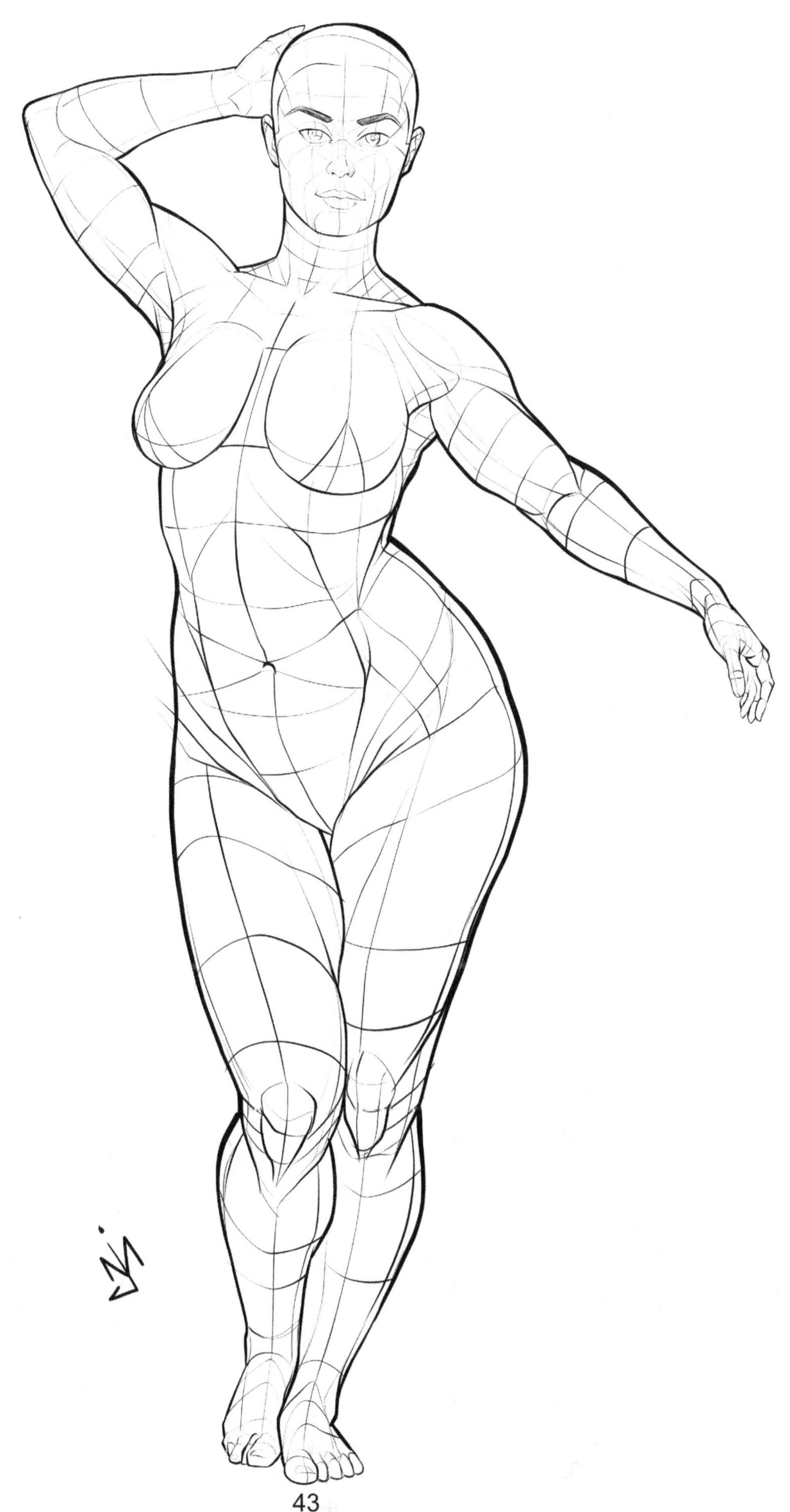

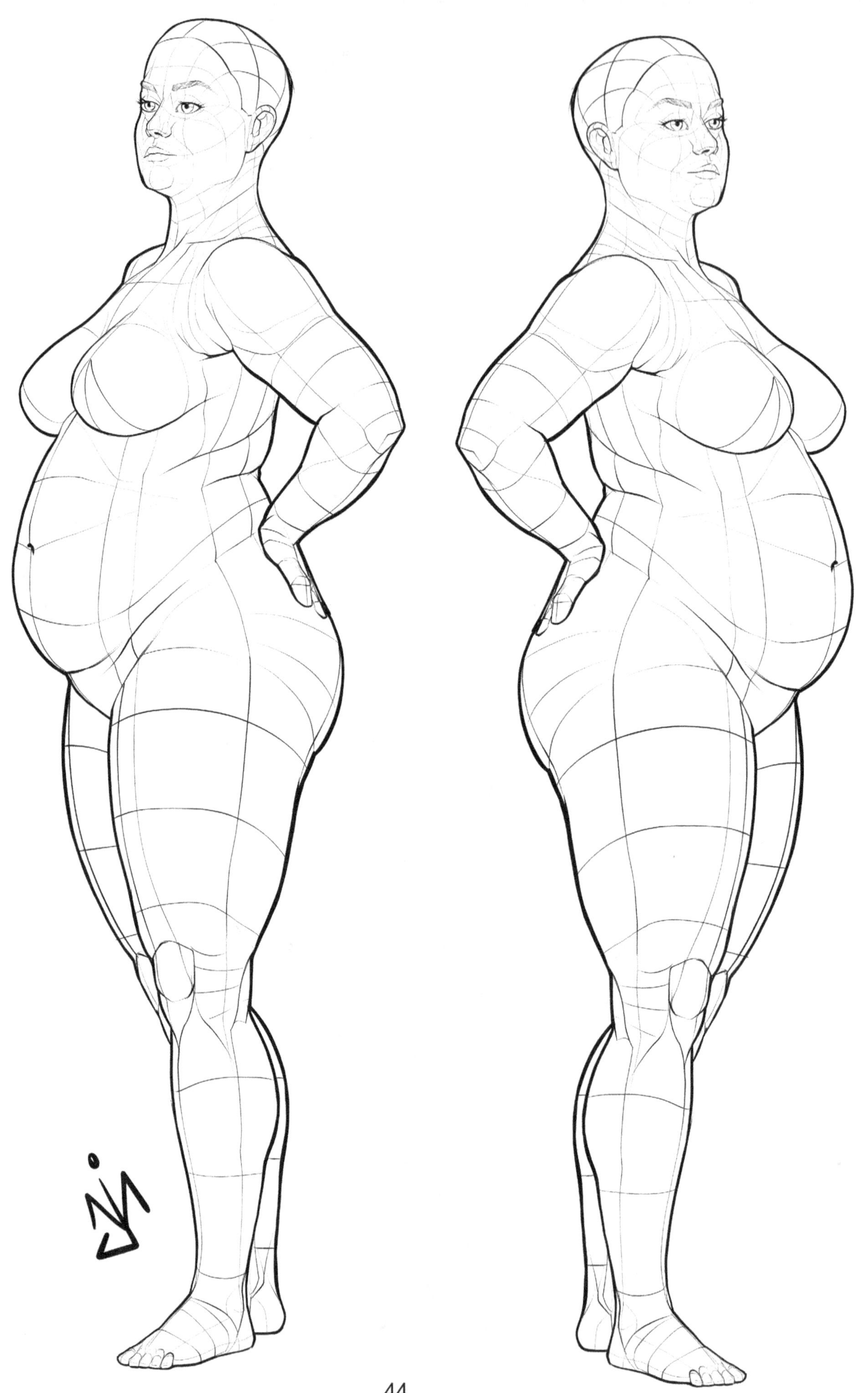

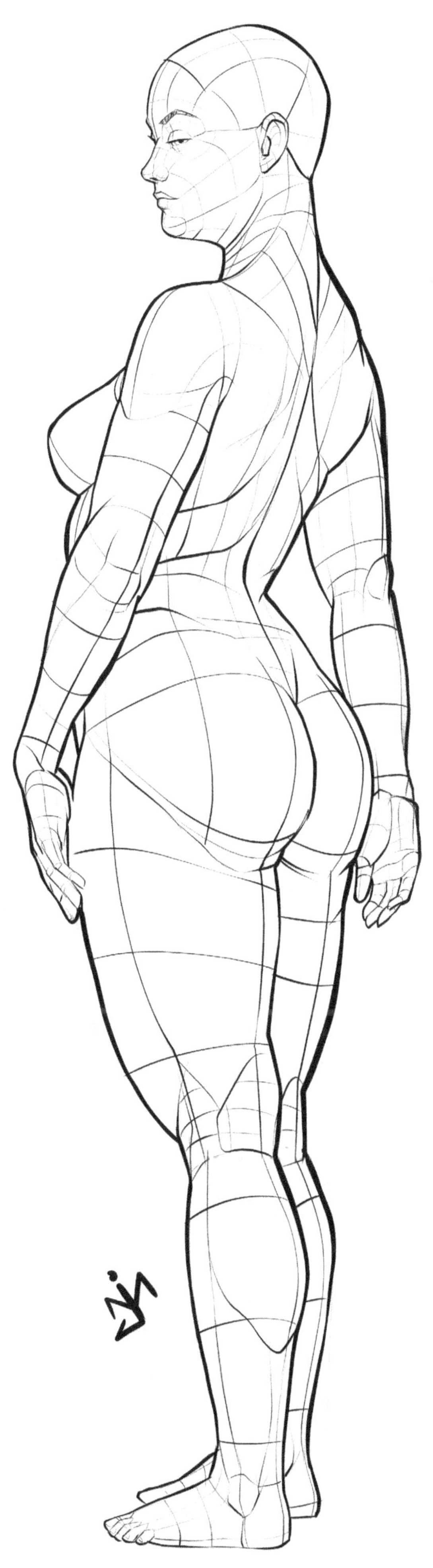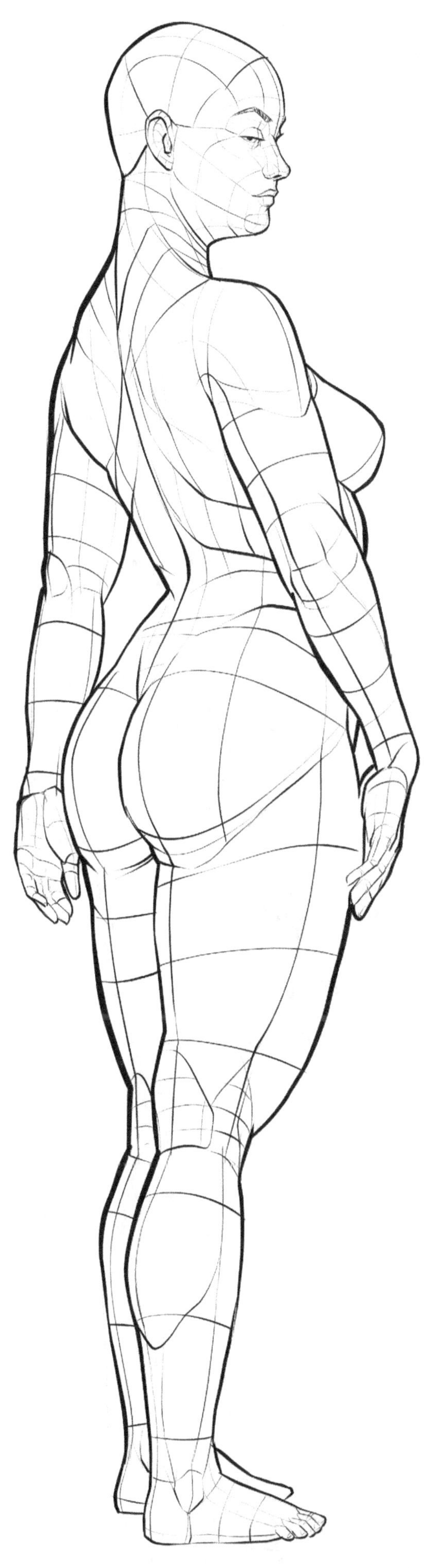

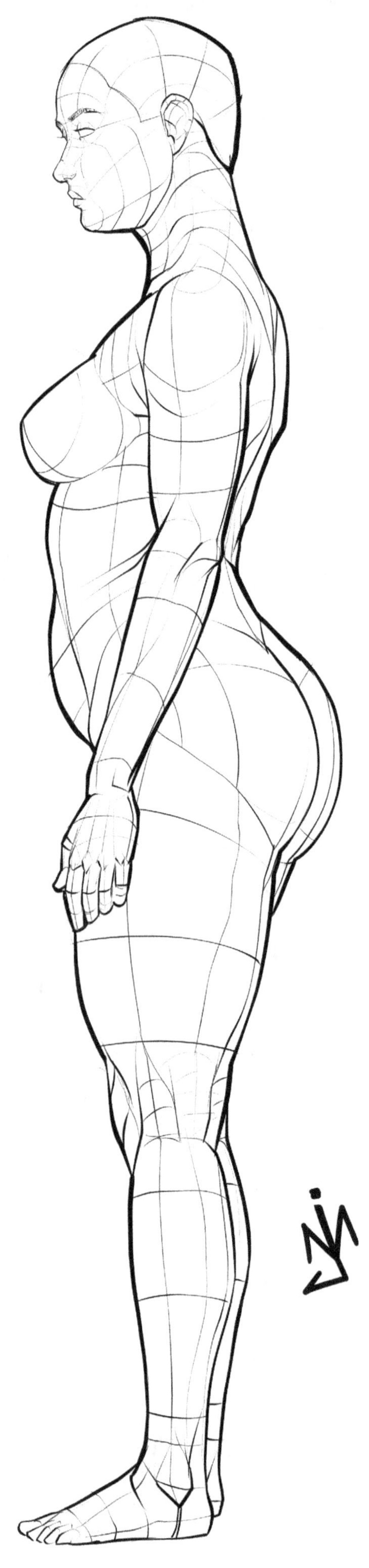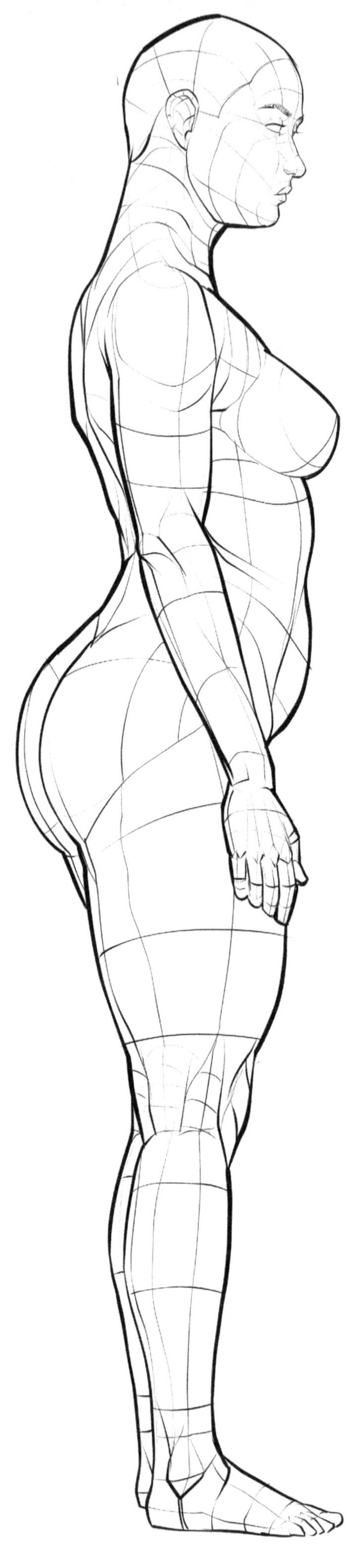

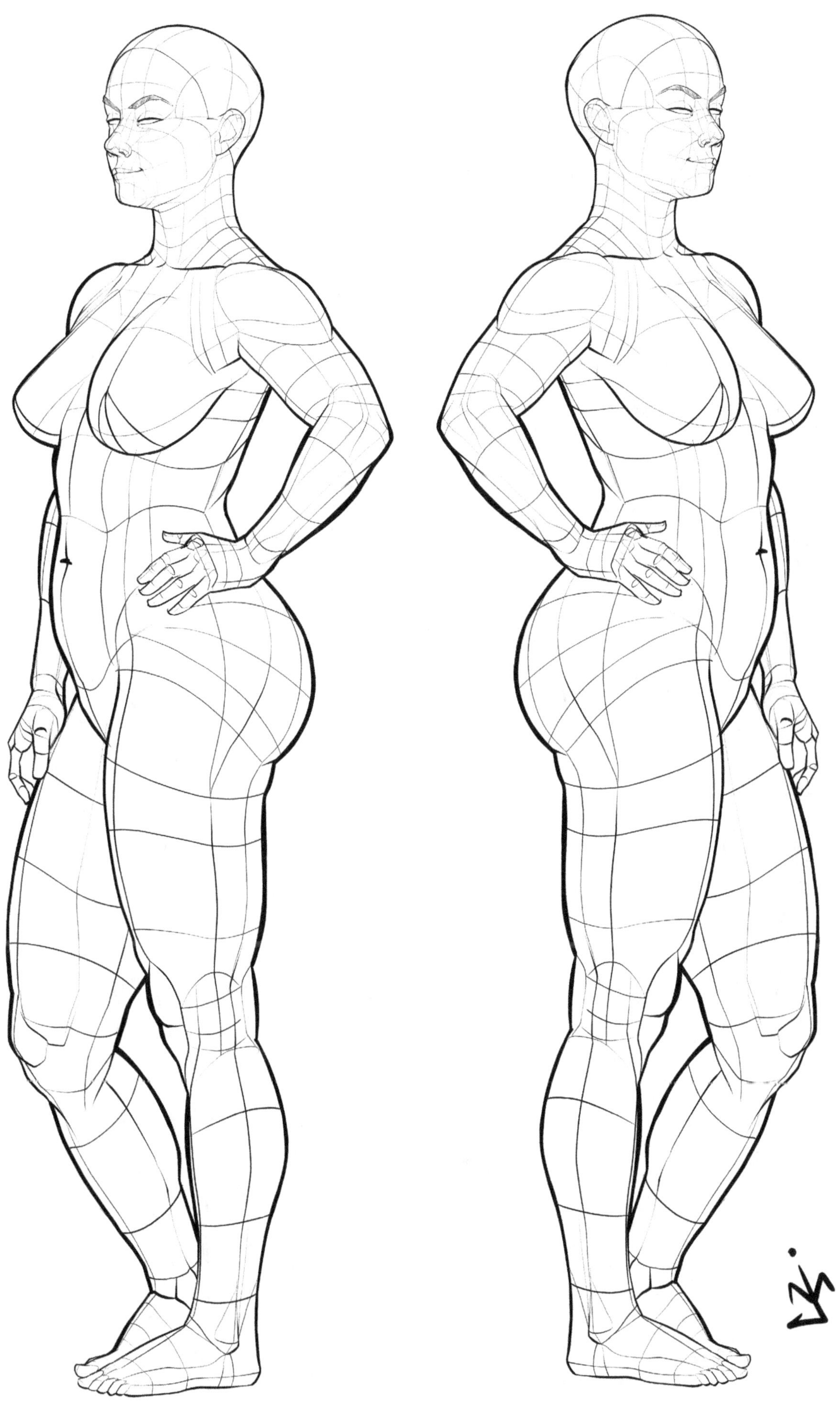

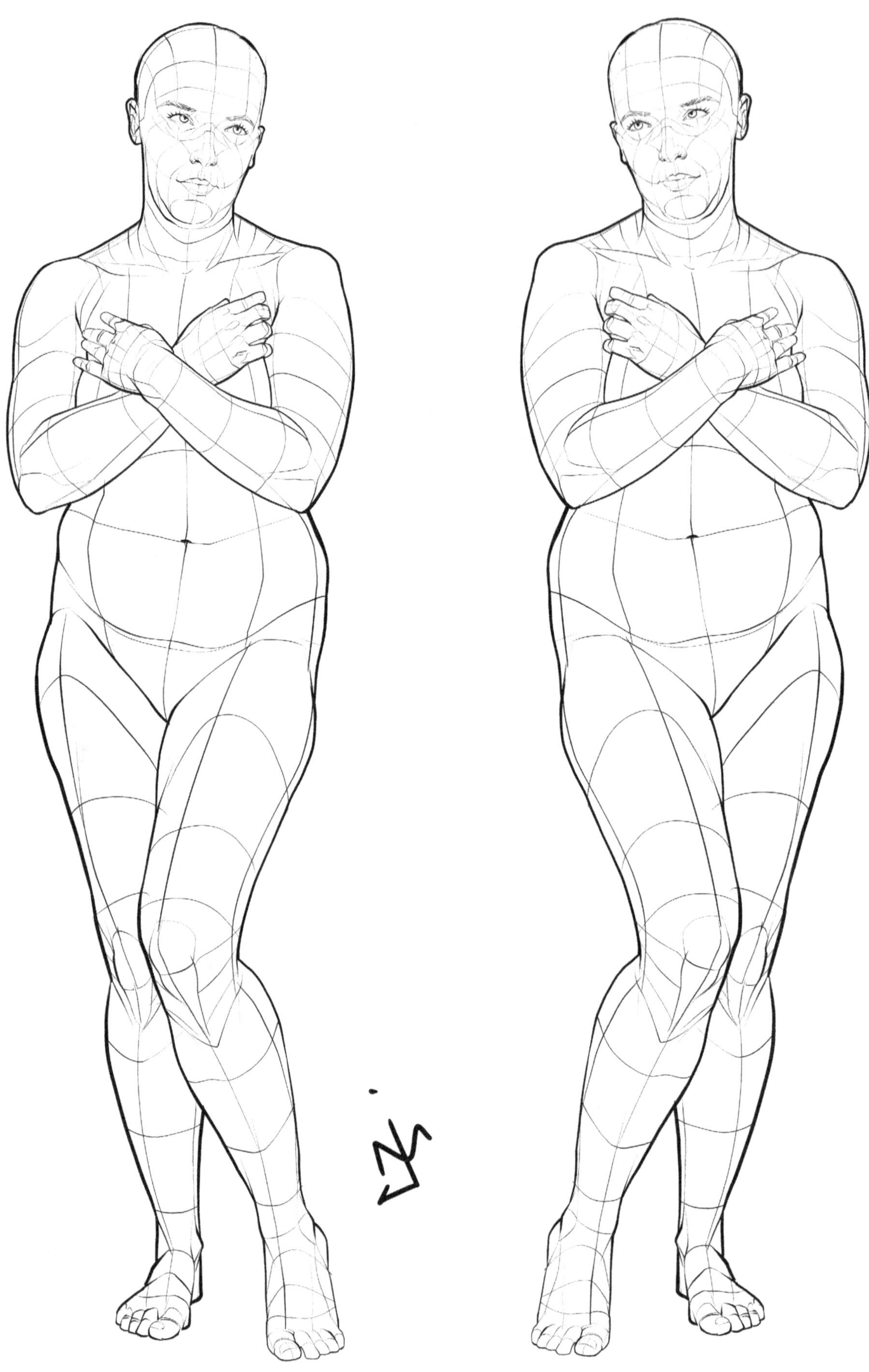

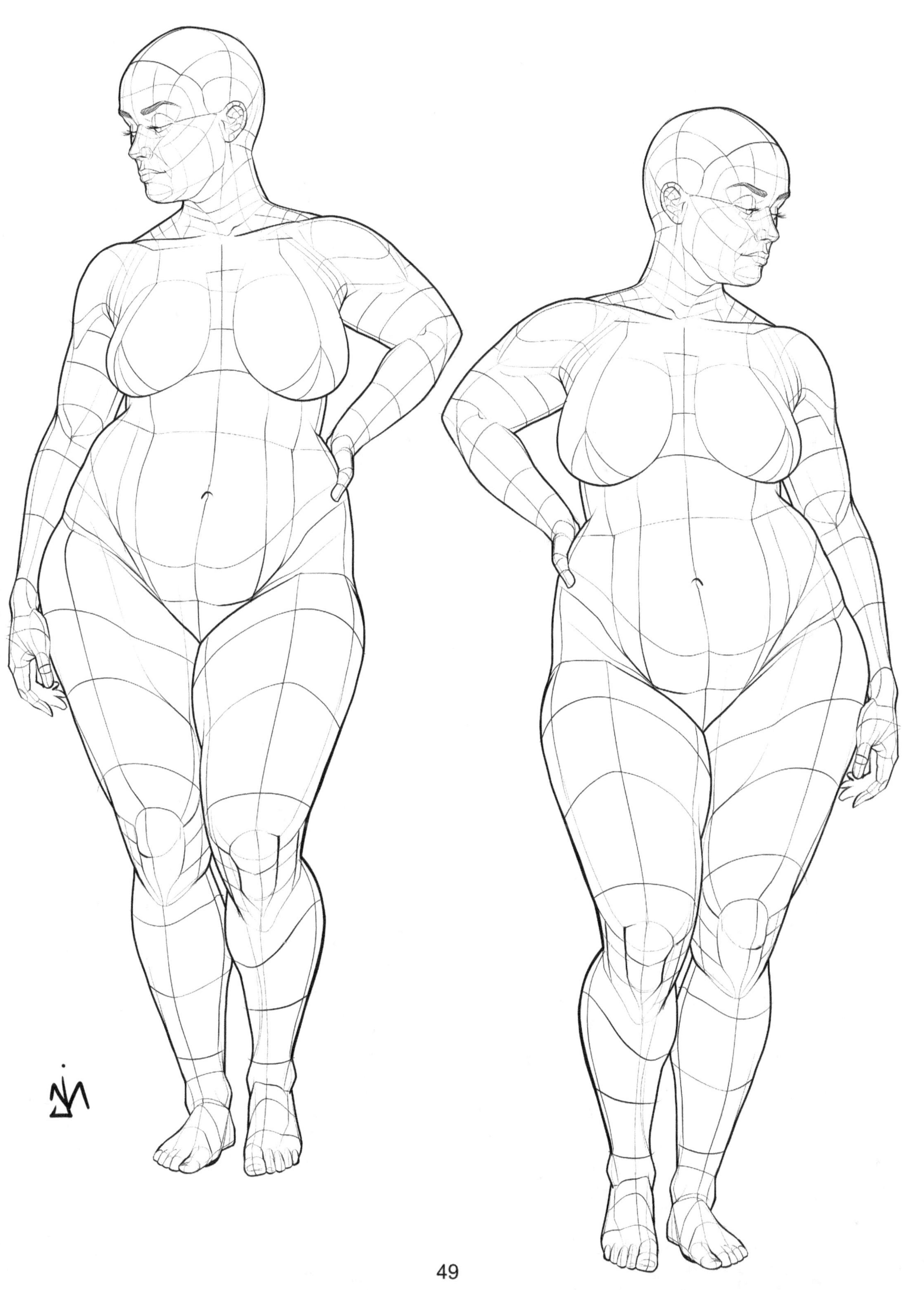

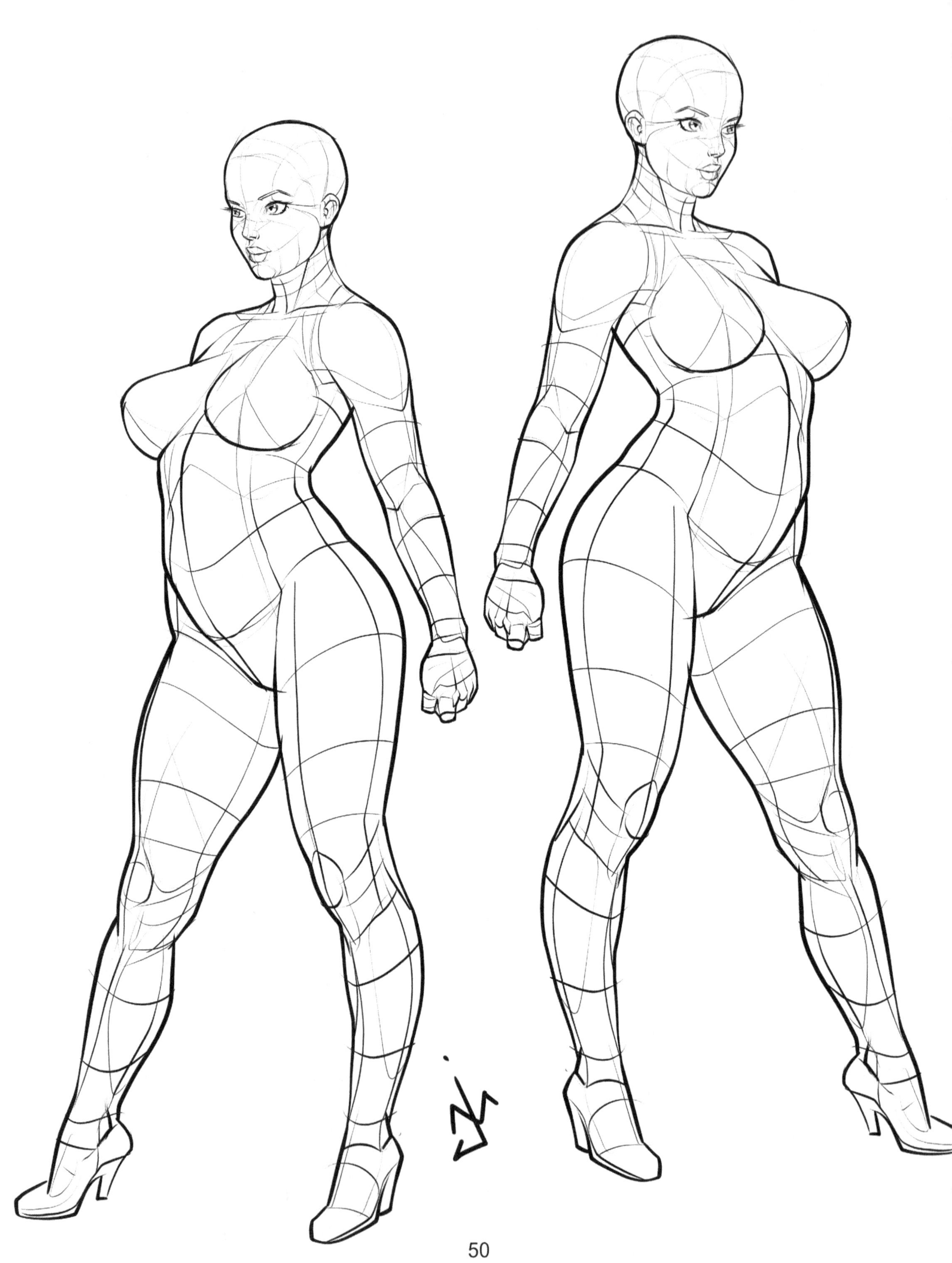

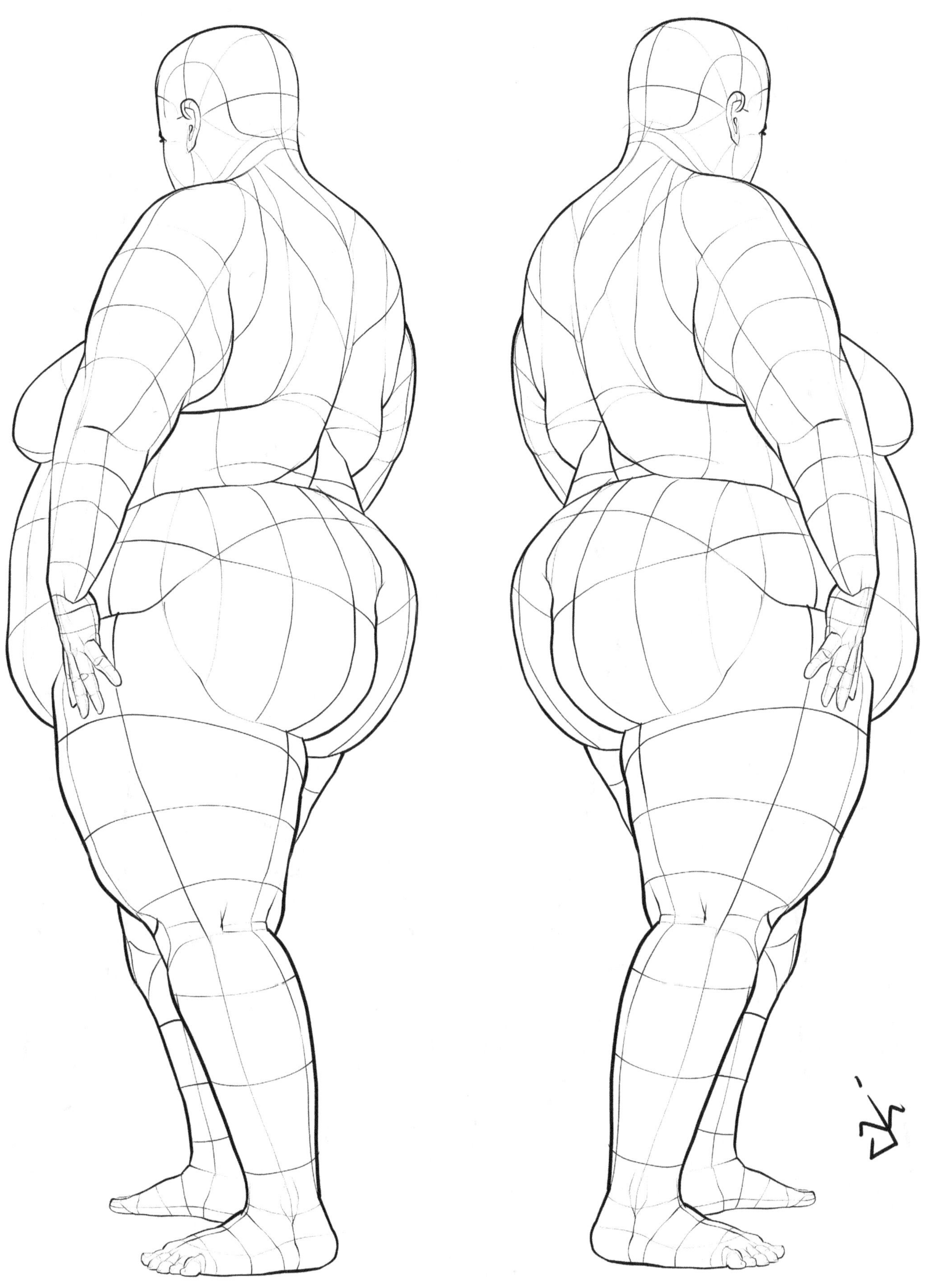

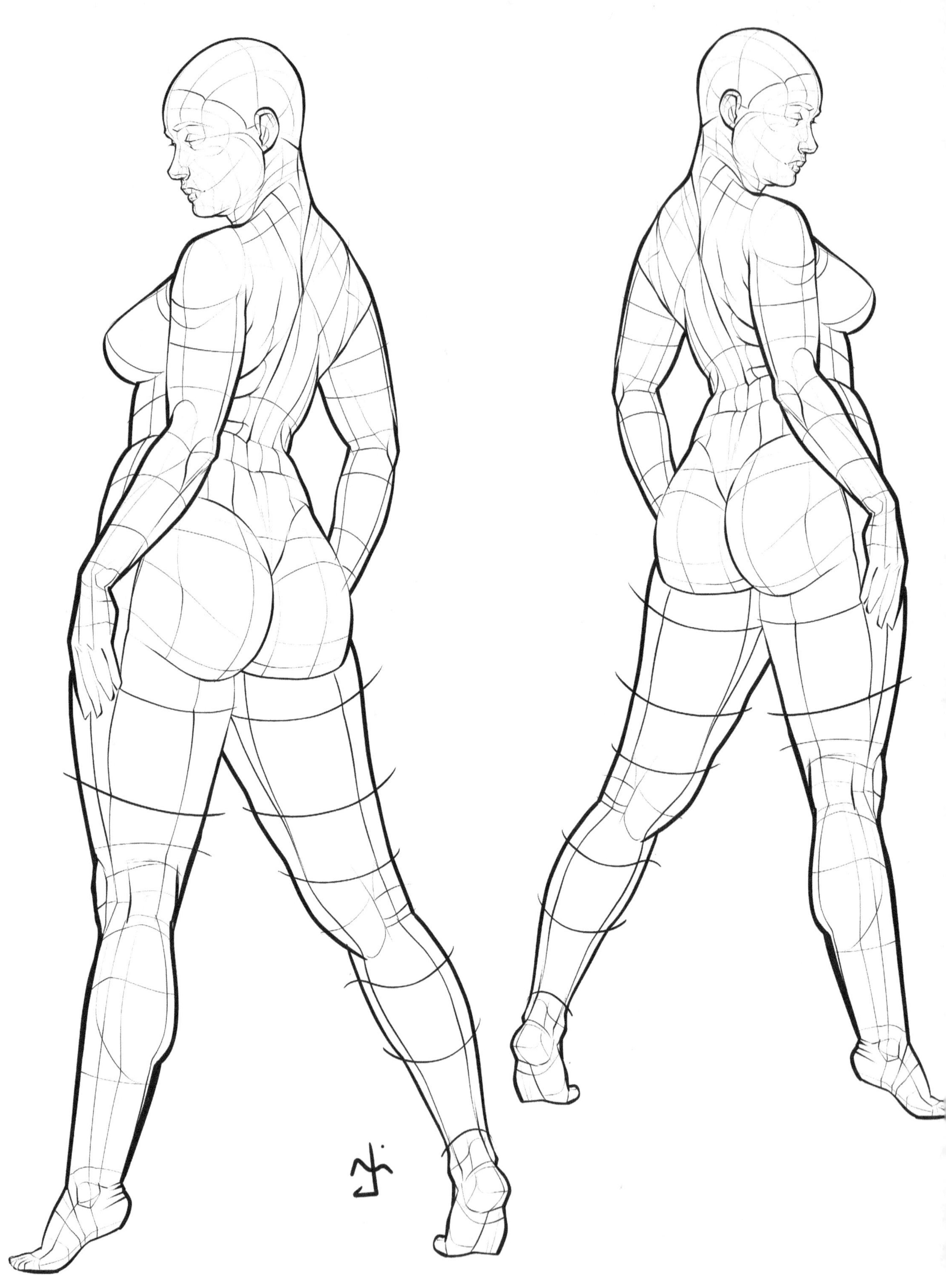

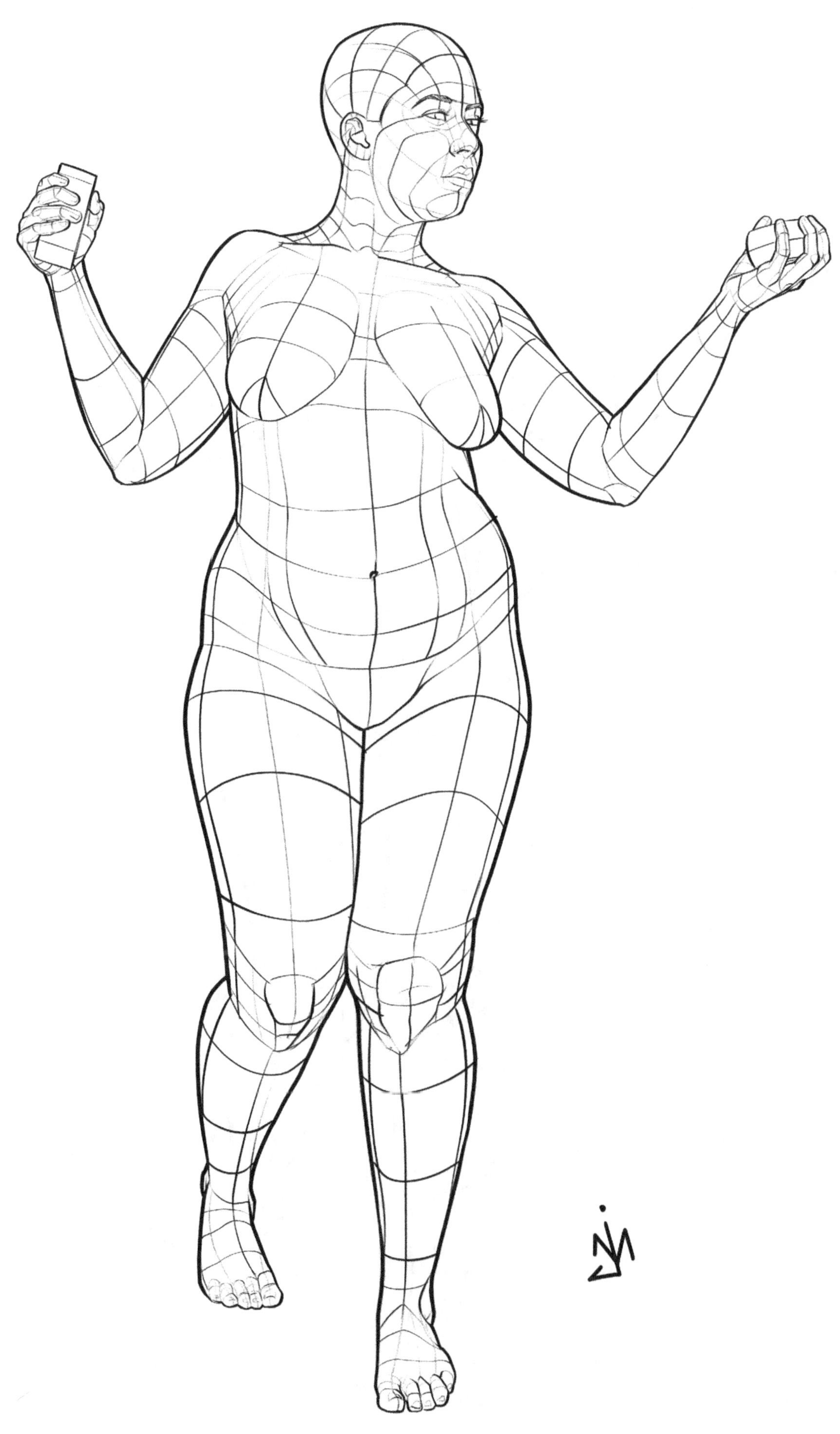

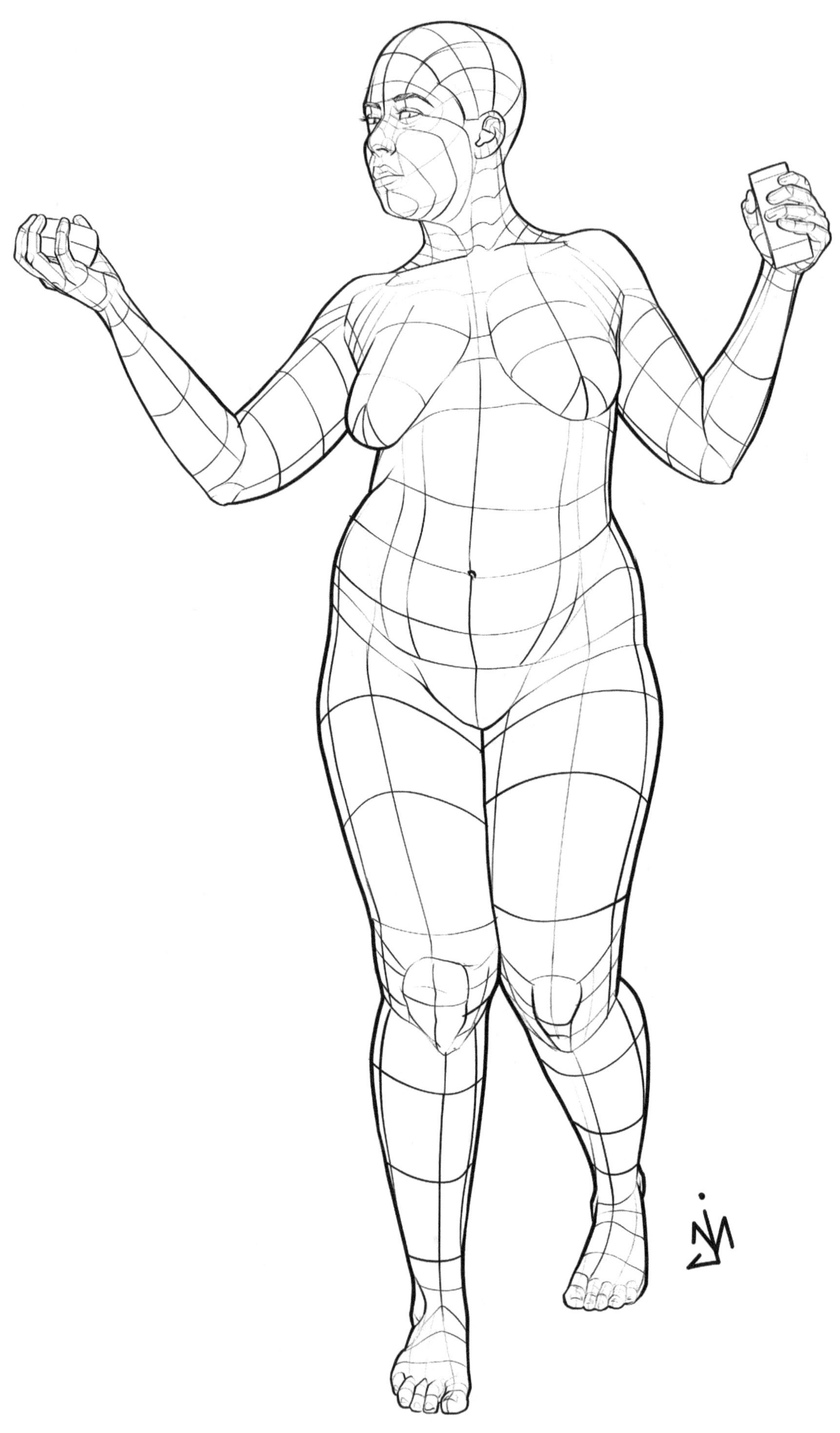

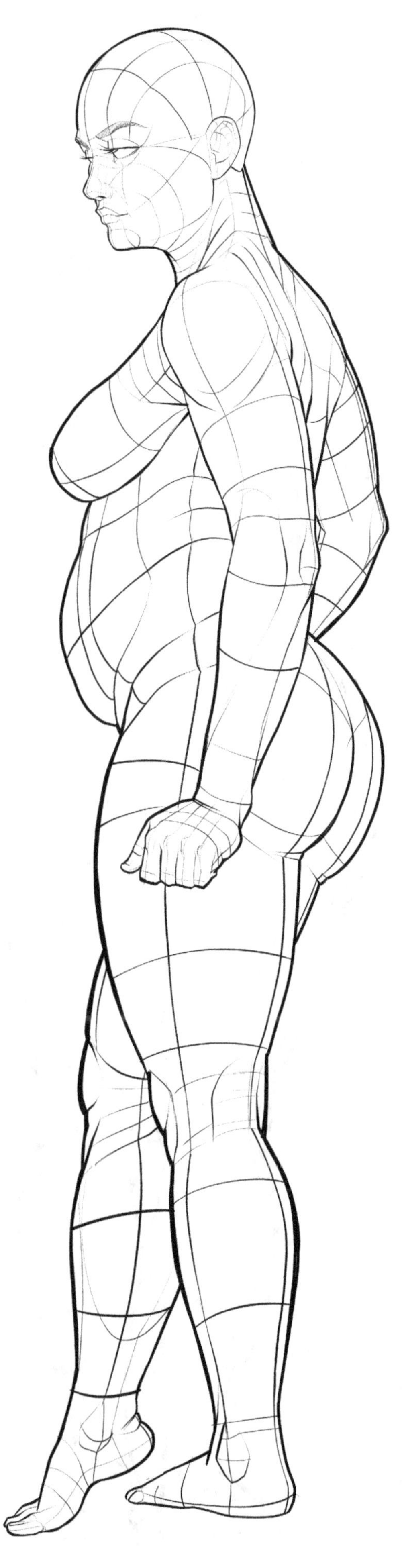
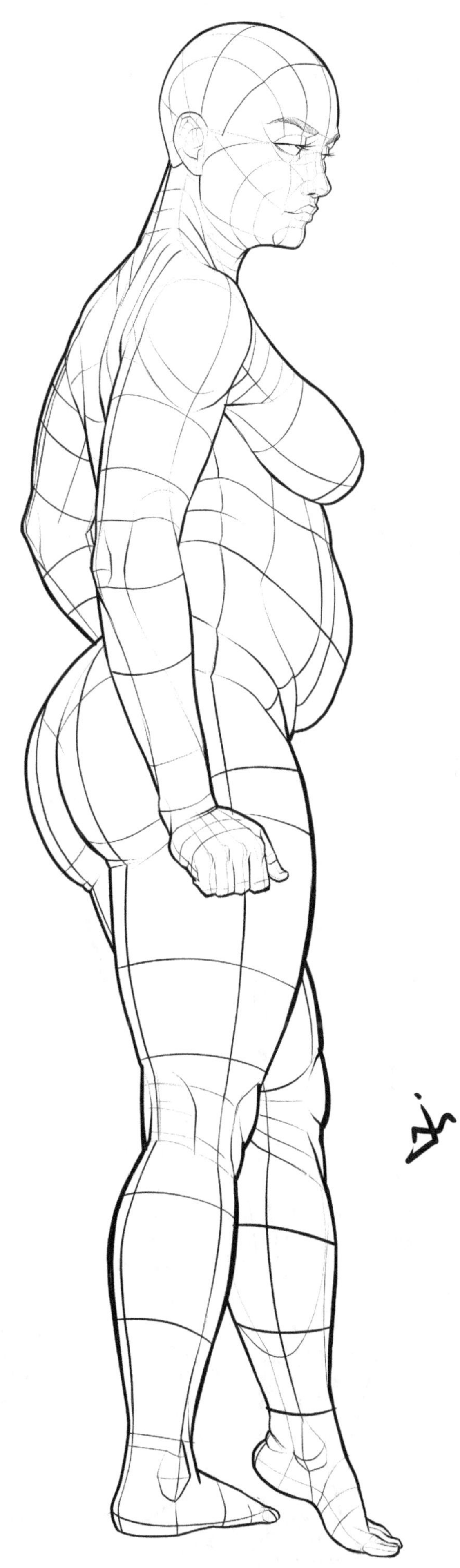

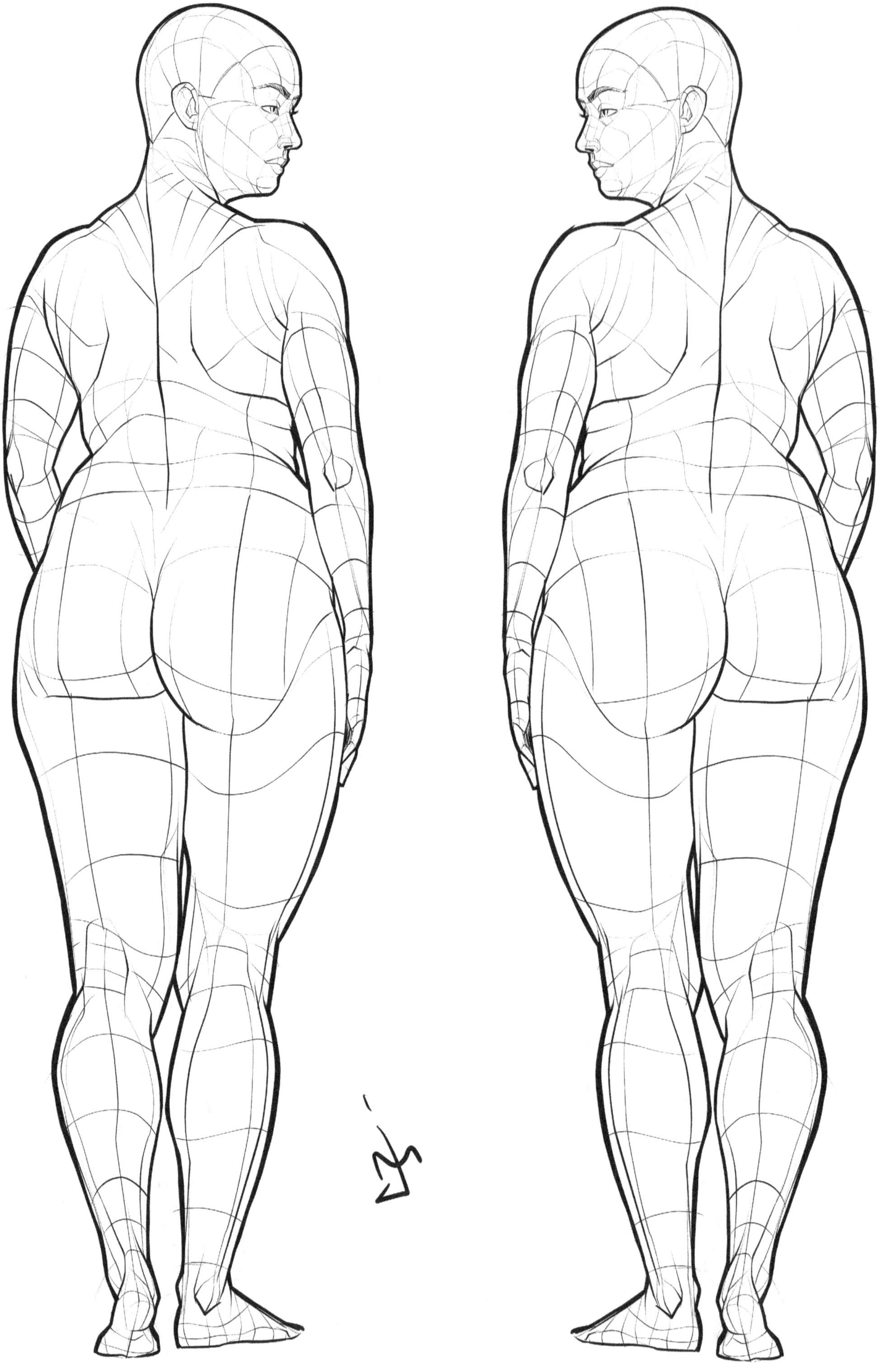

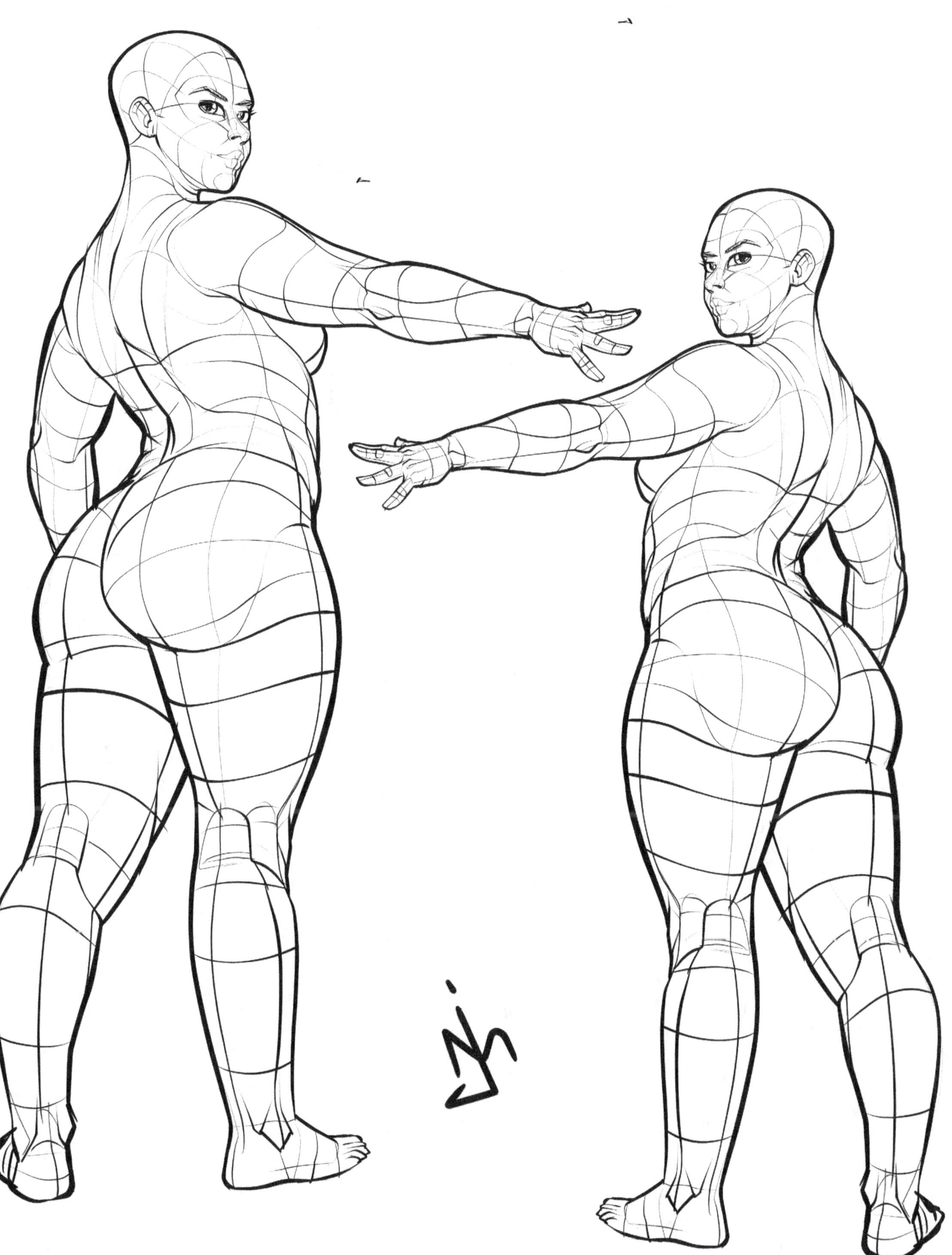

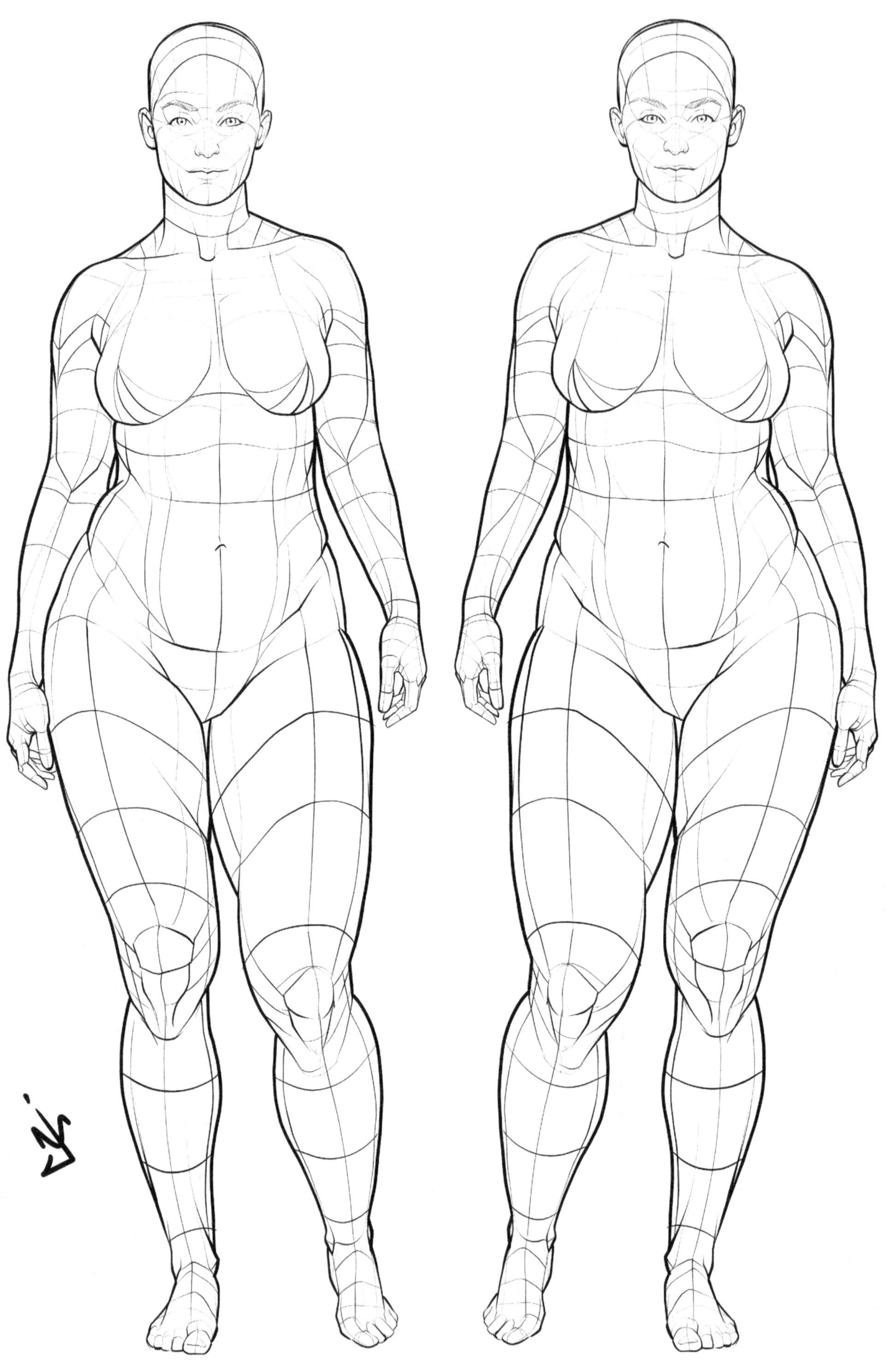

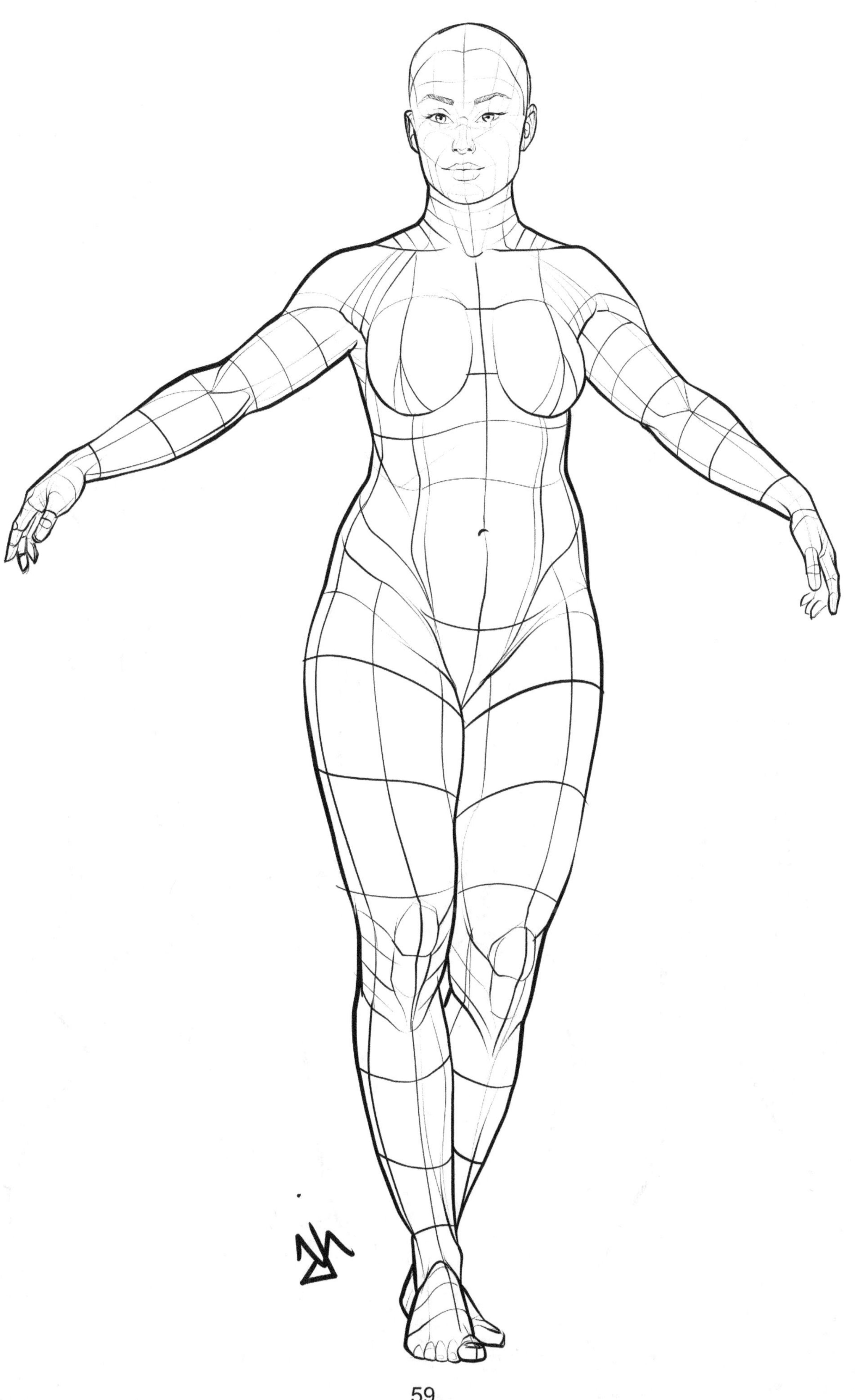

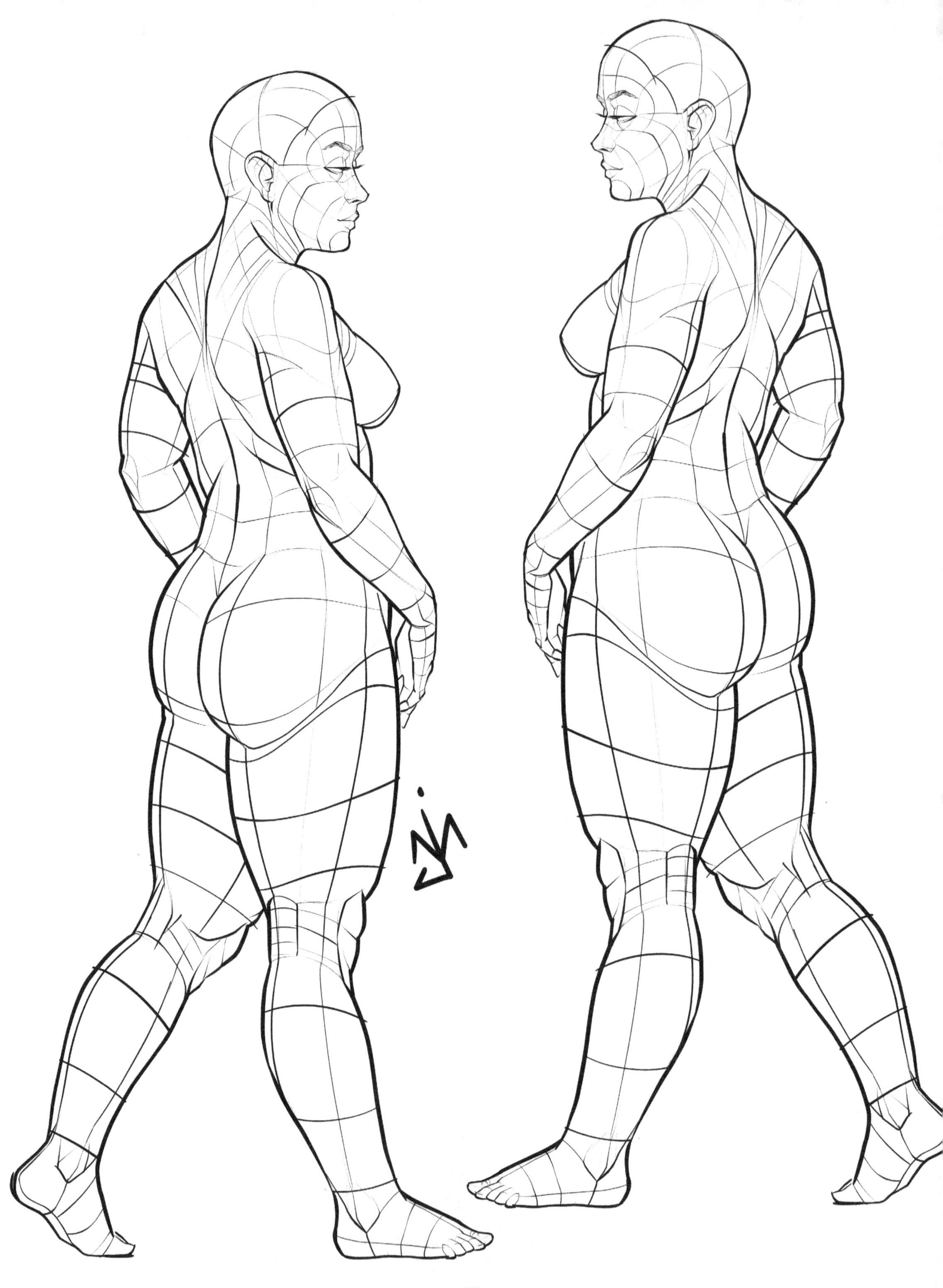

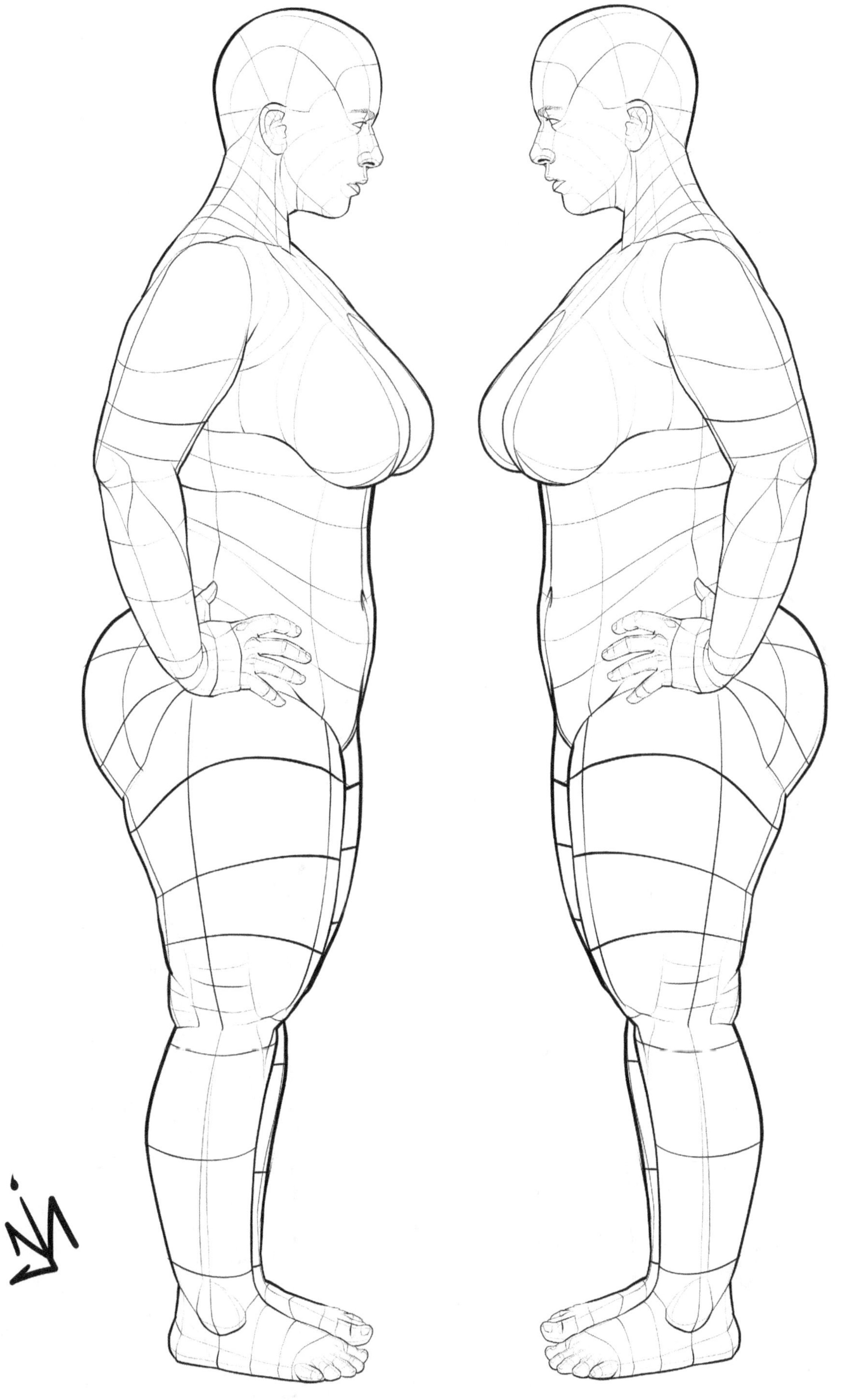

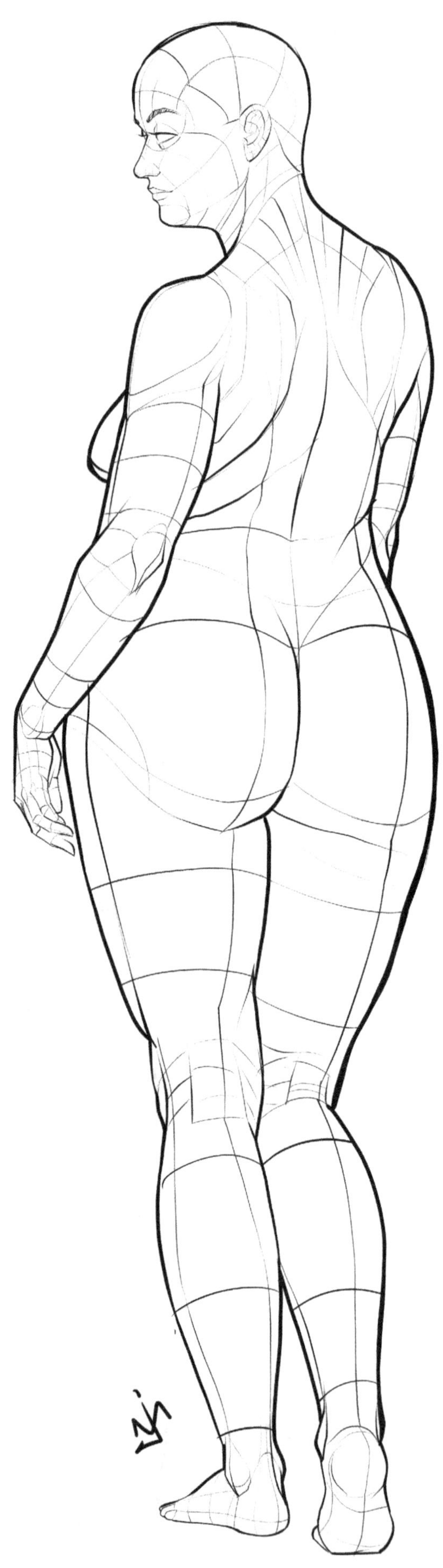
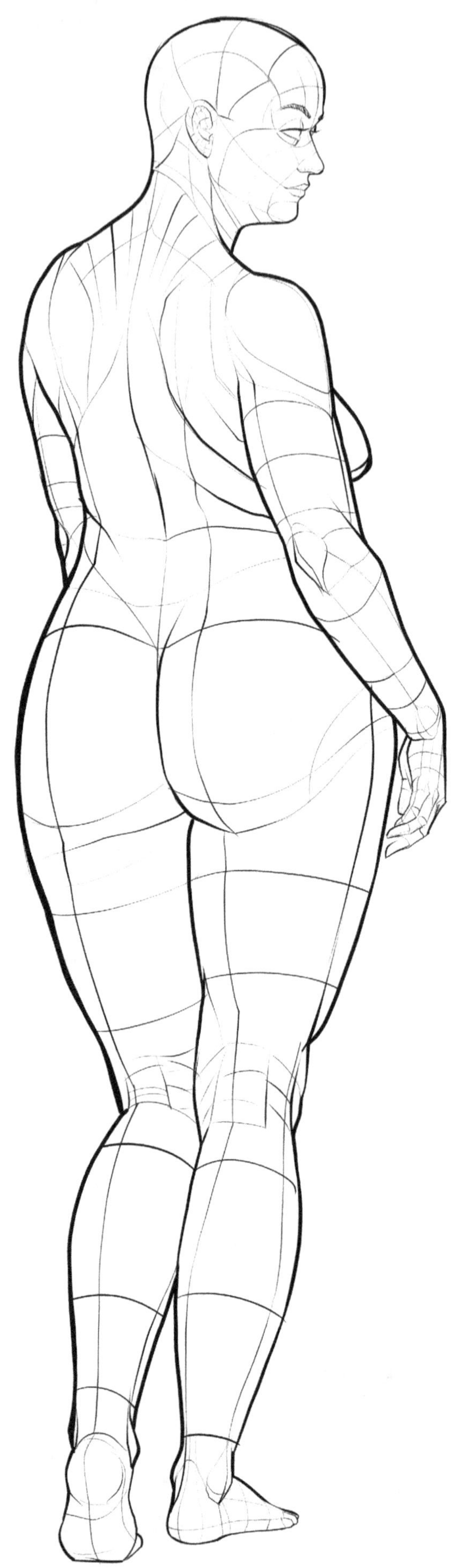

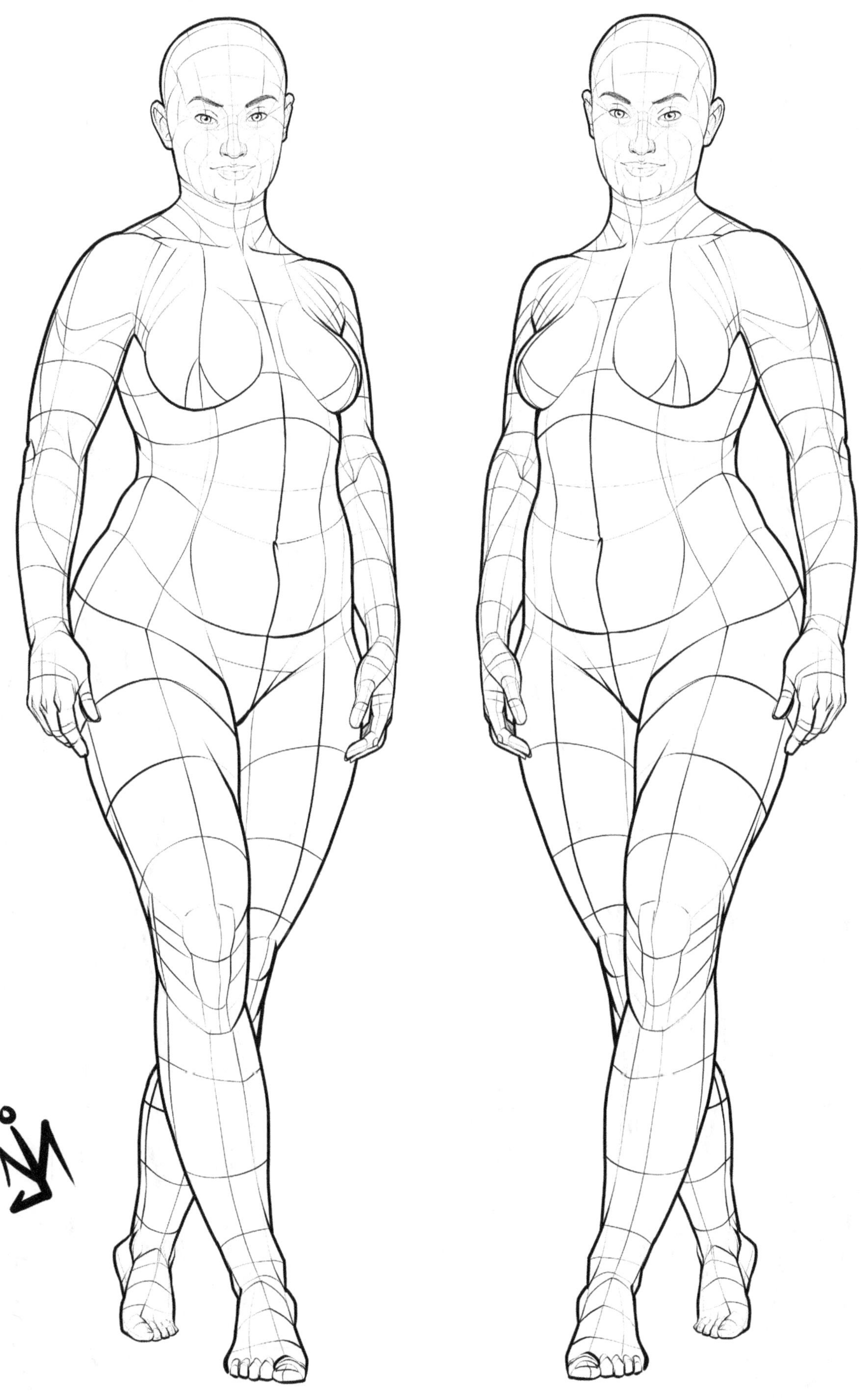

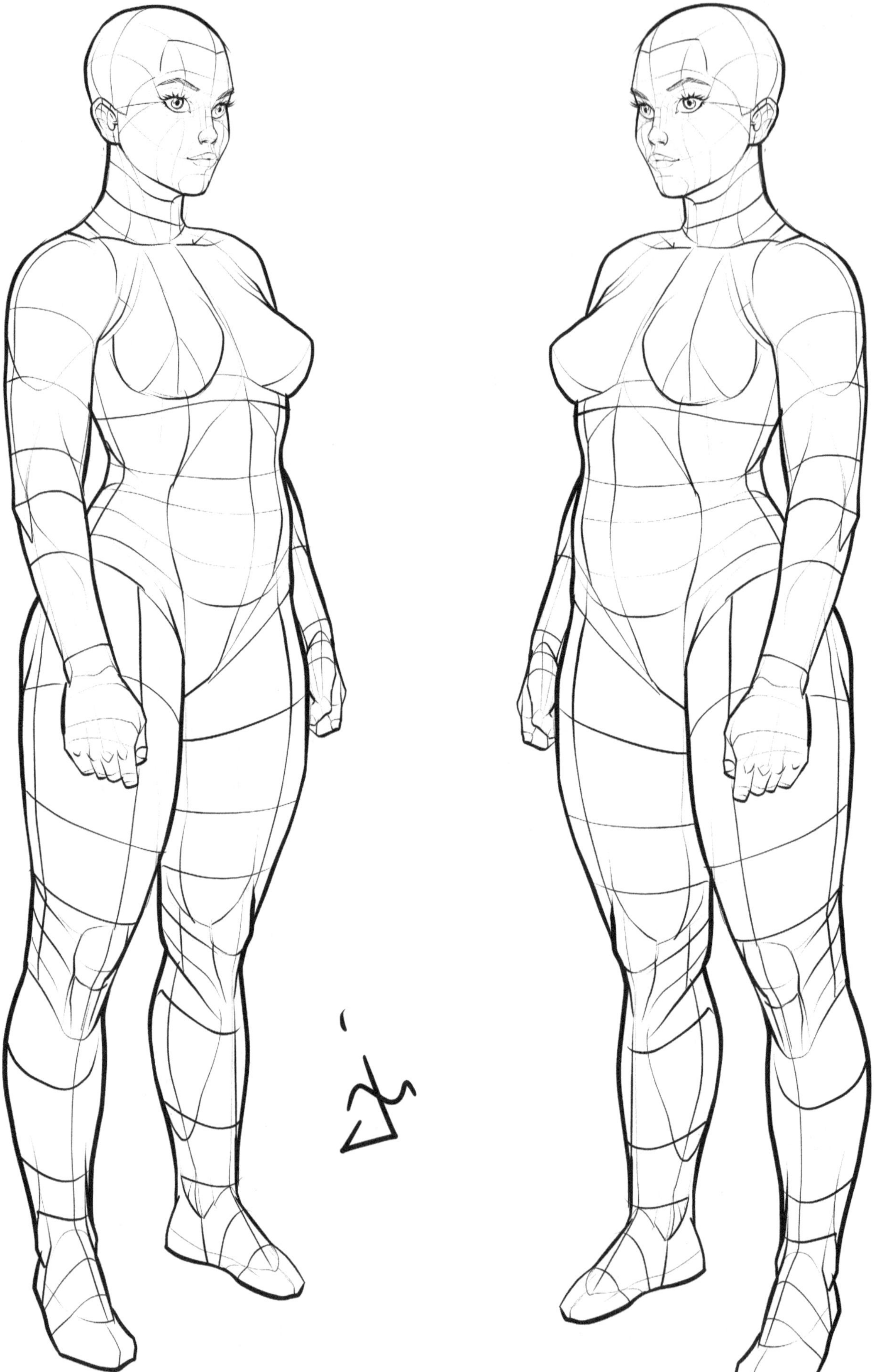

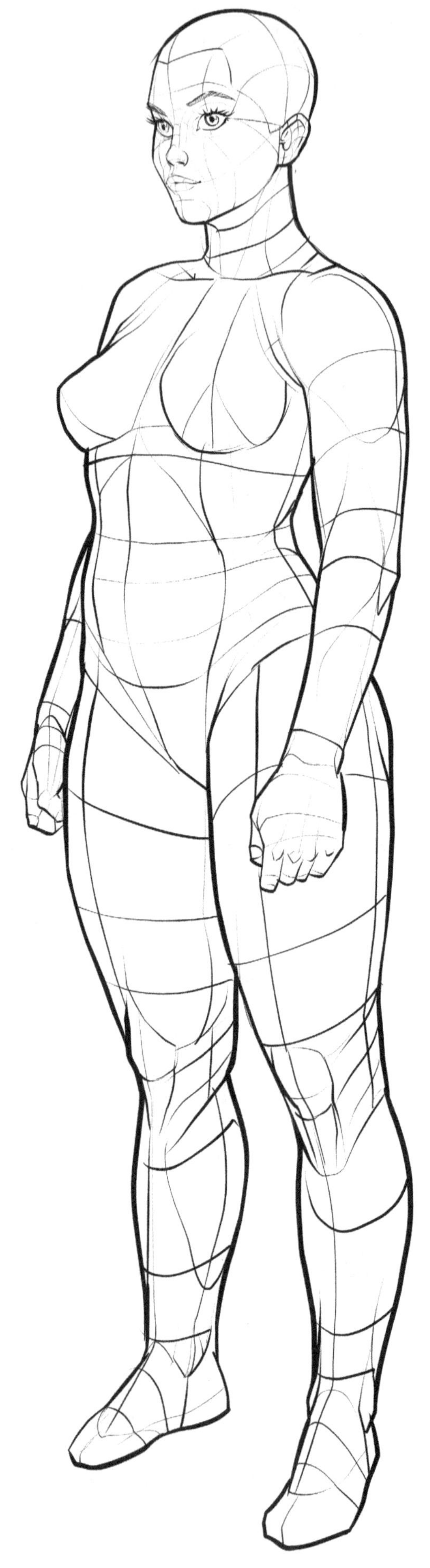

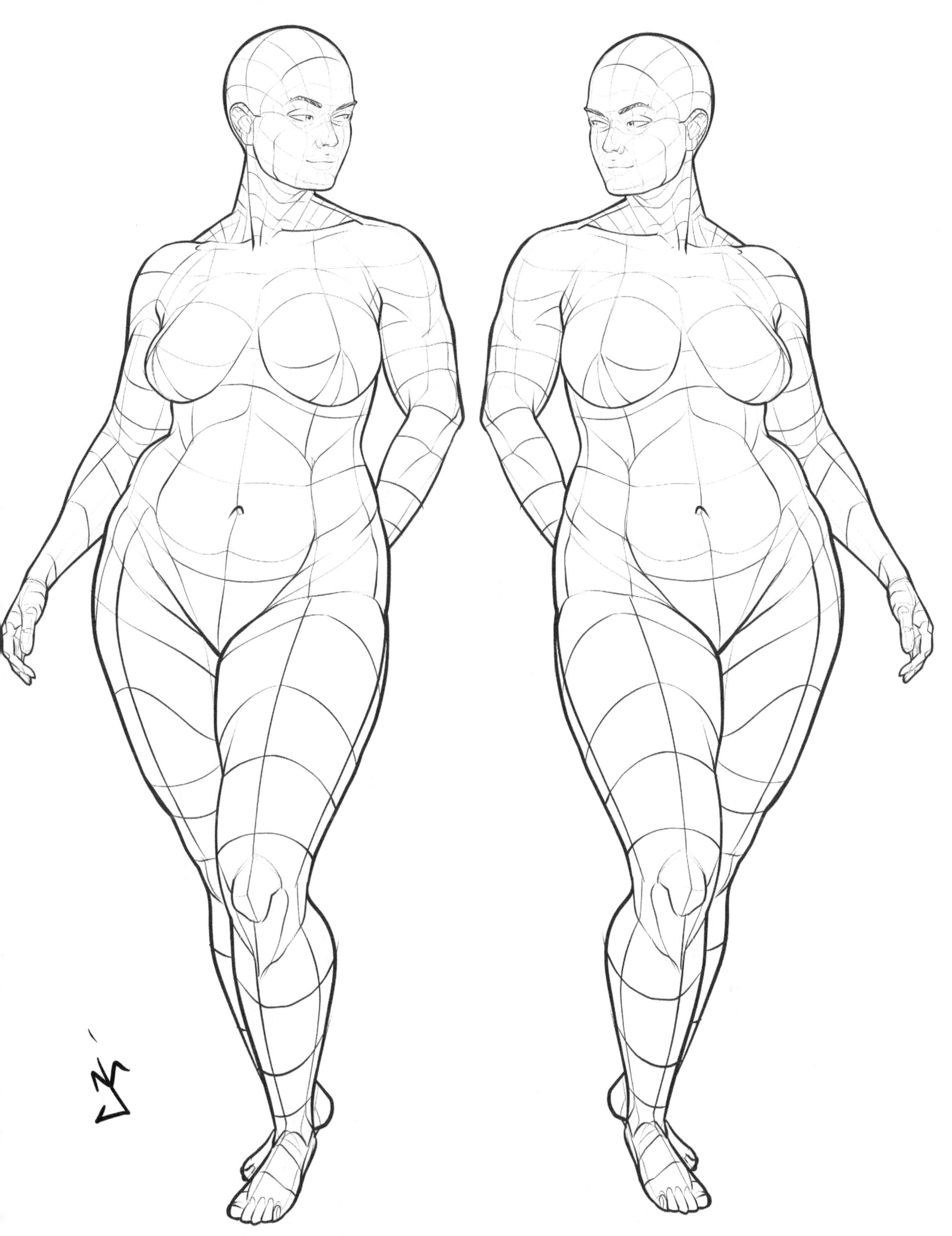

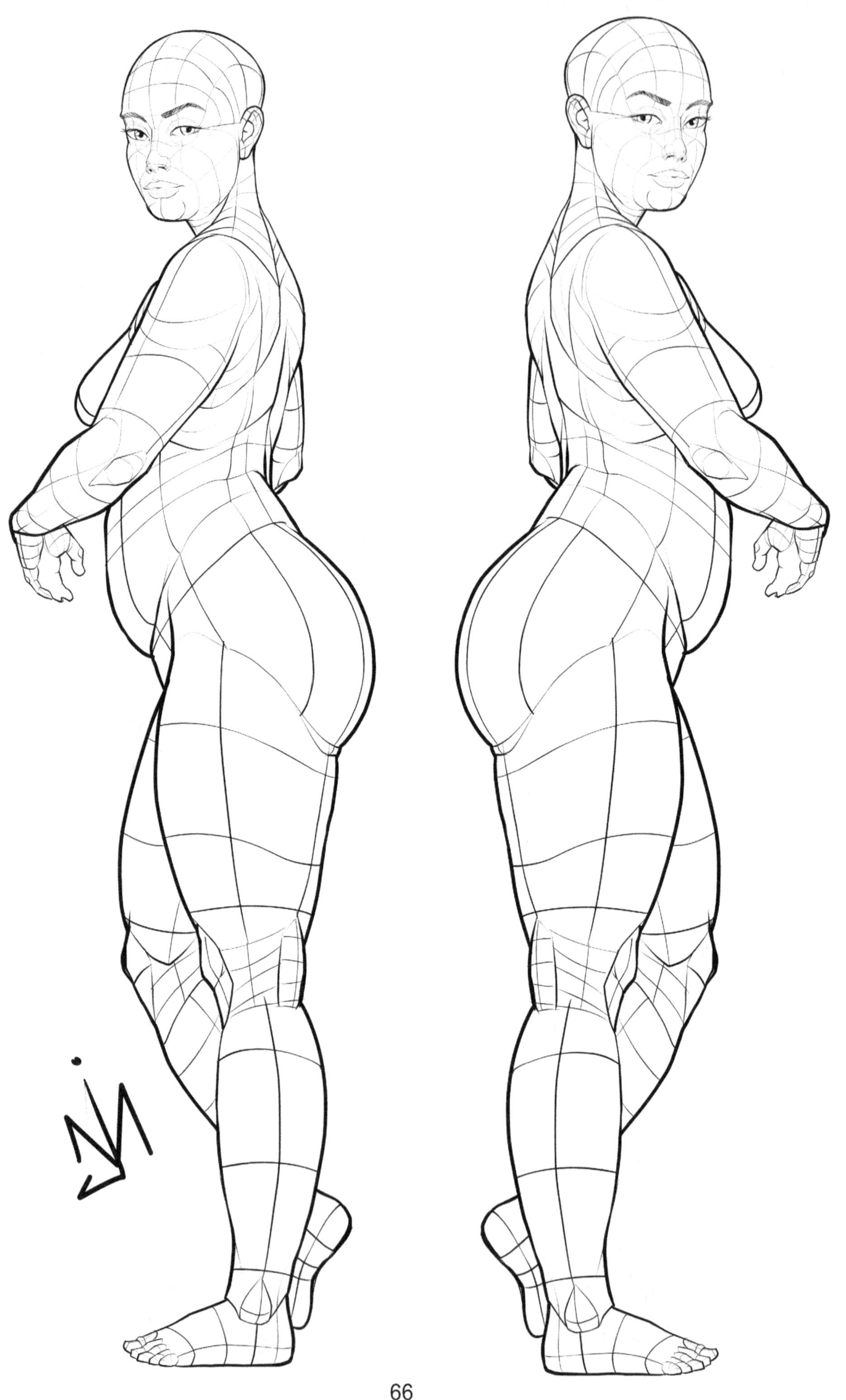

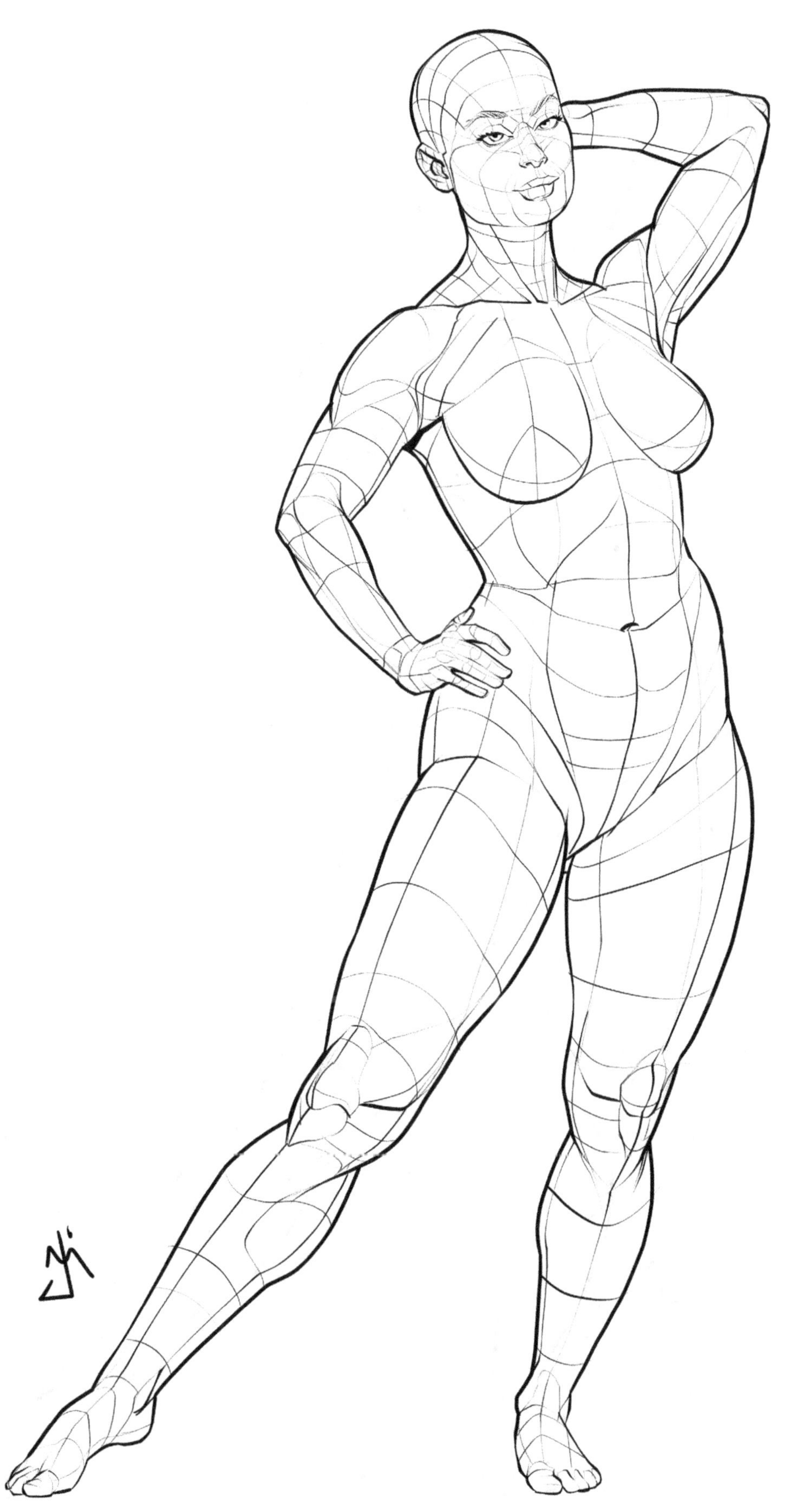

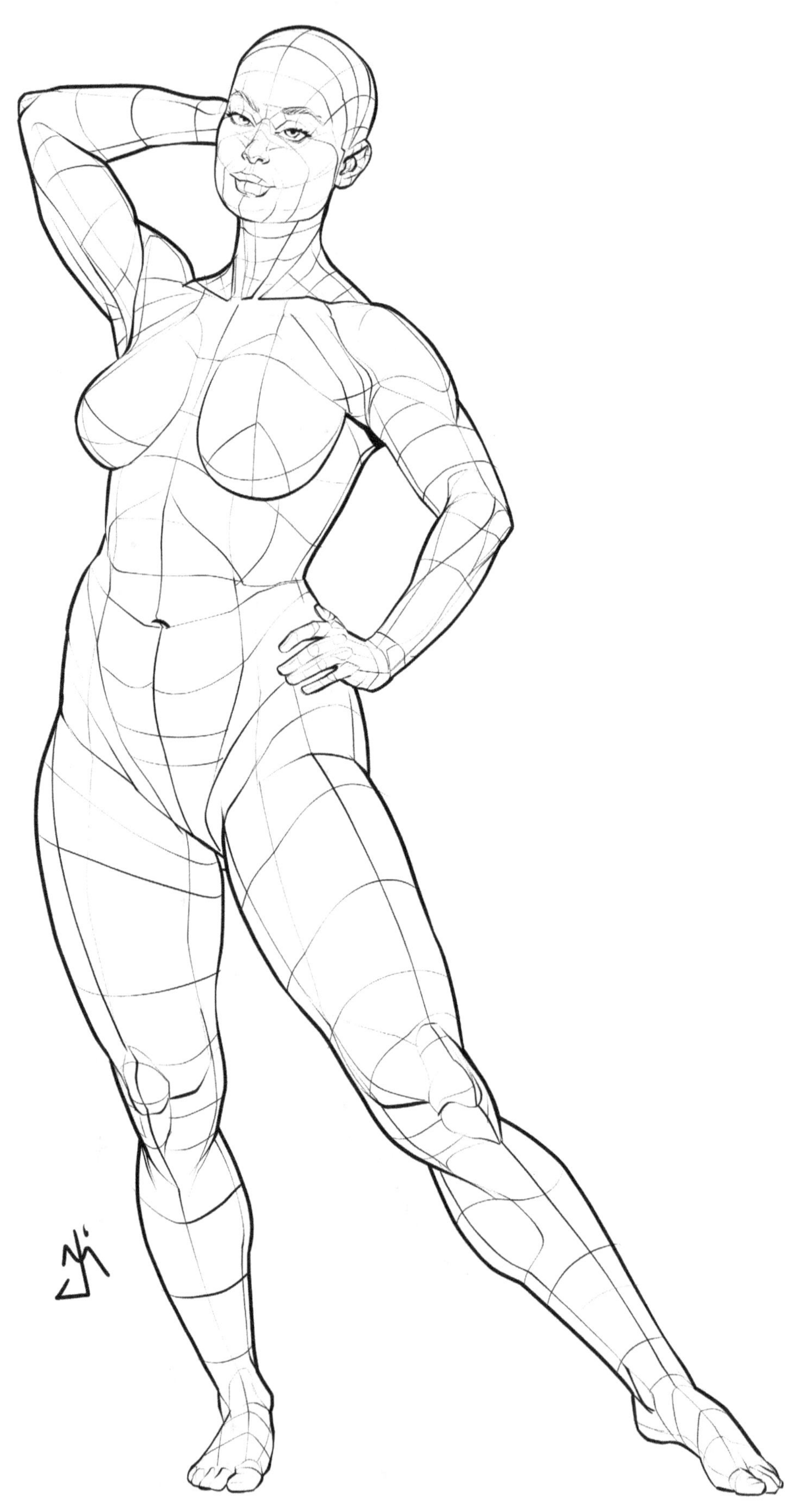

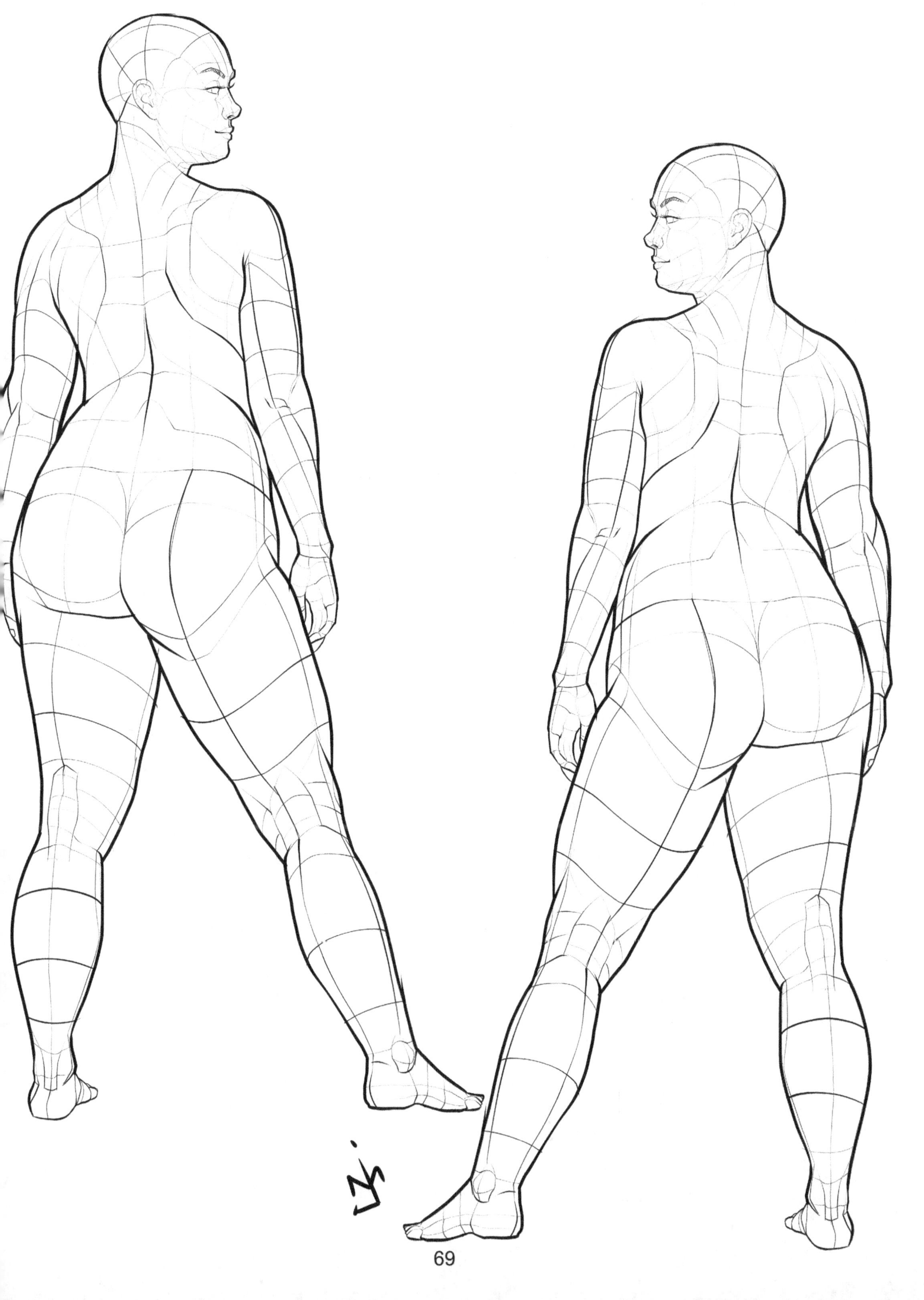

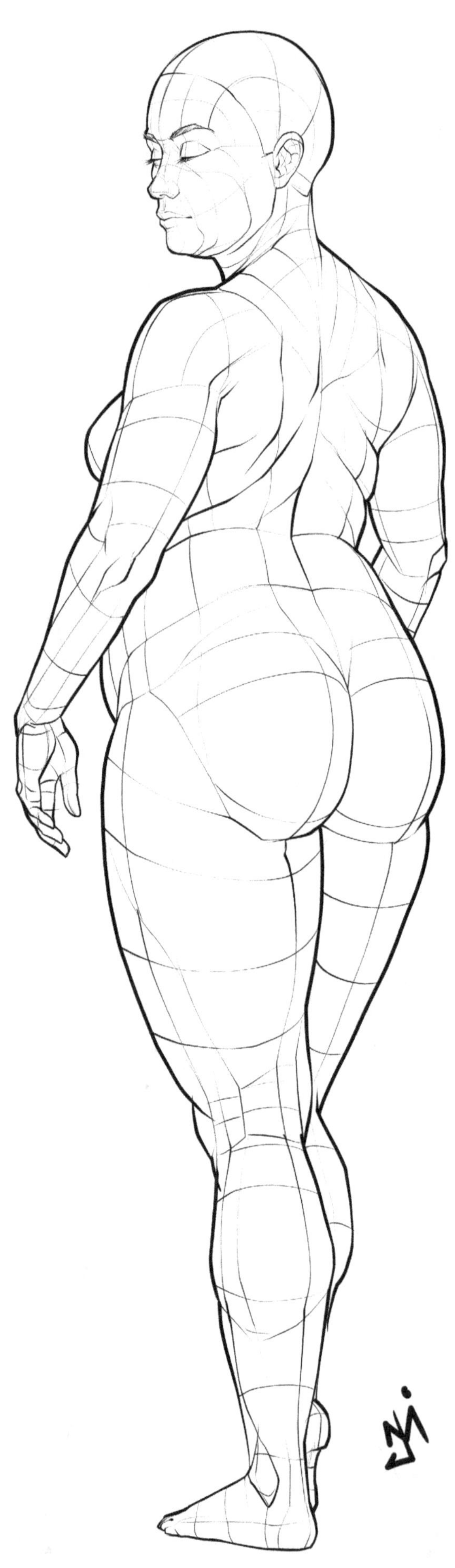
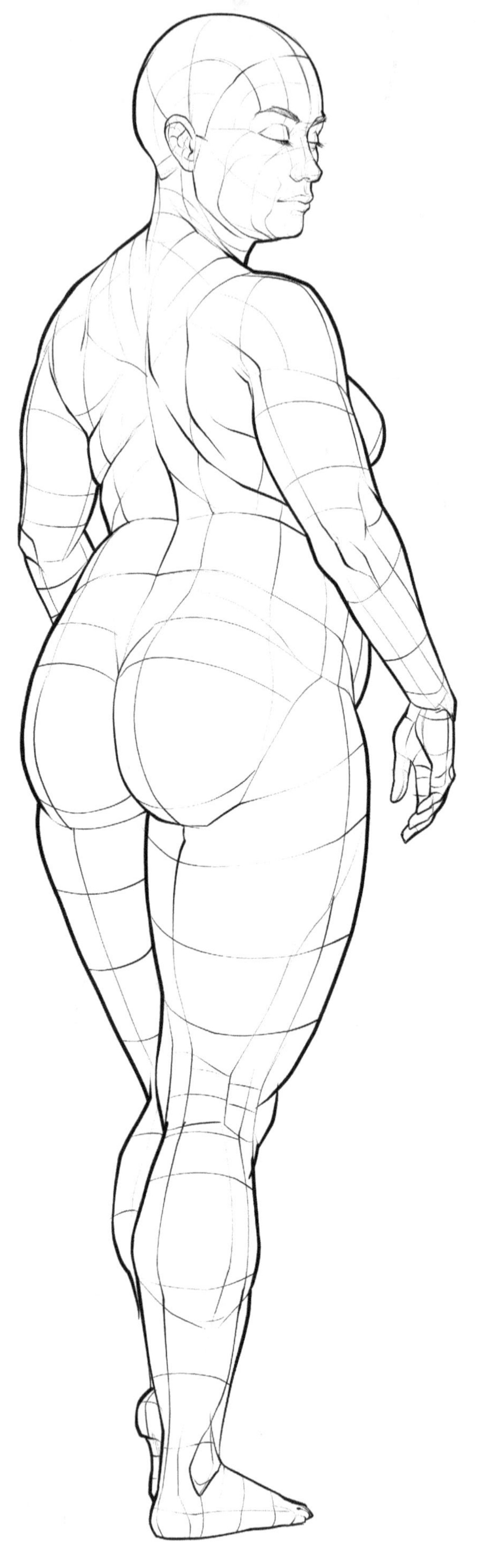

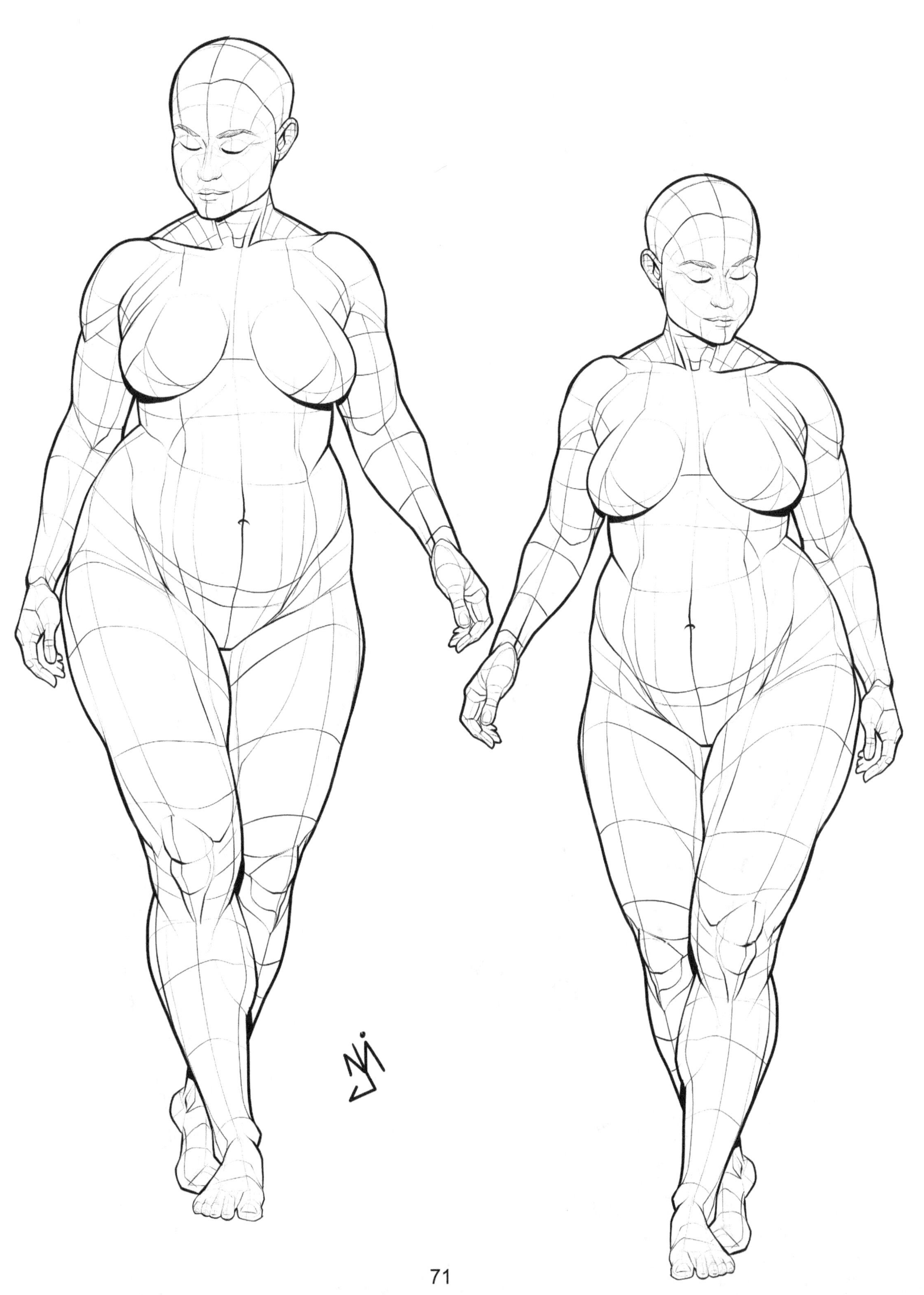

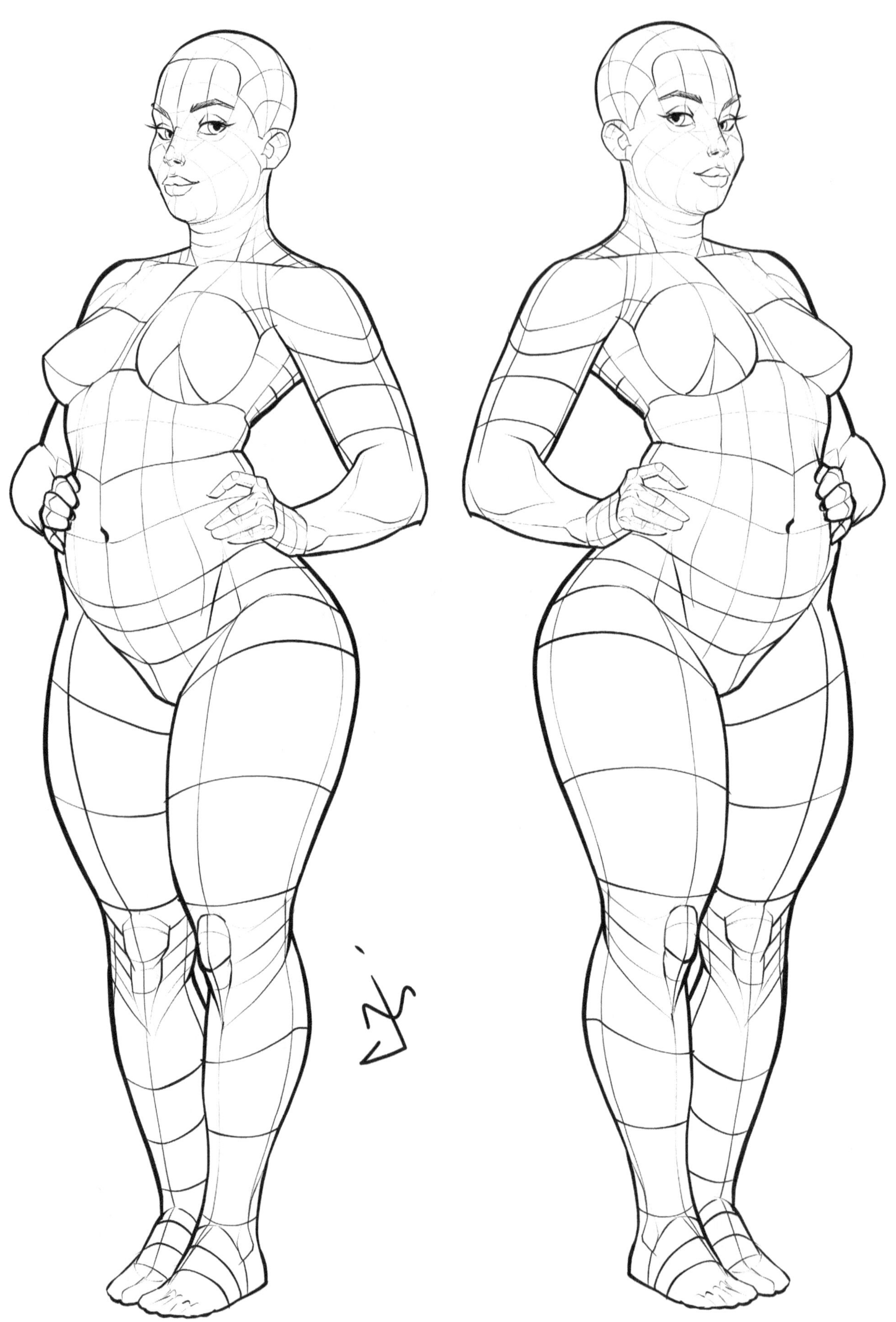

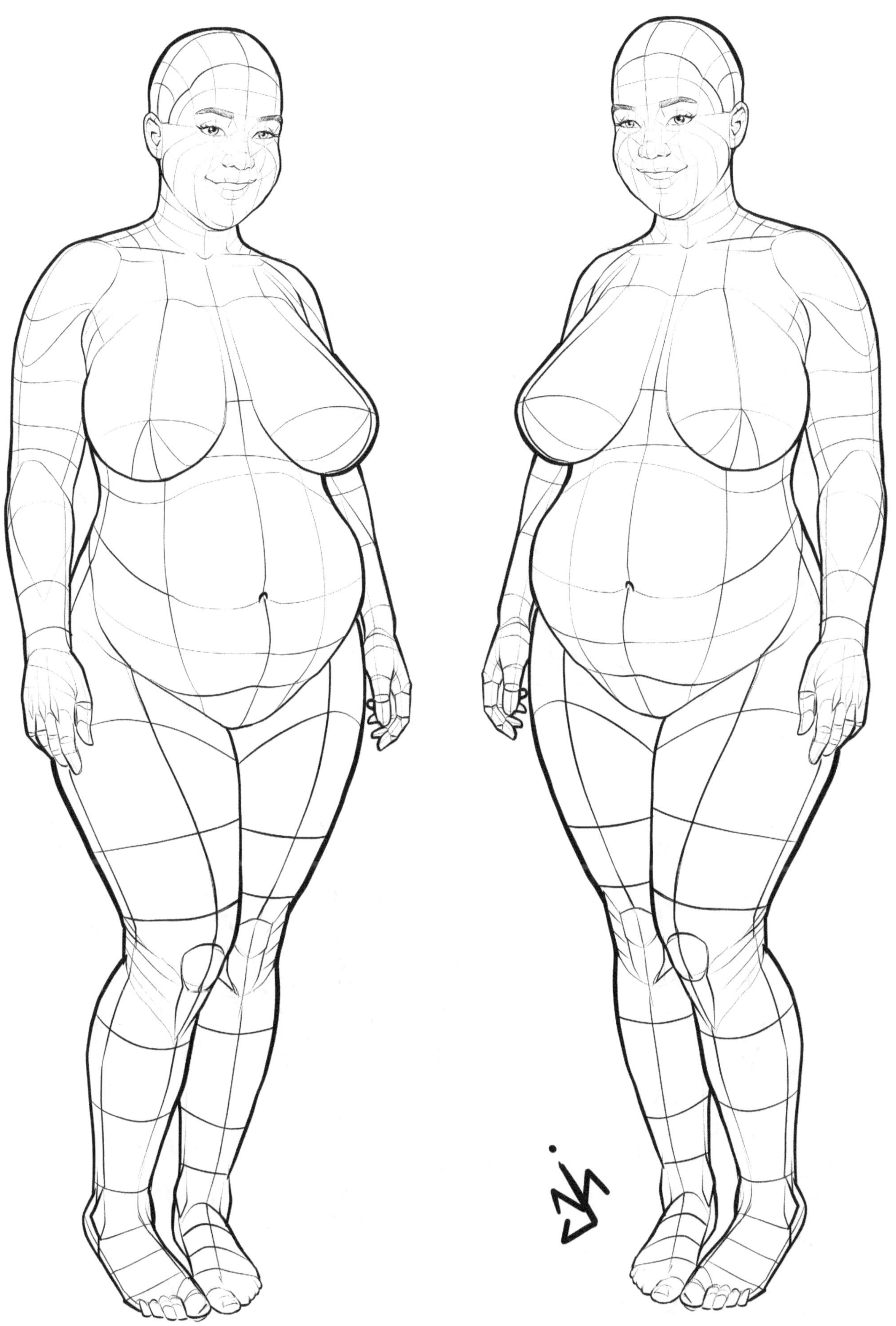

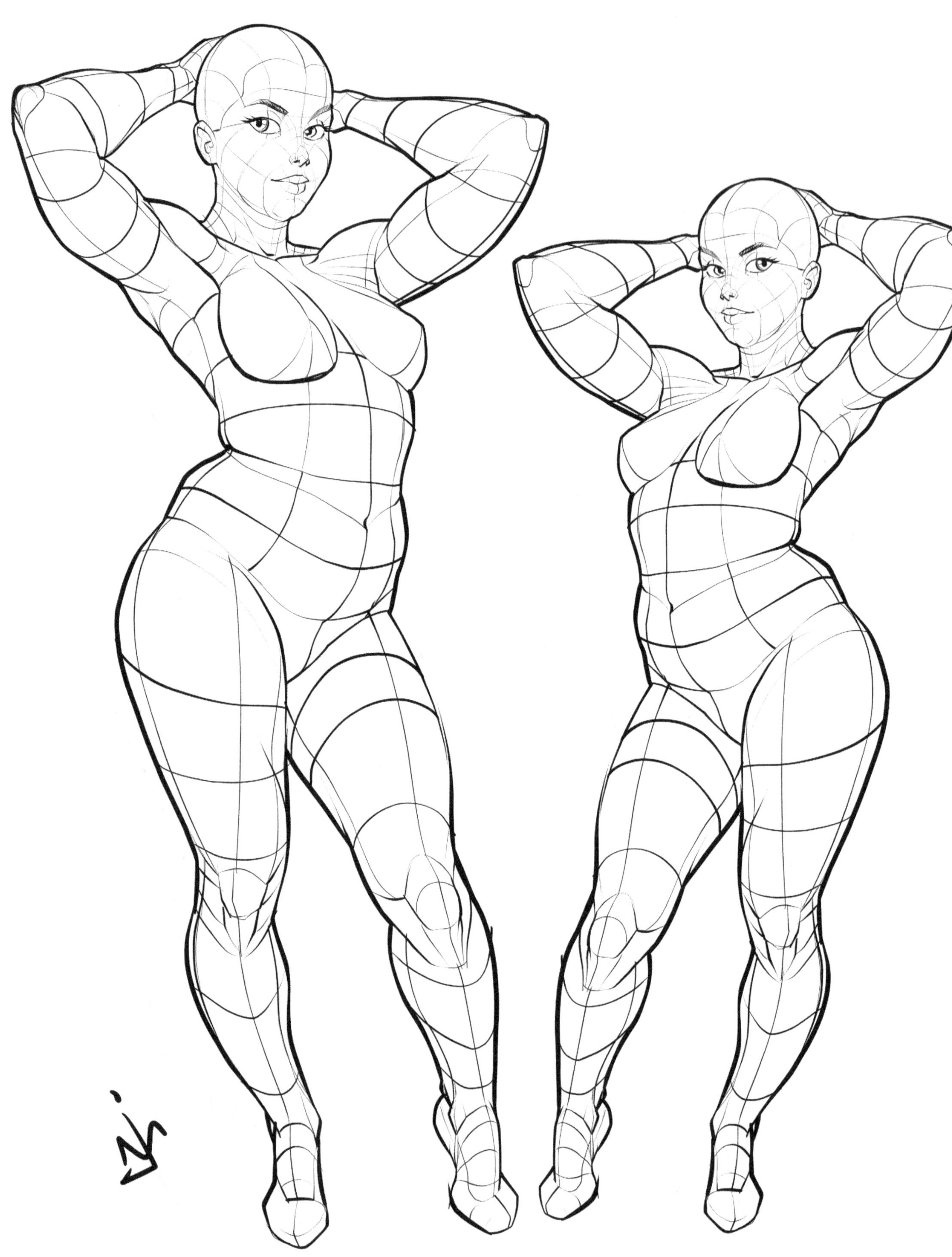

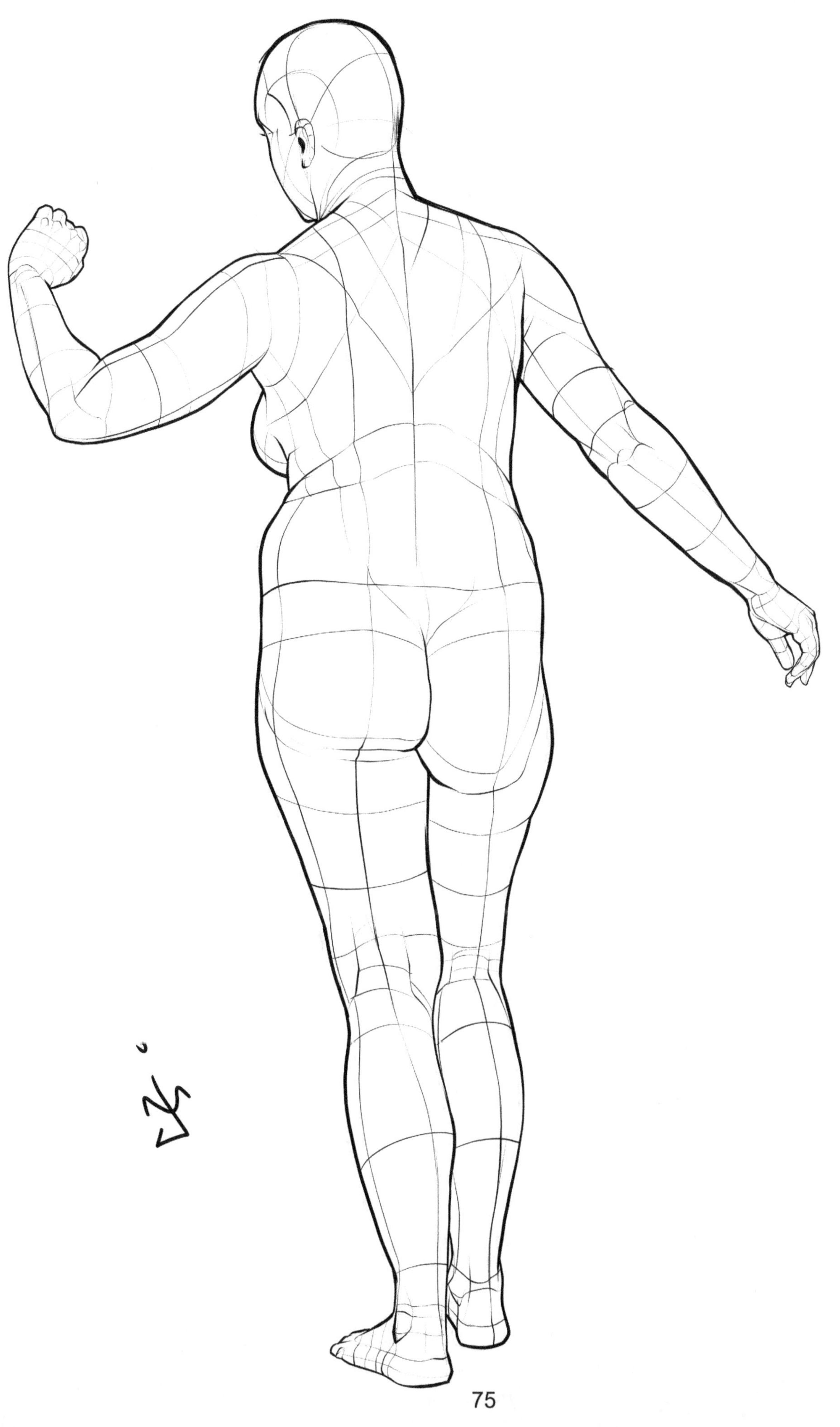

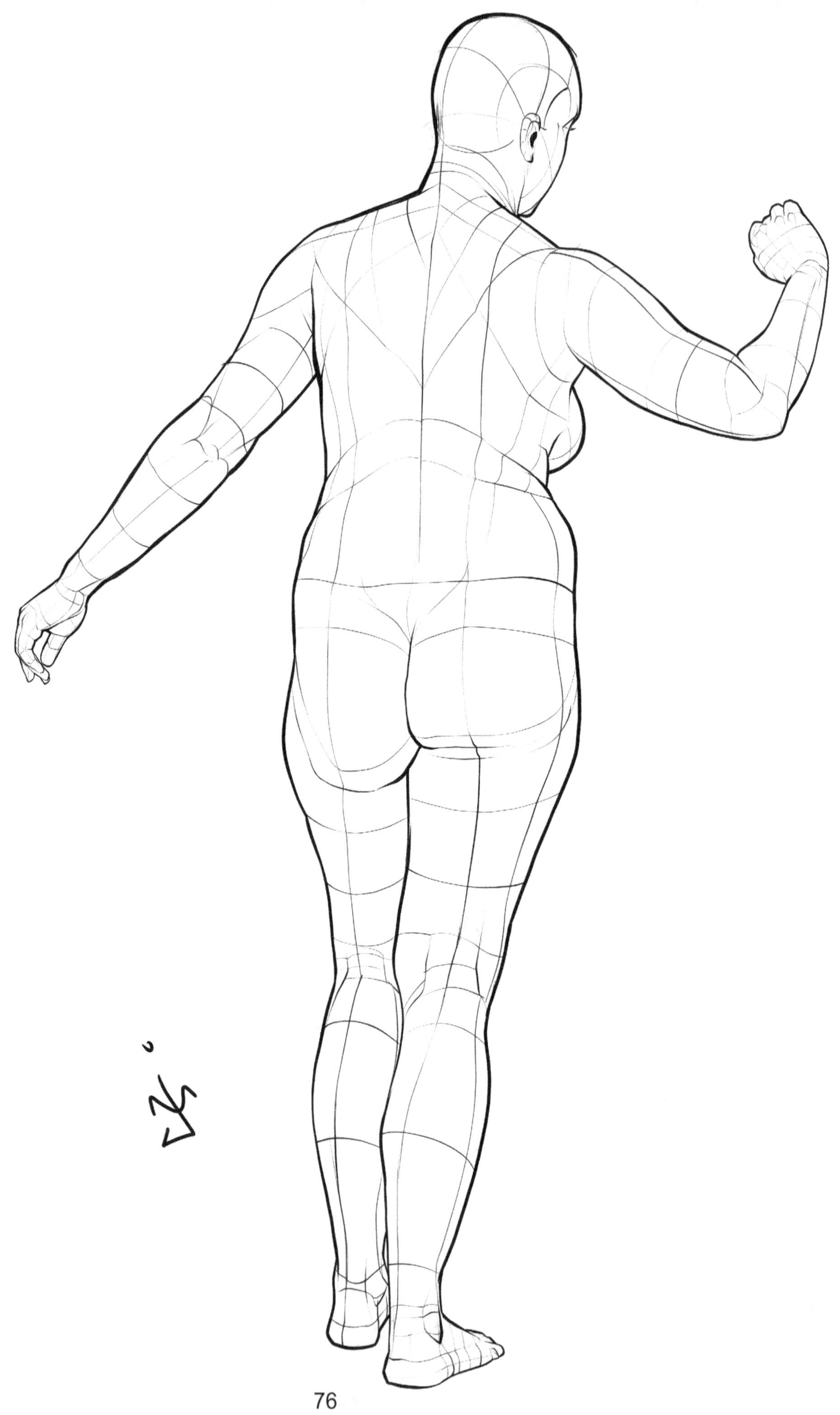

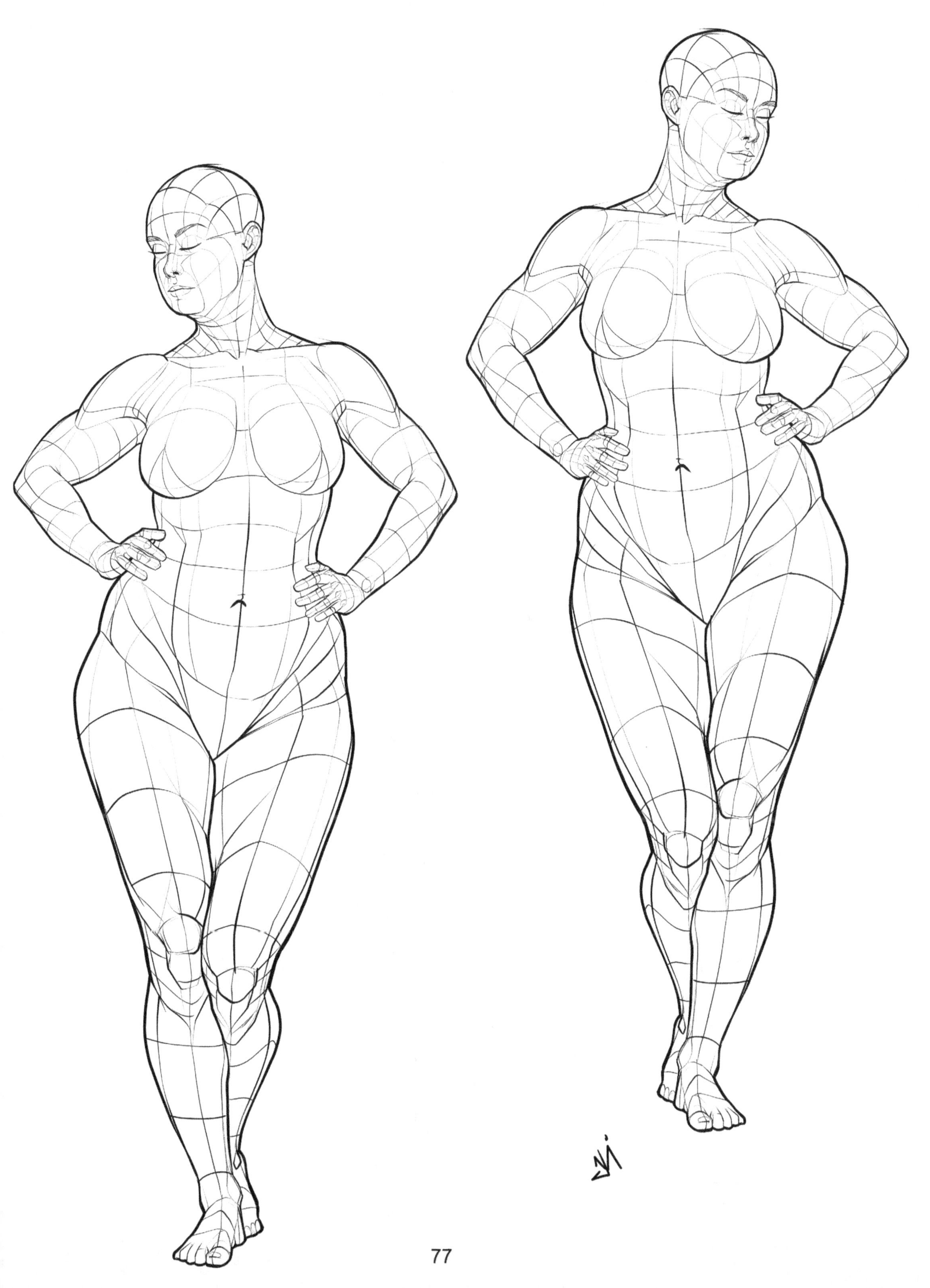

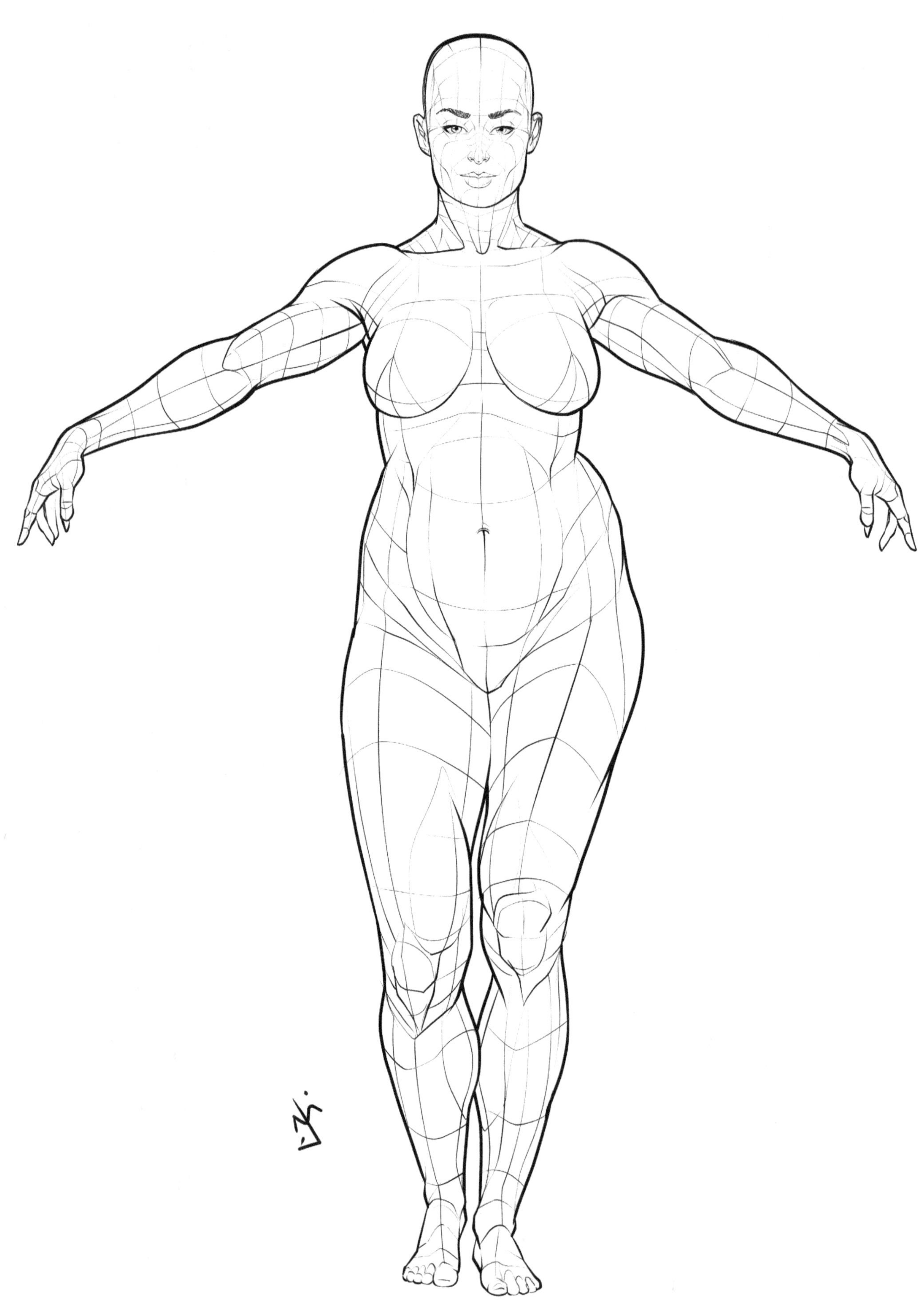

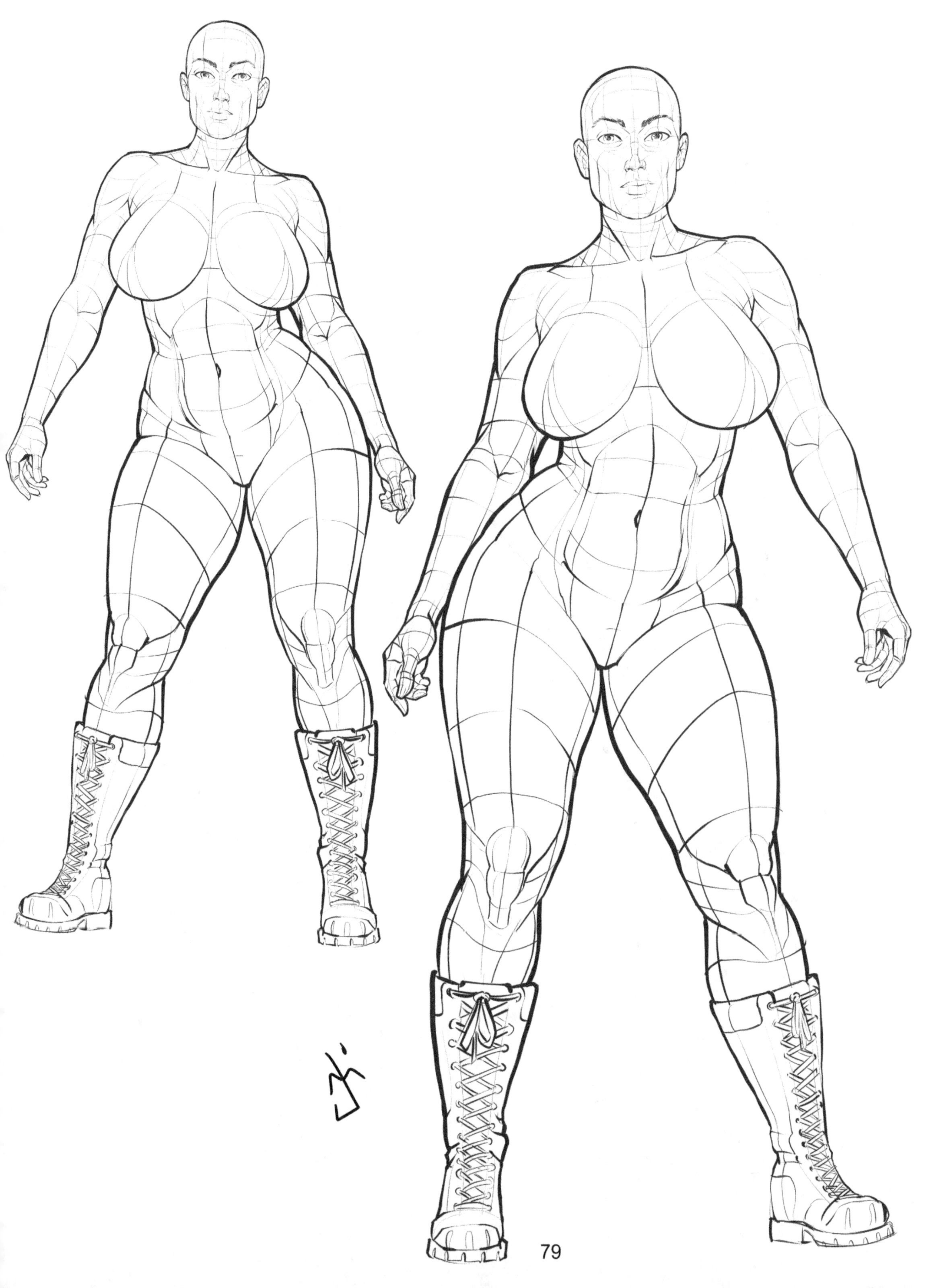

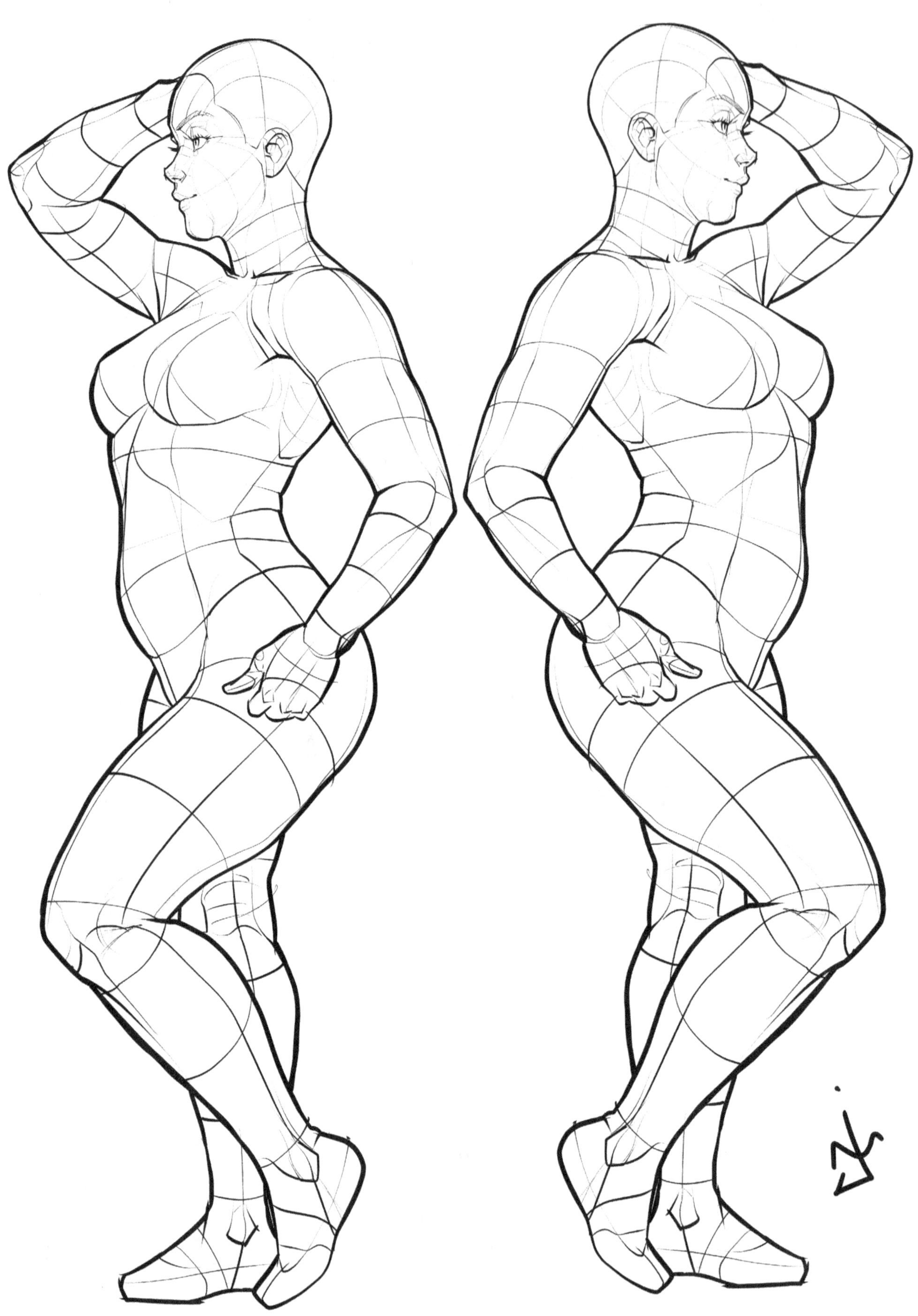

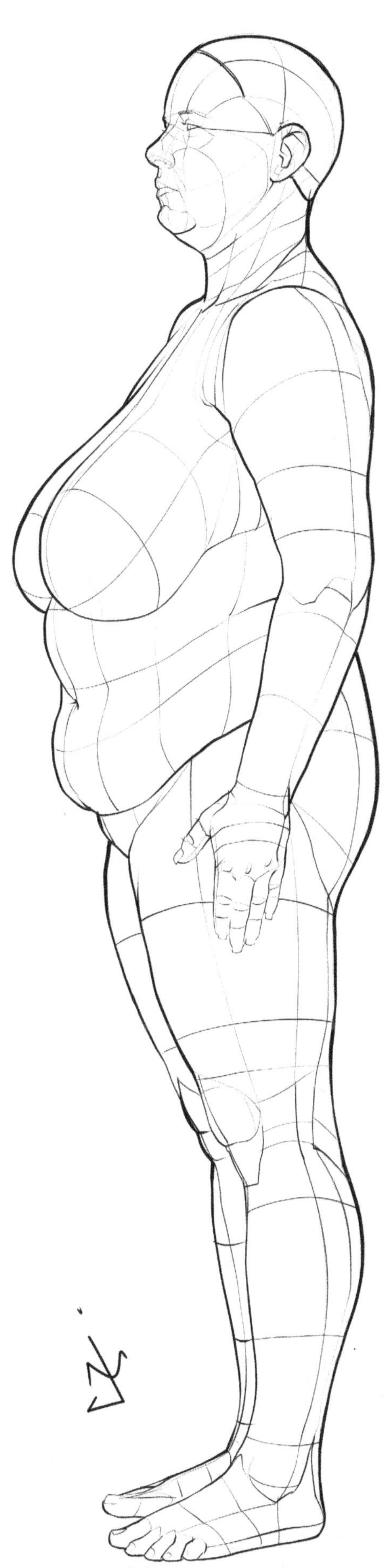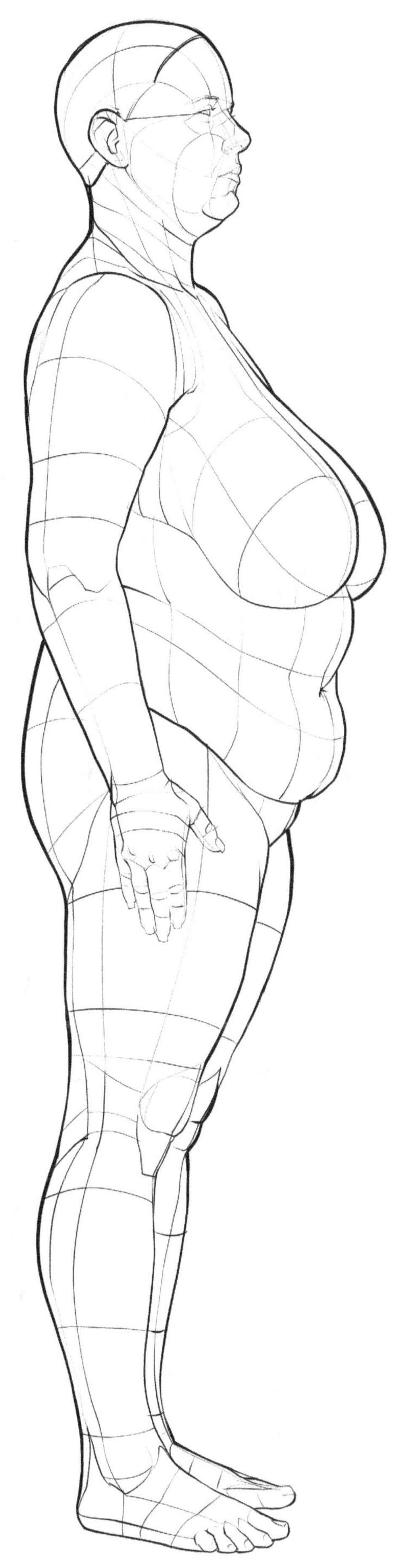

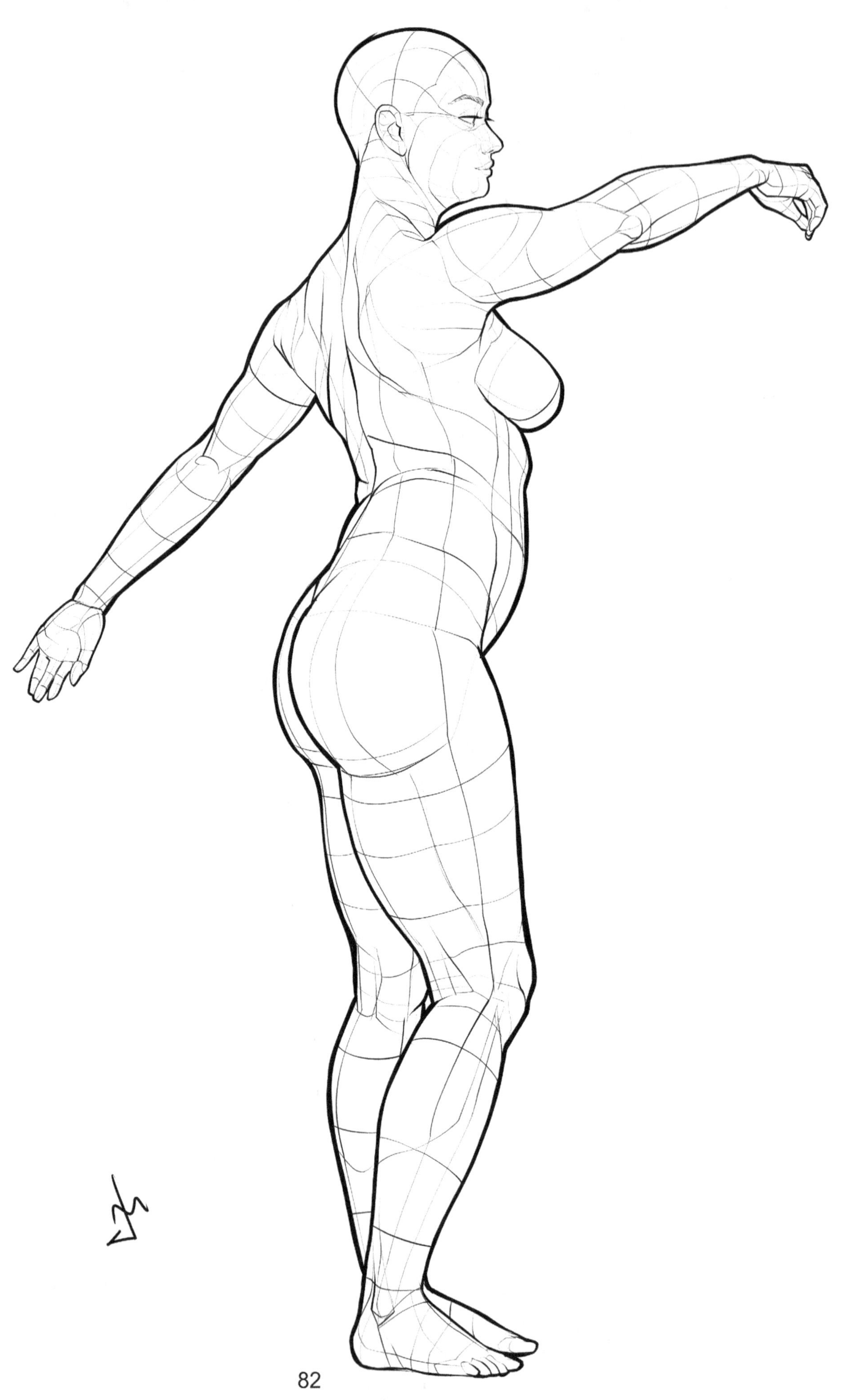

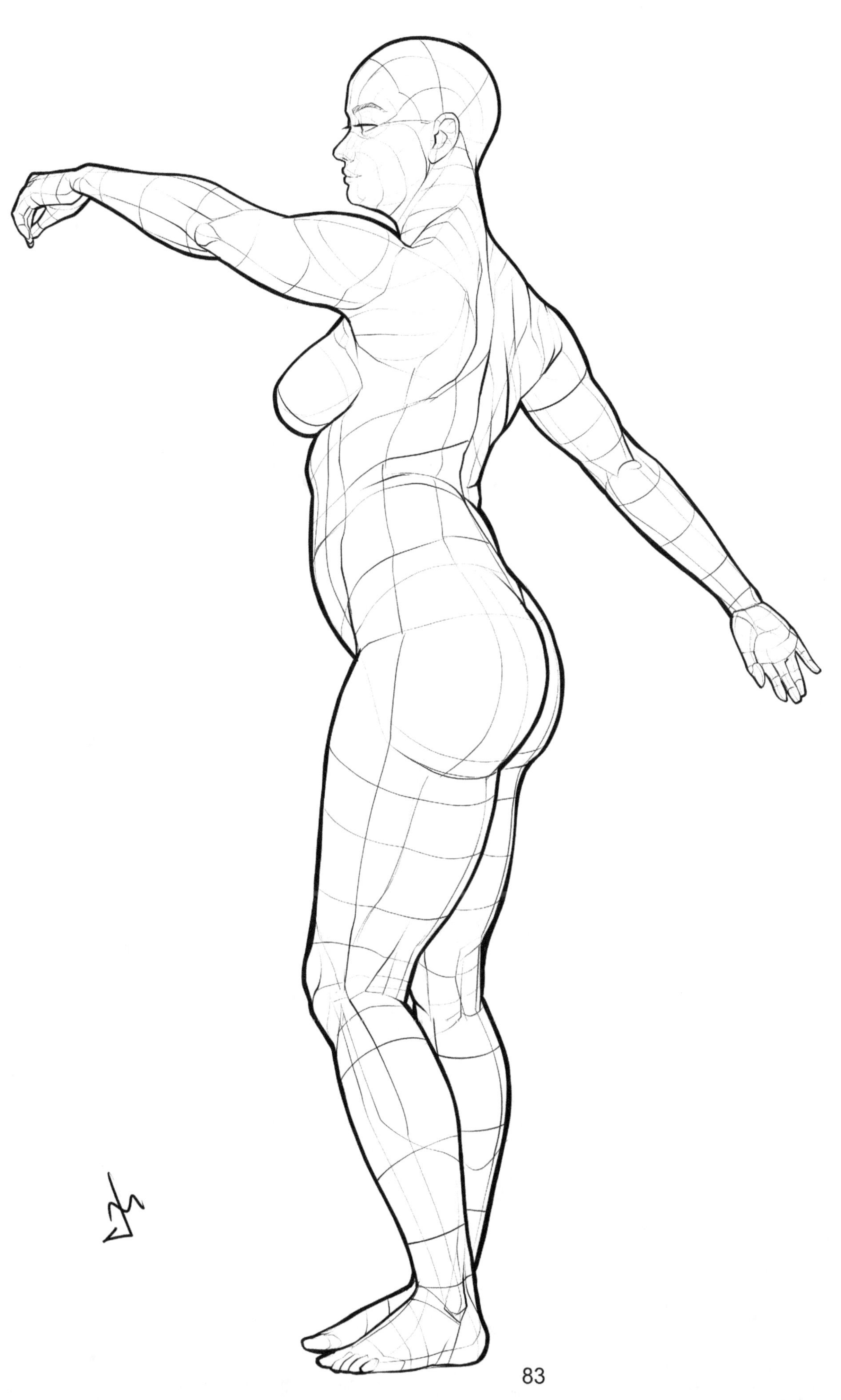

Active Poses

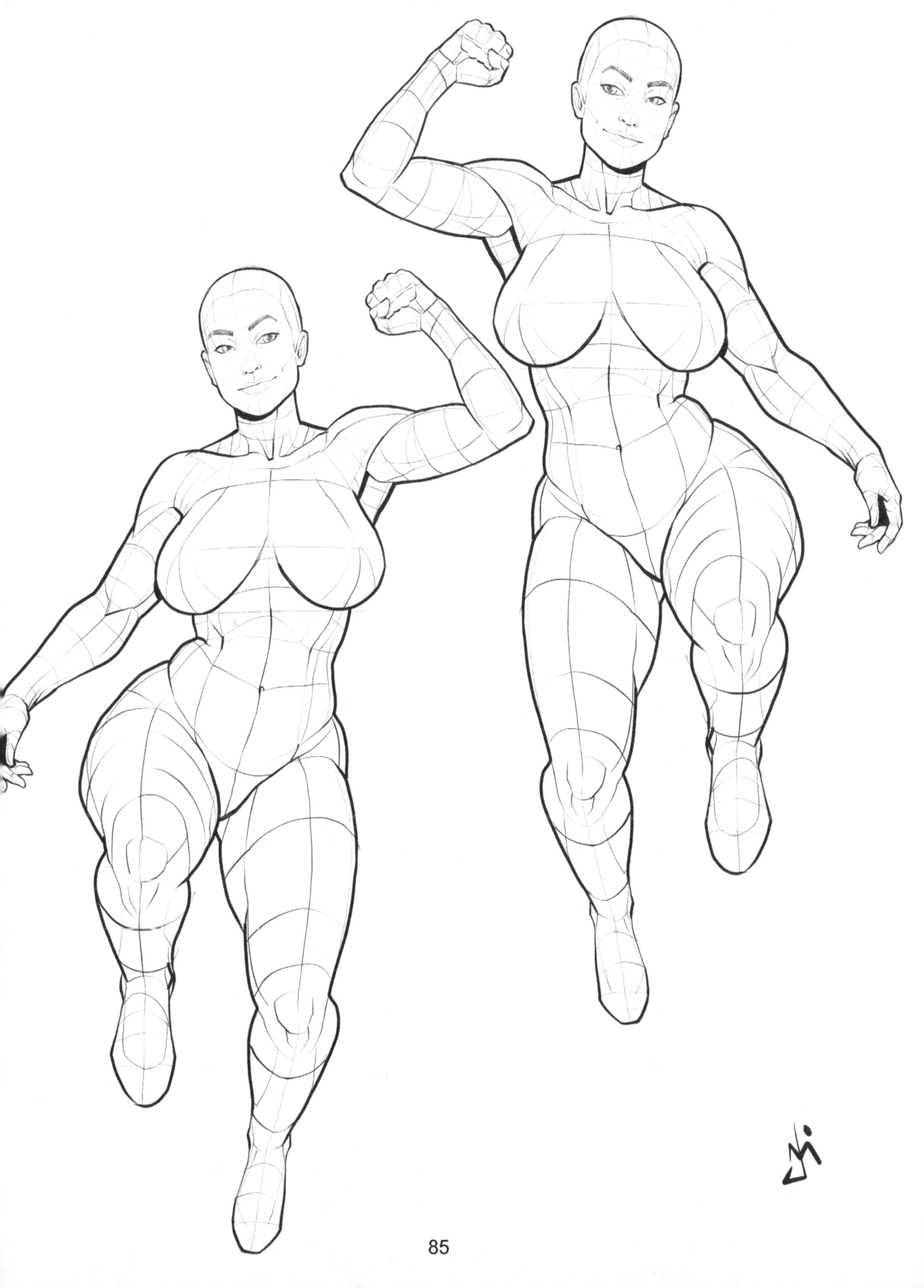

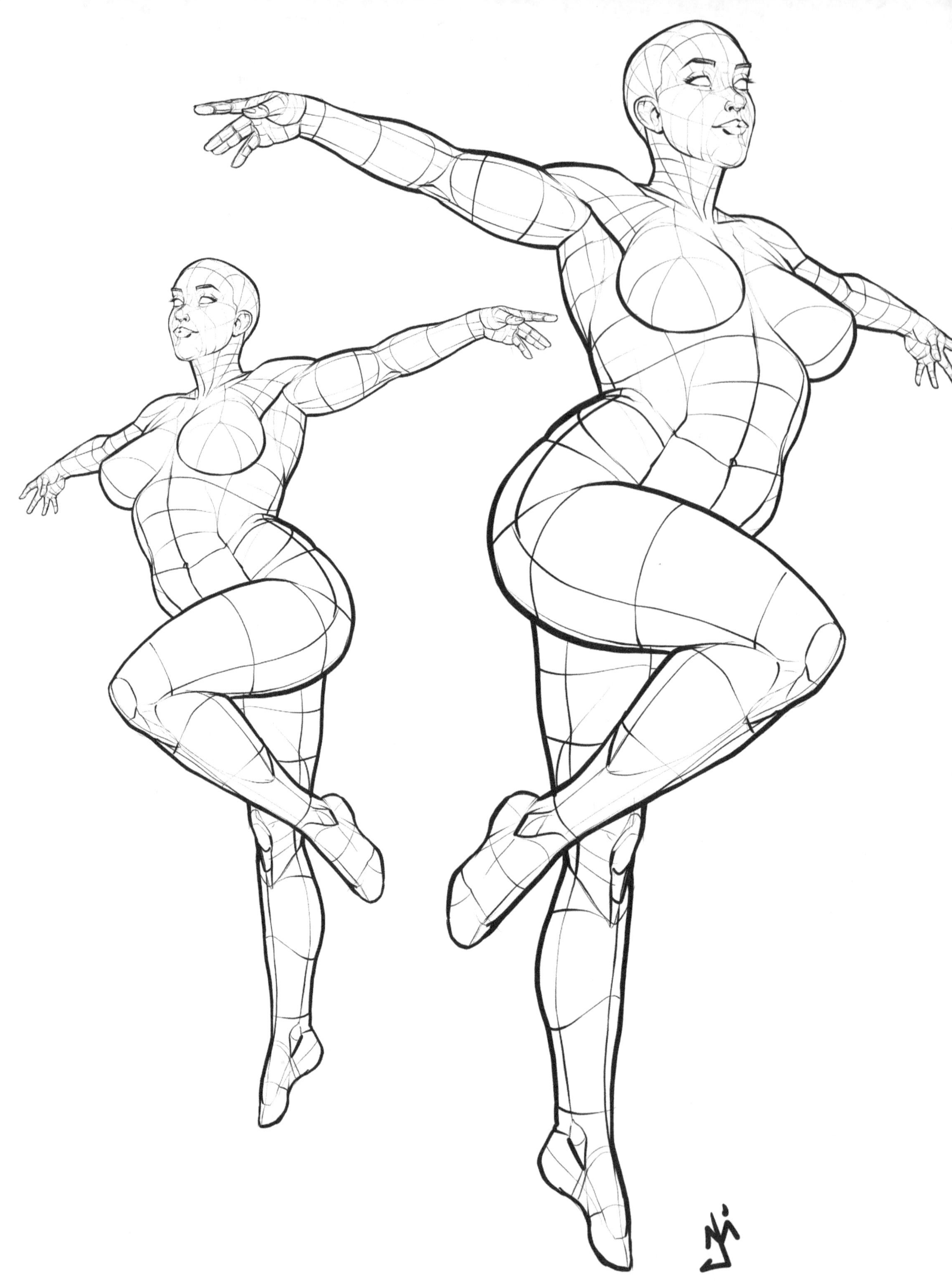

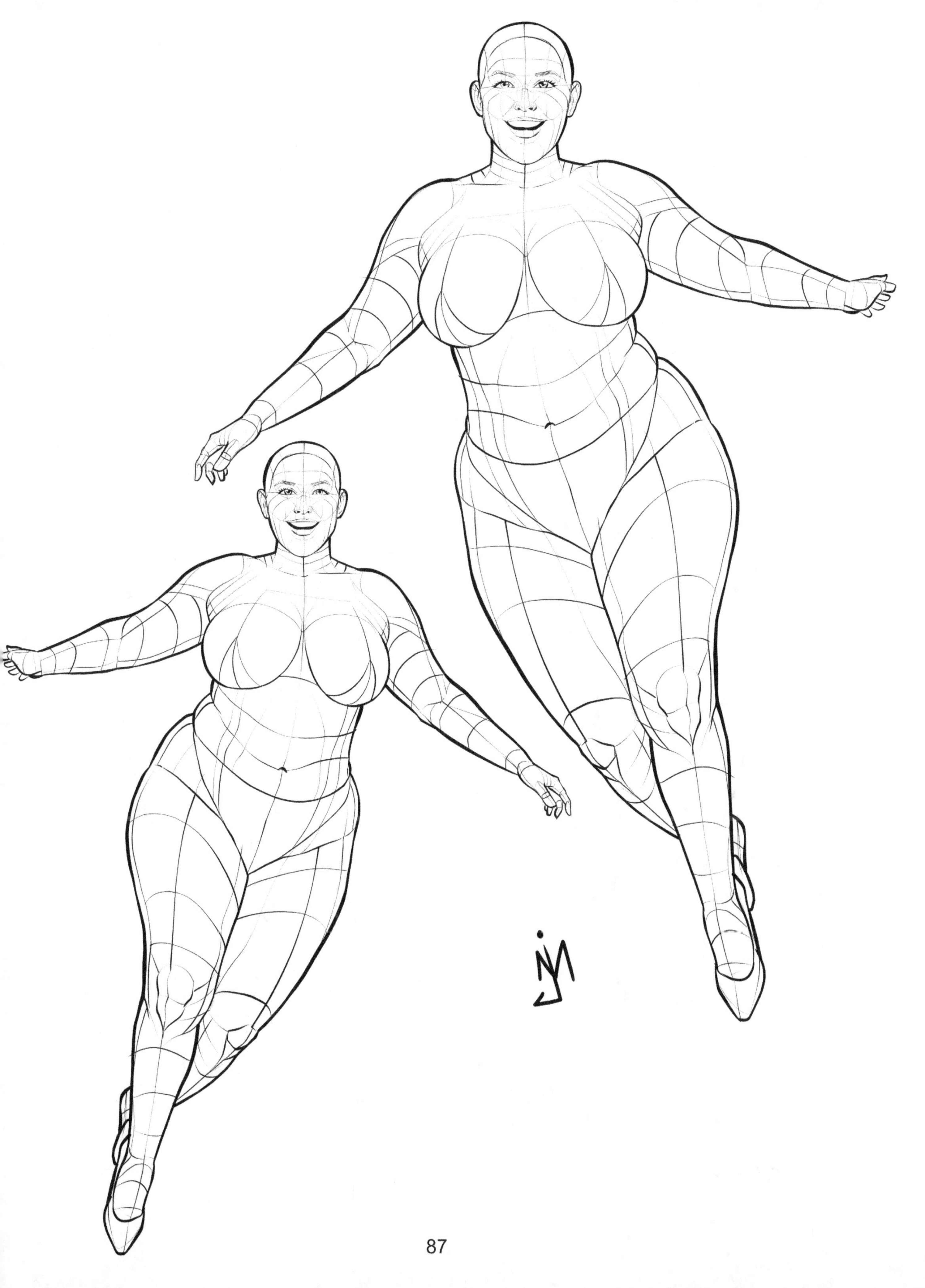

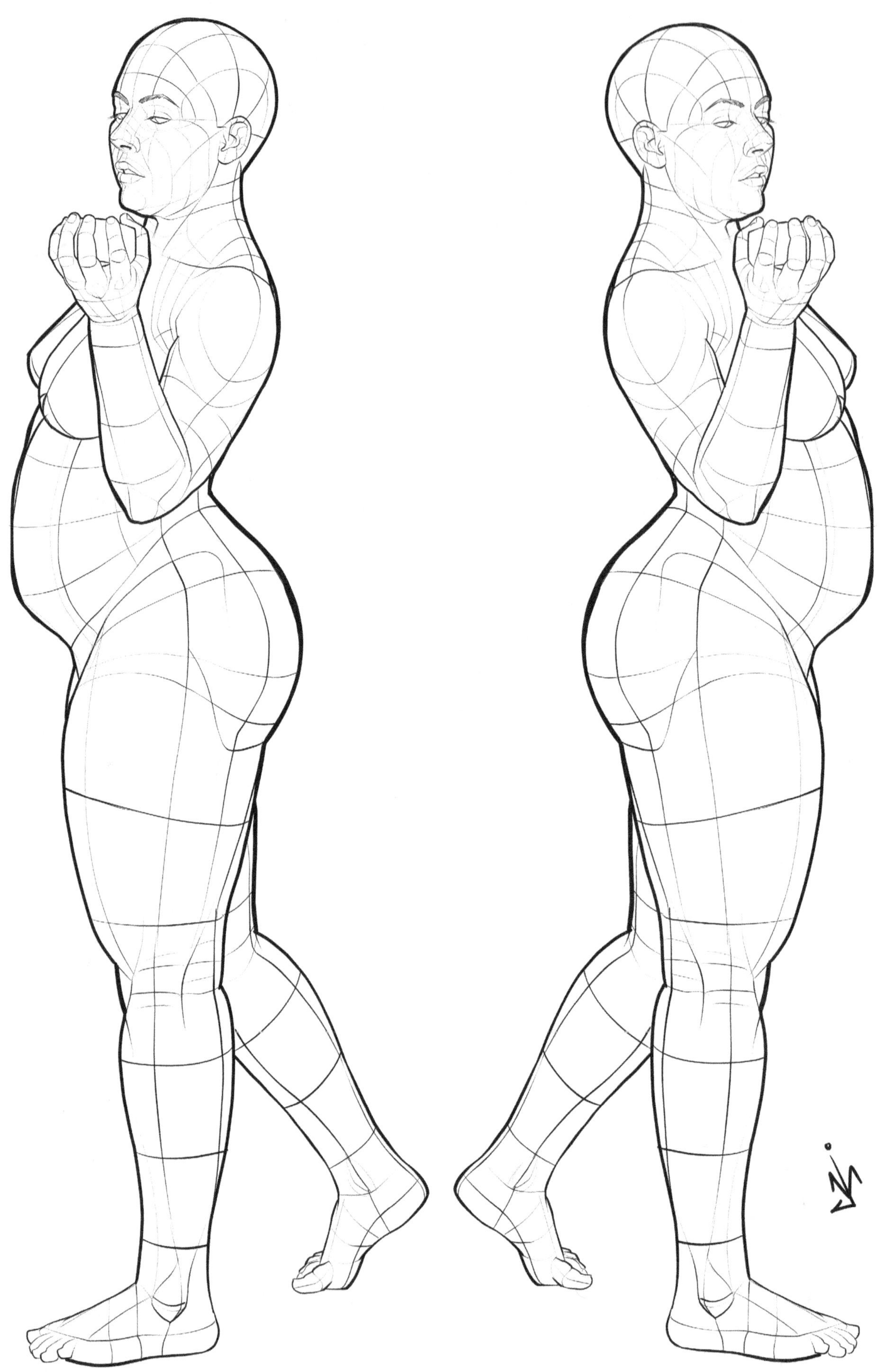

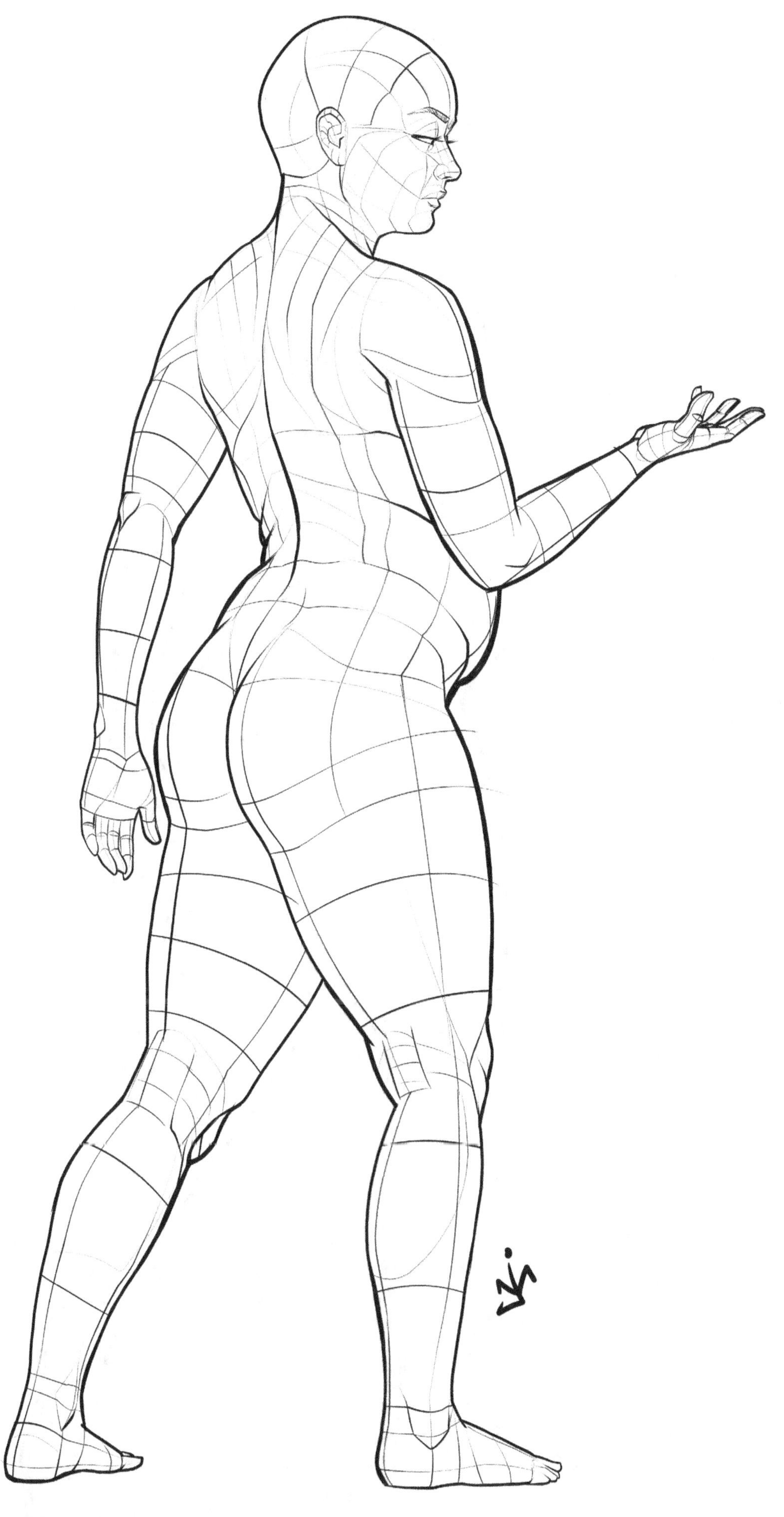

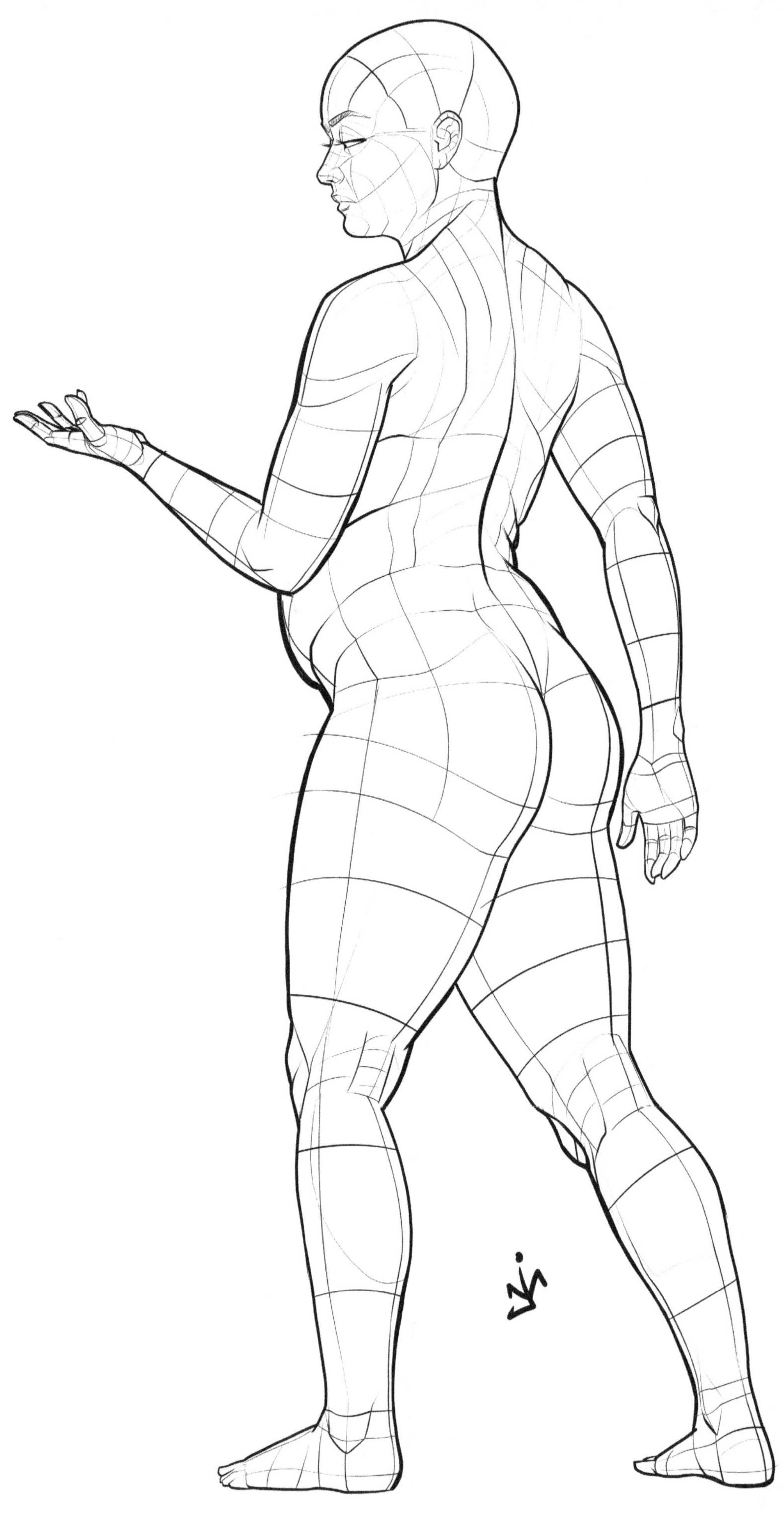

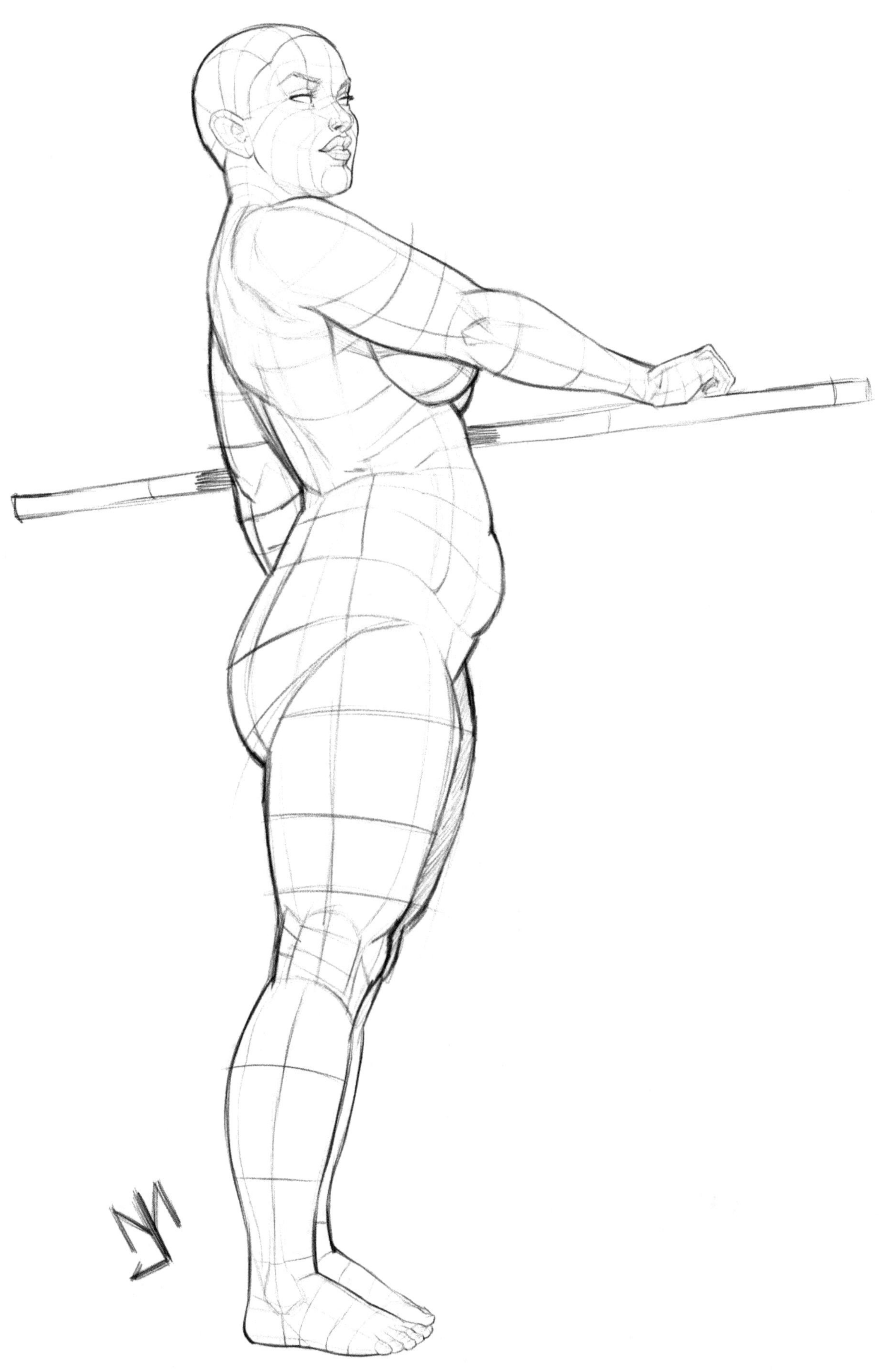

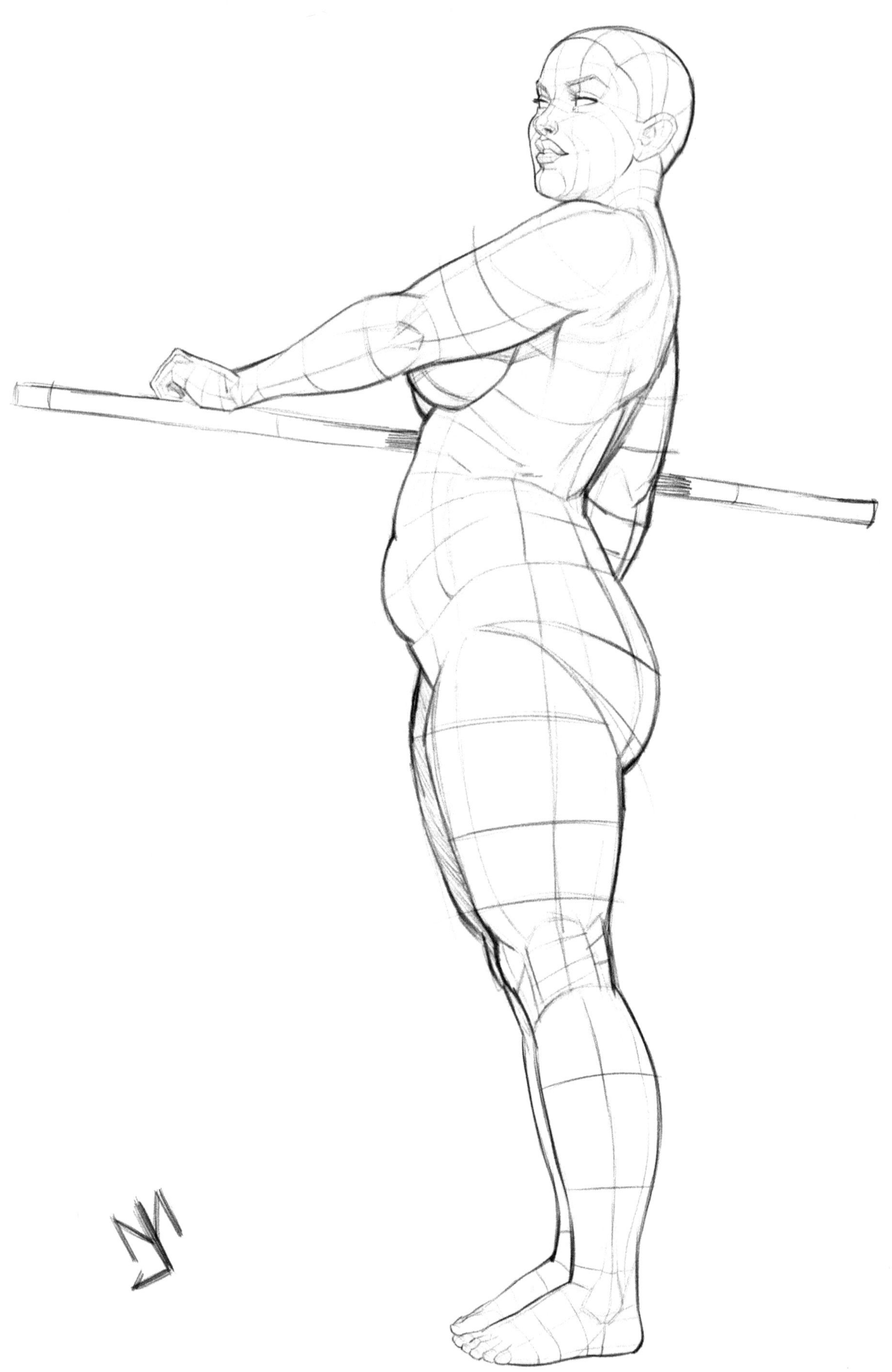

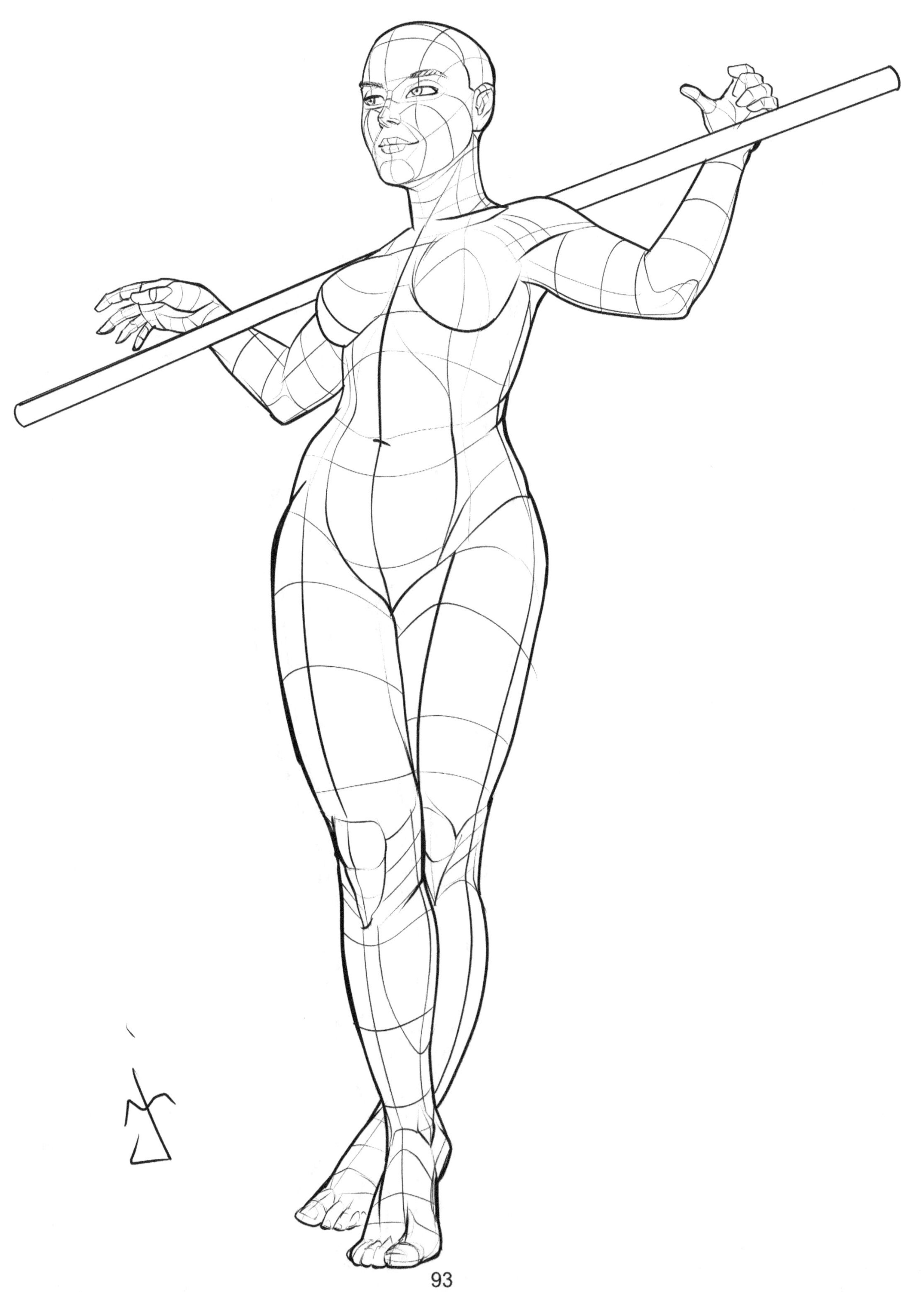

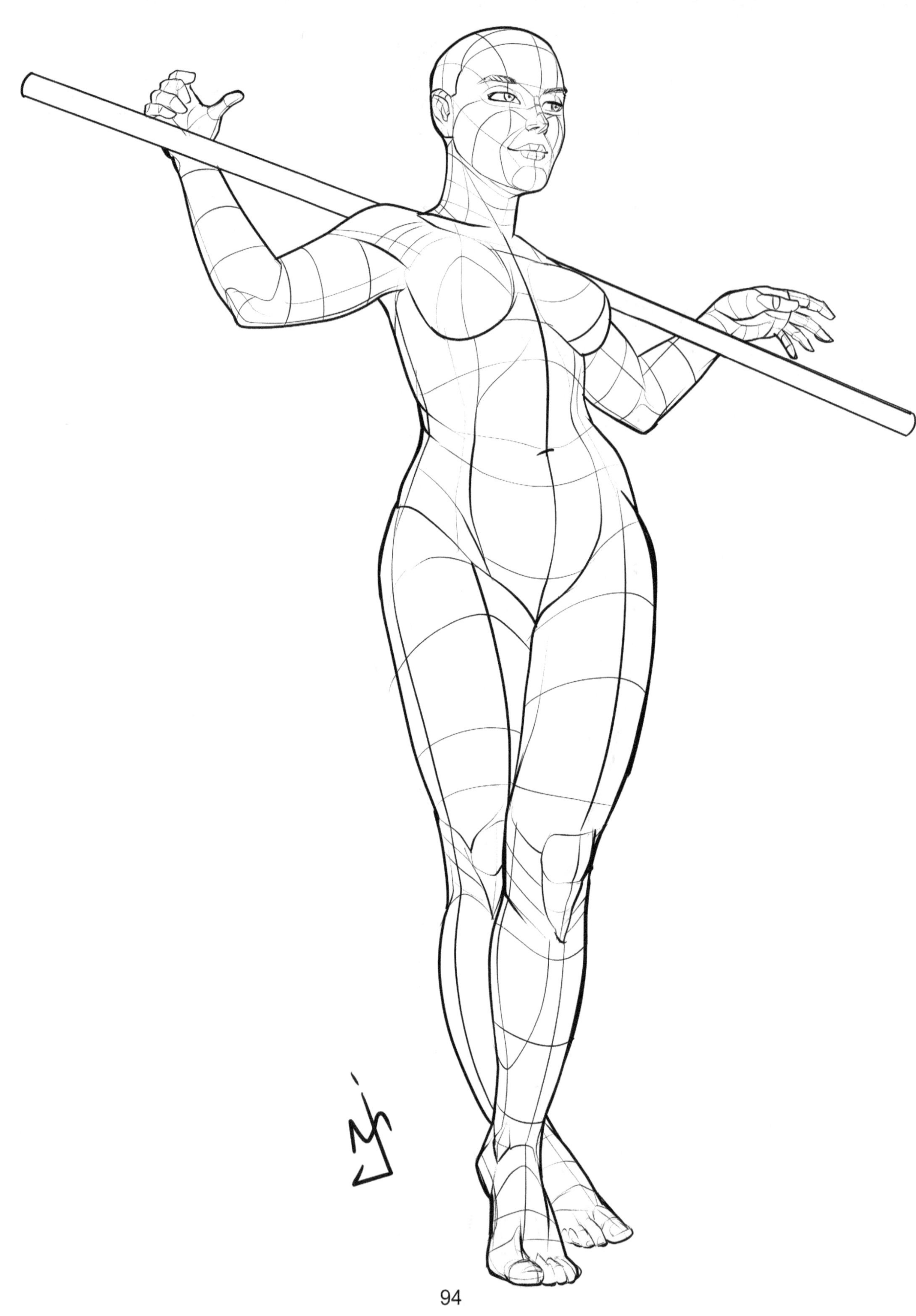

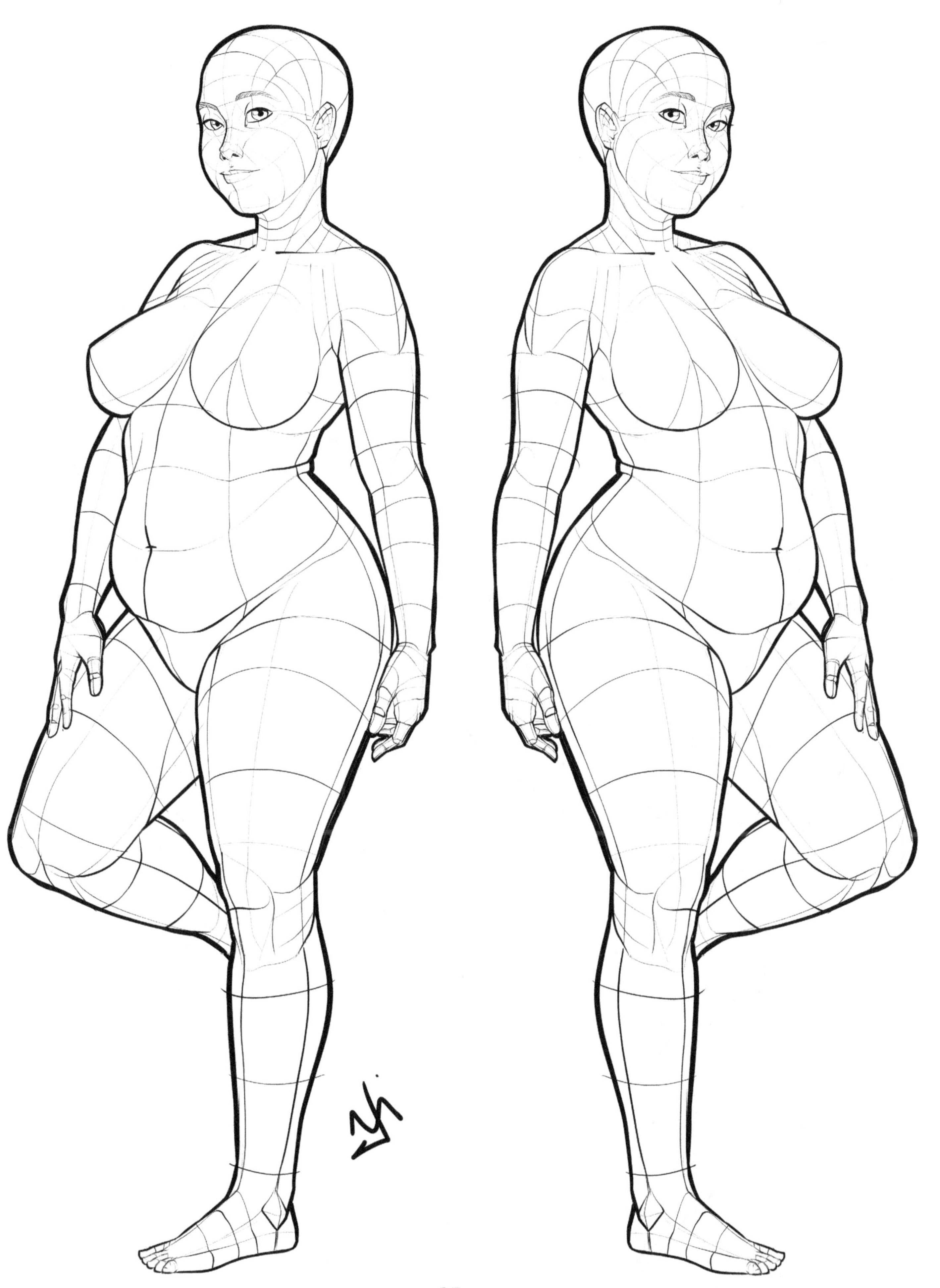

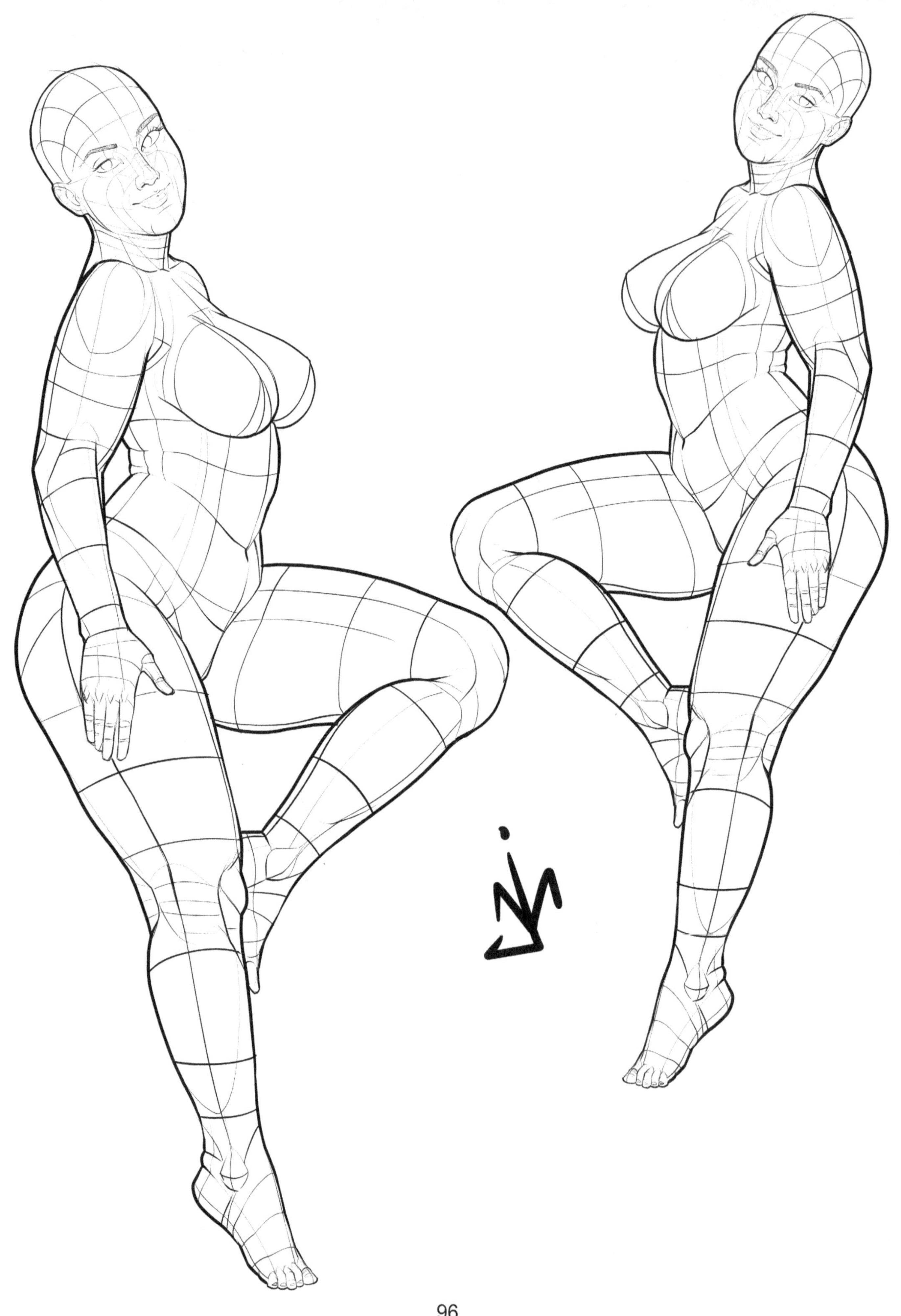

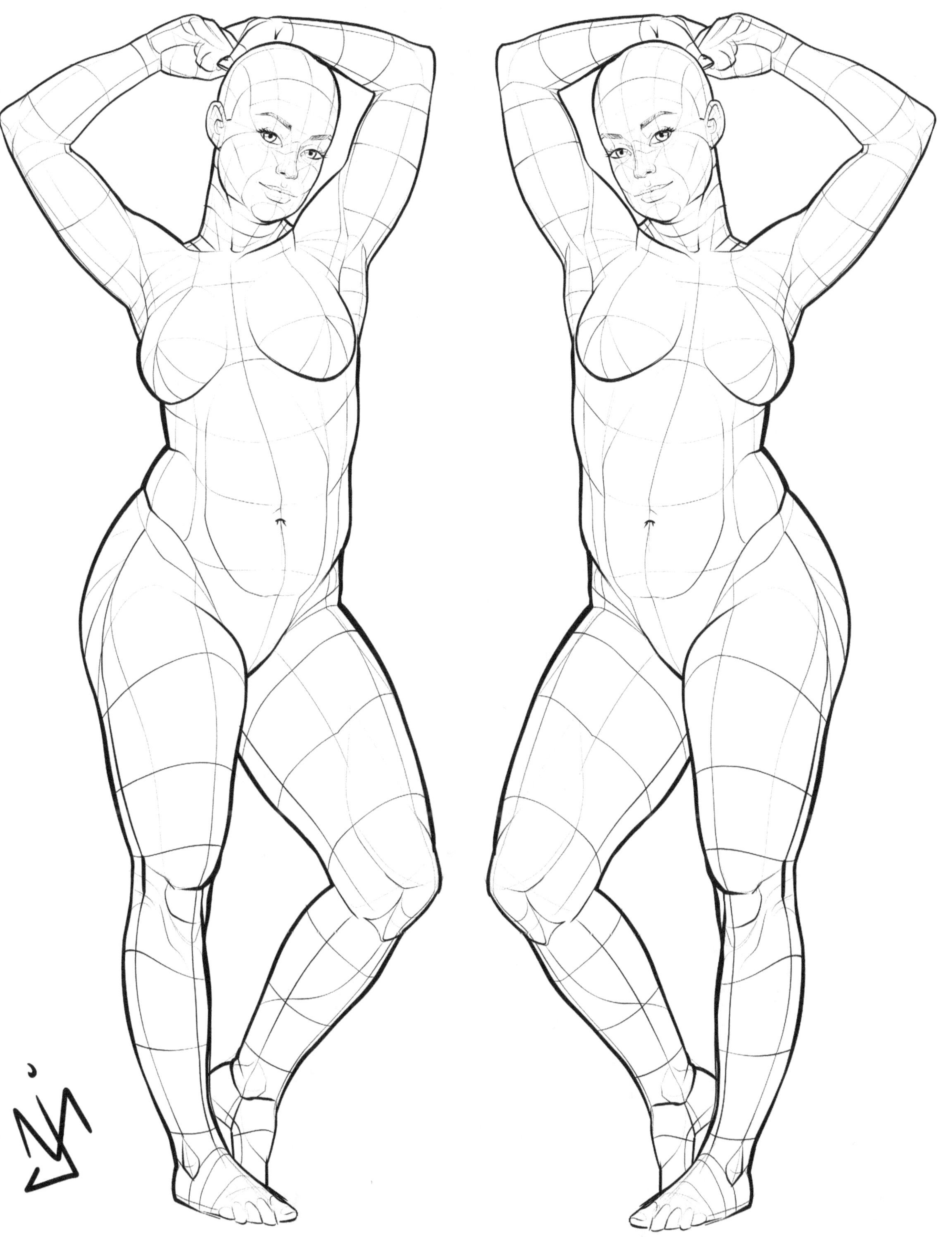

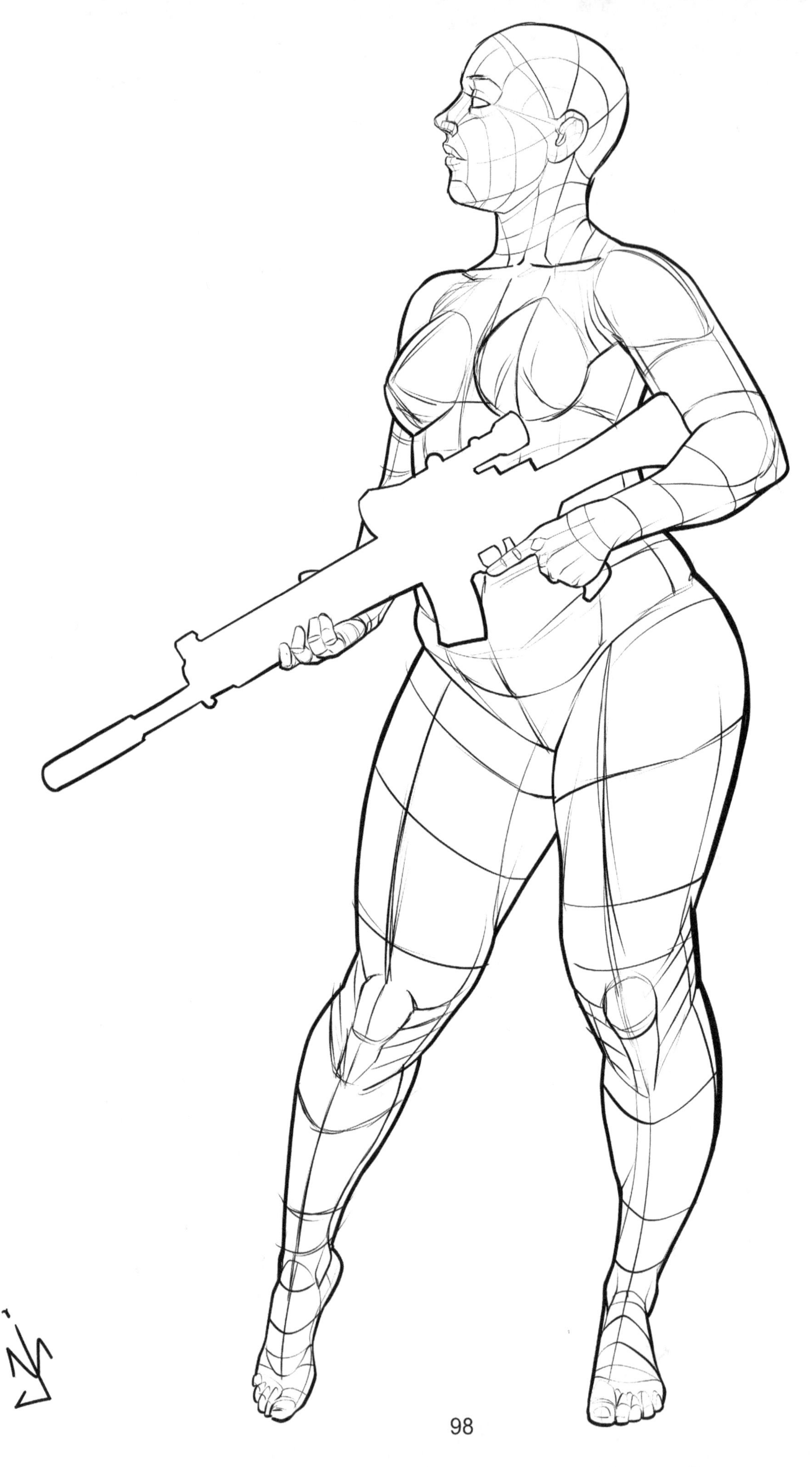

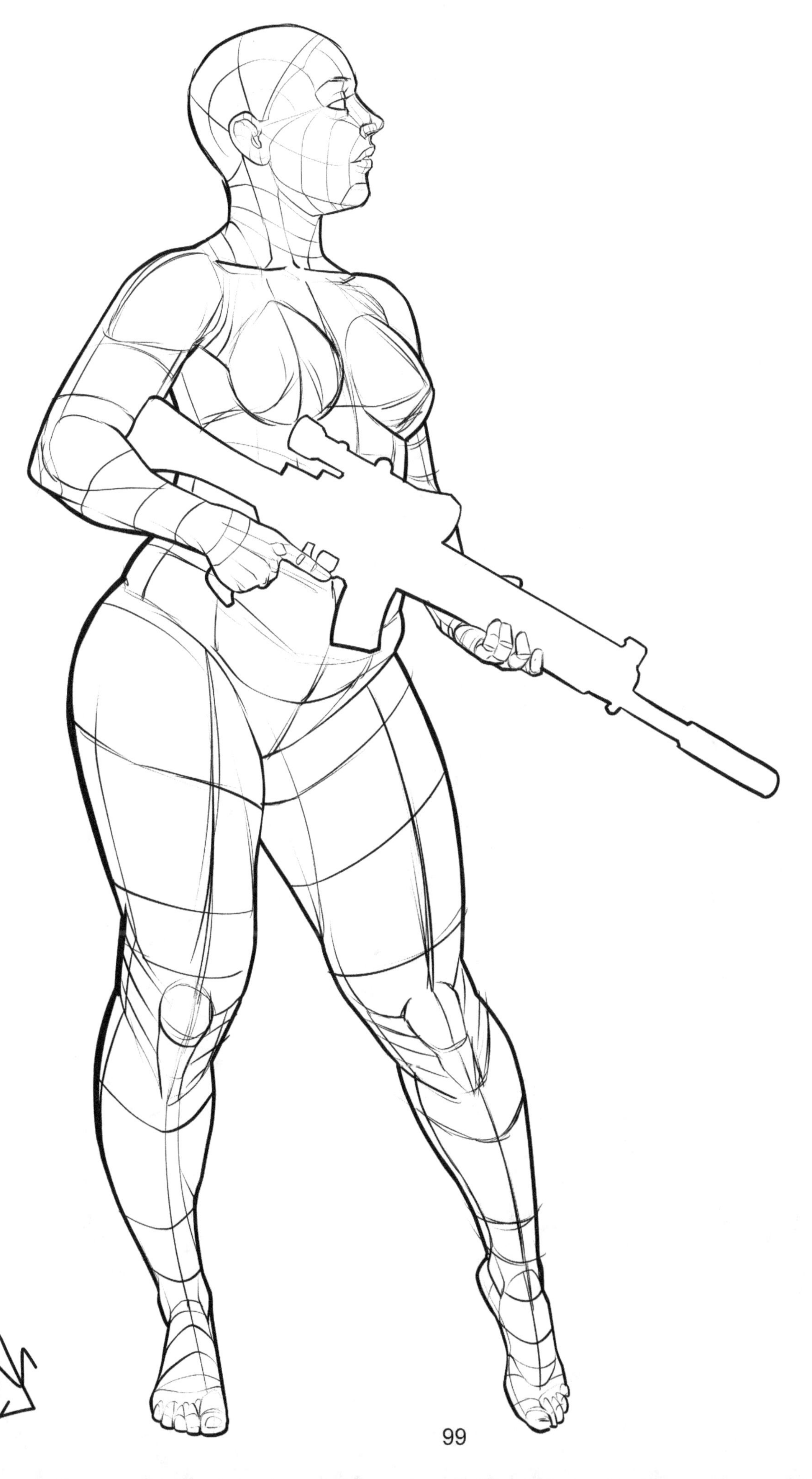

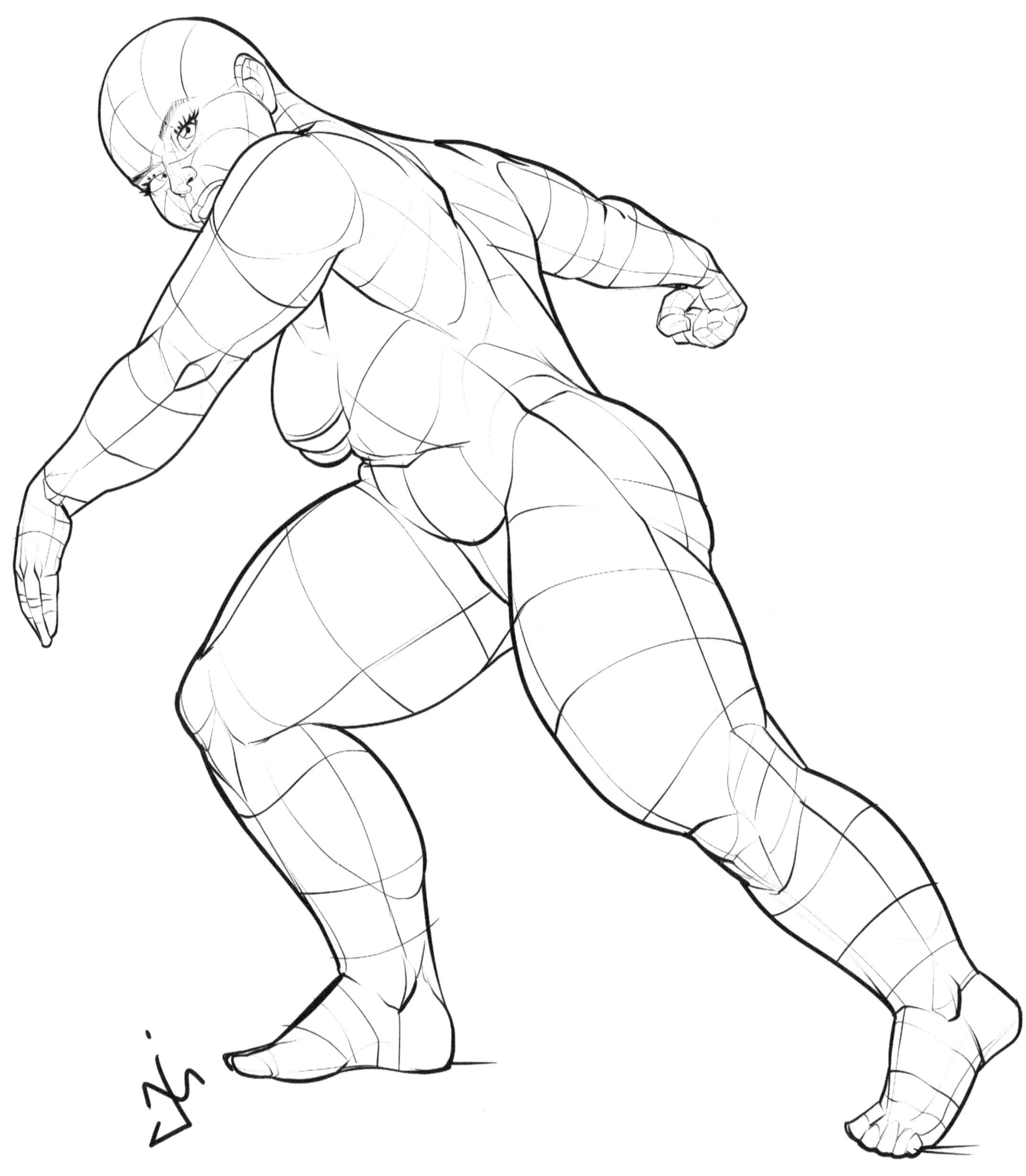

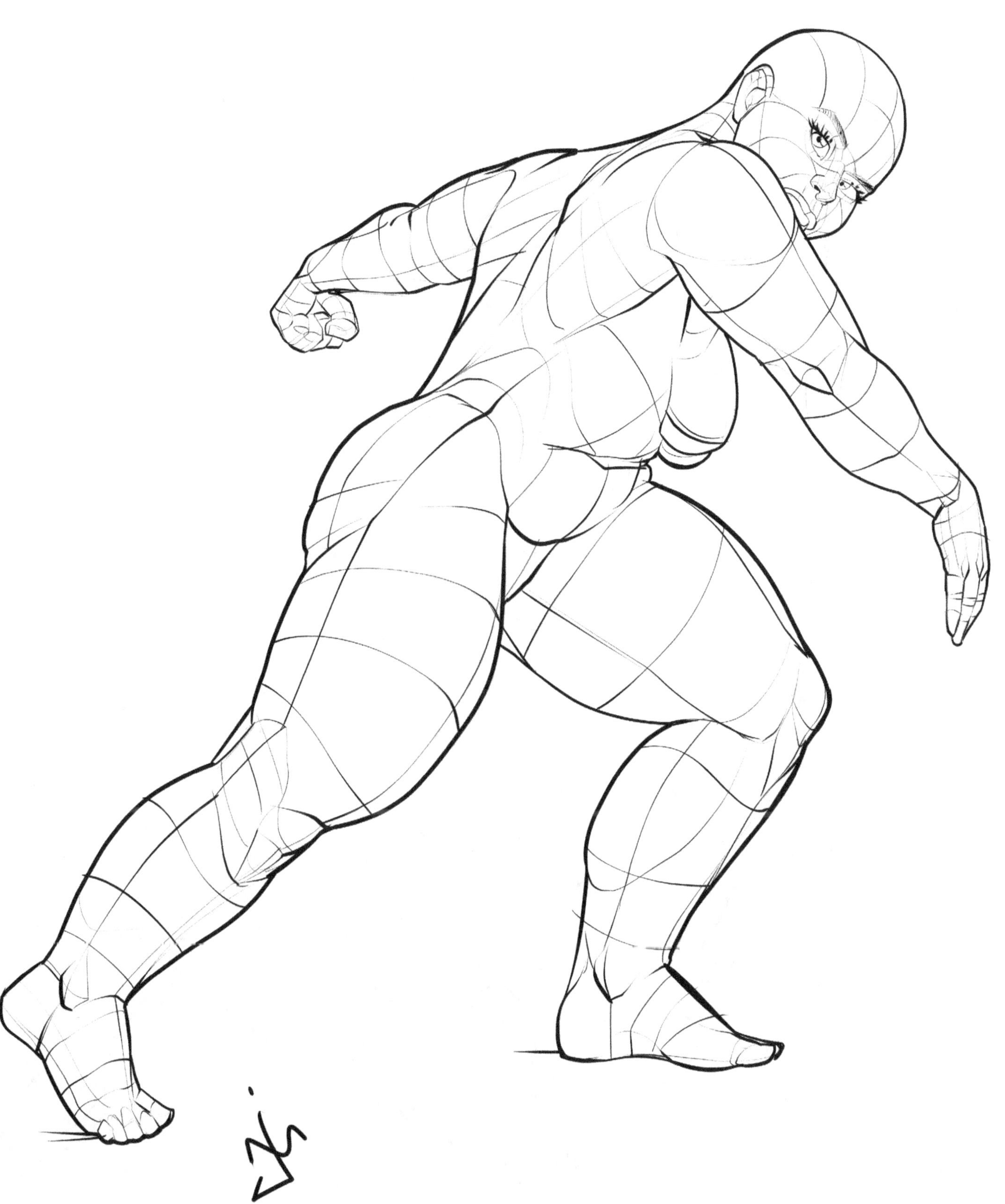

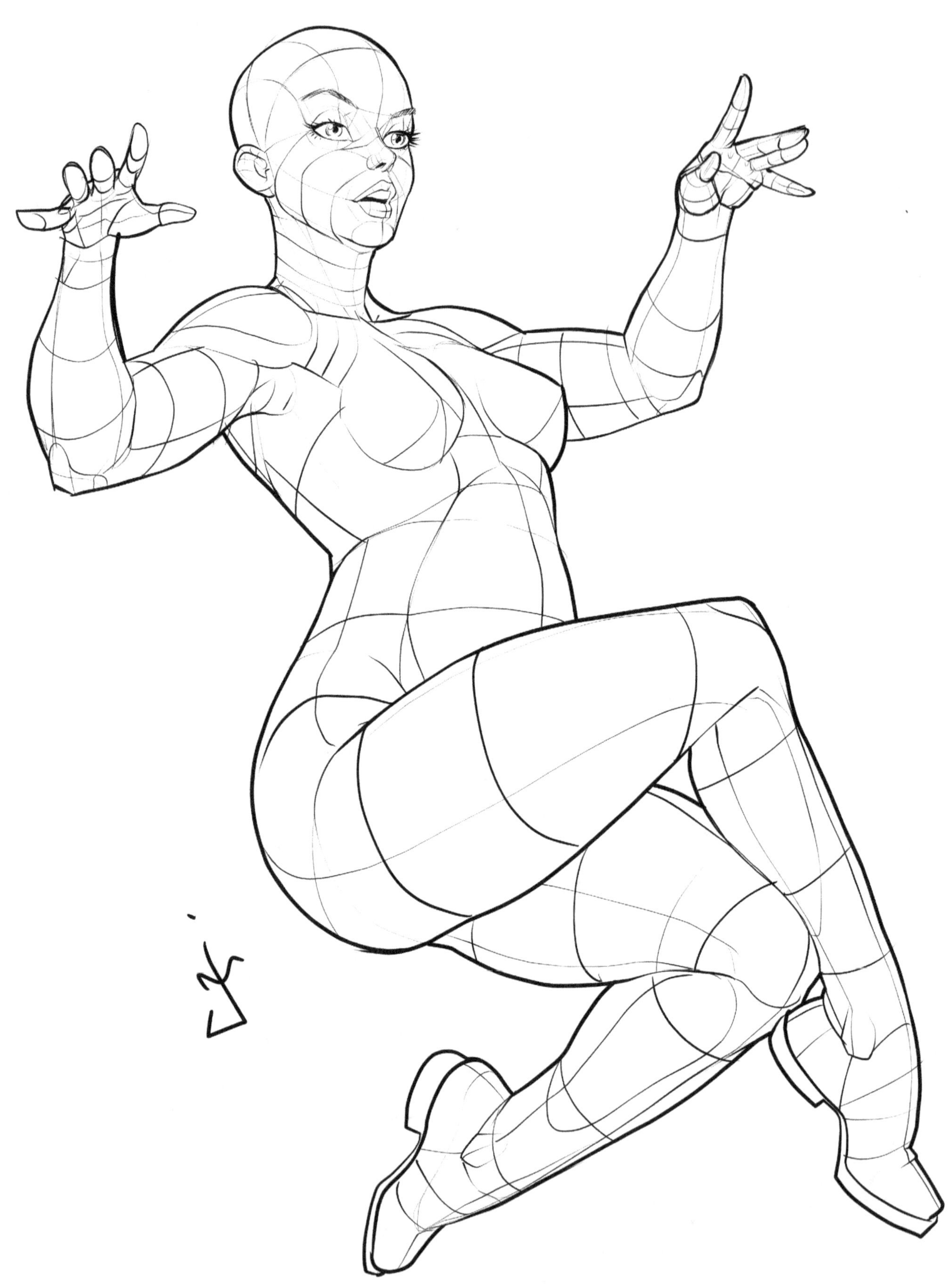

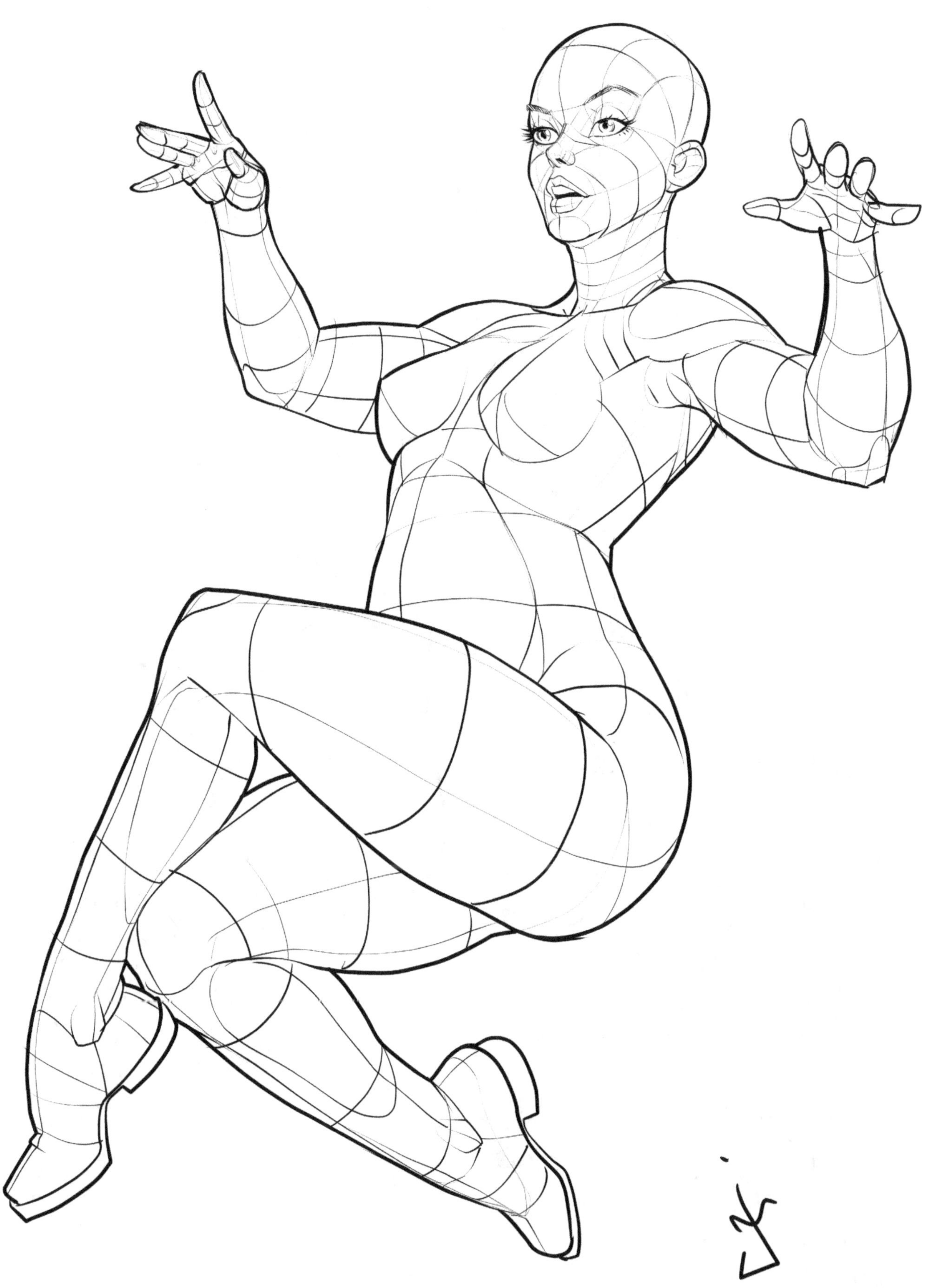

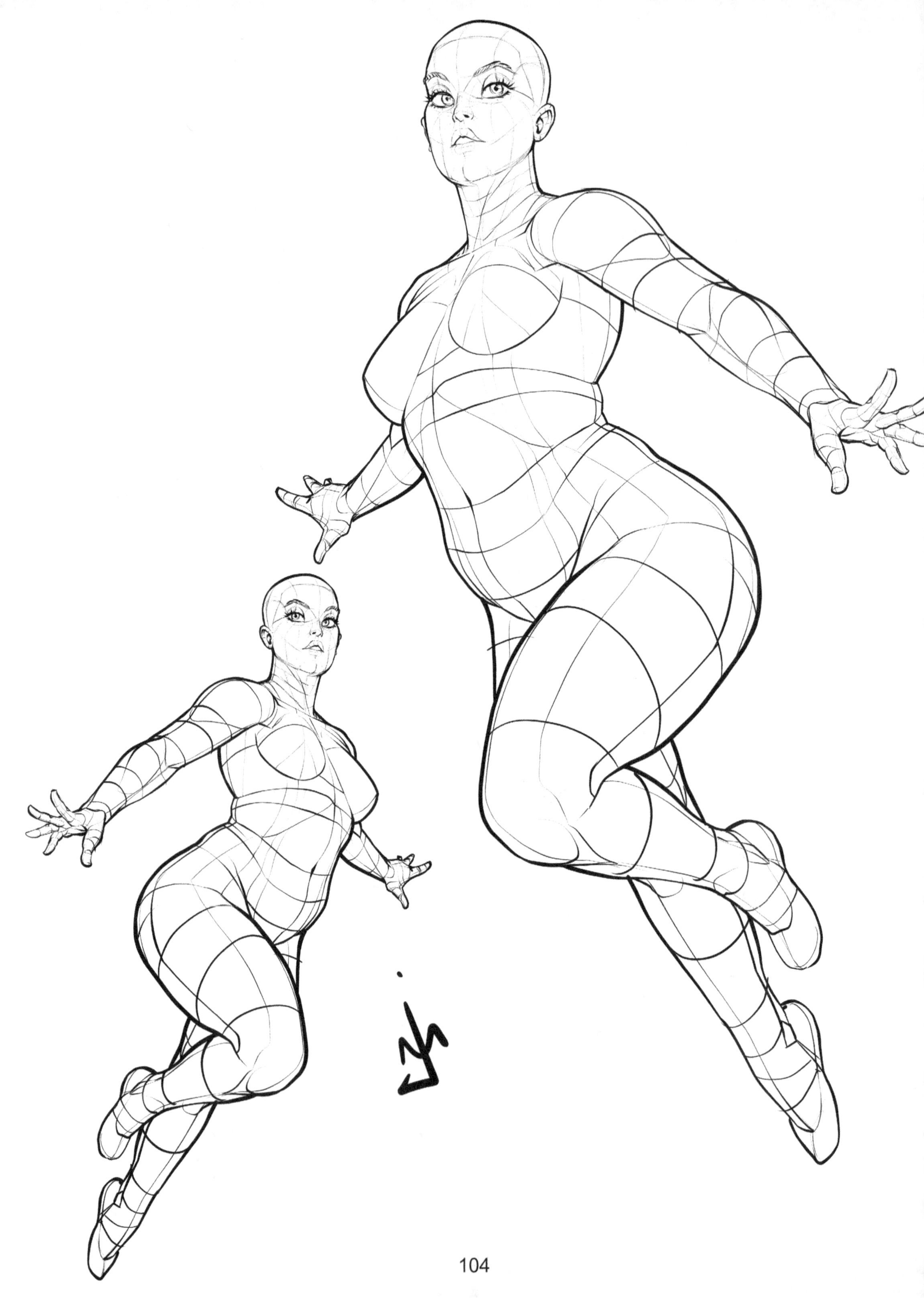

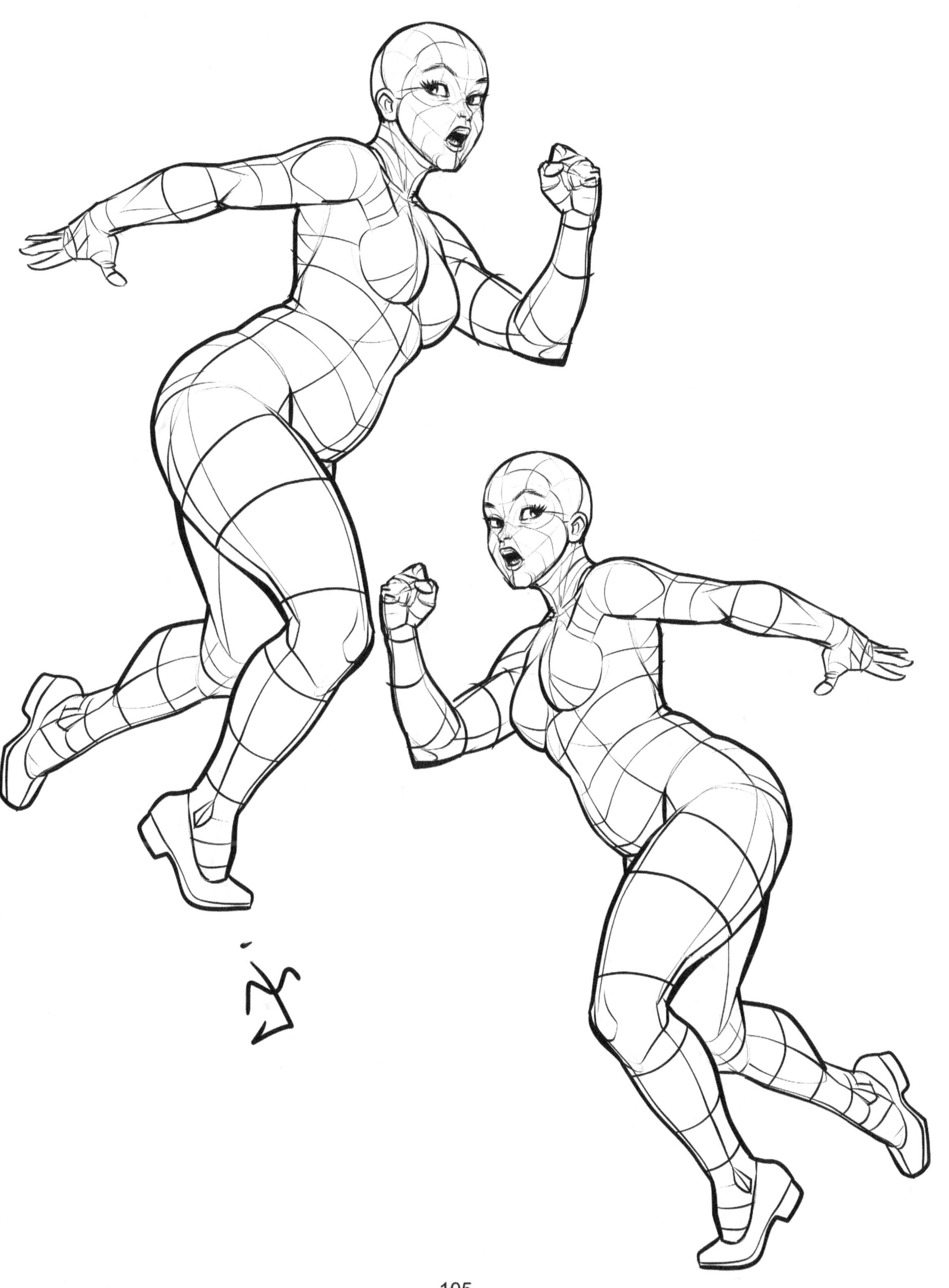

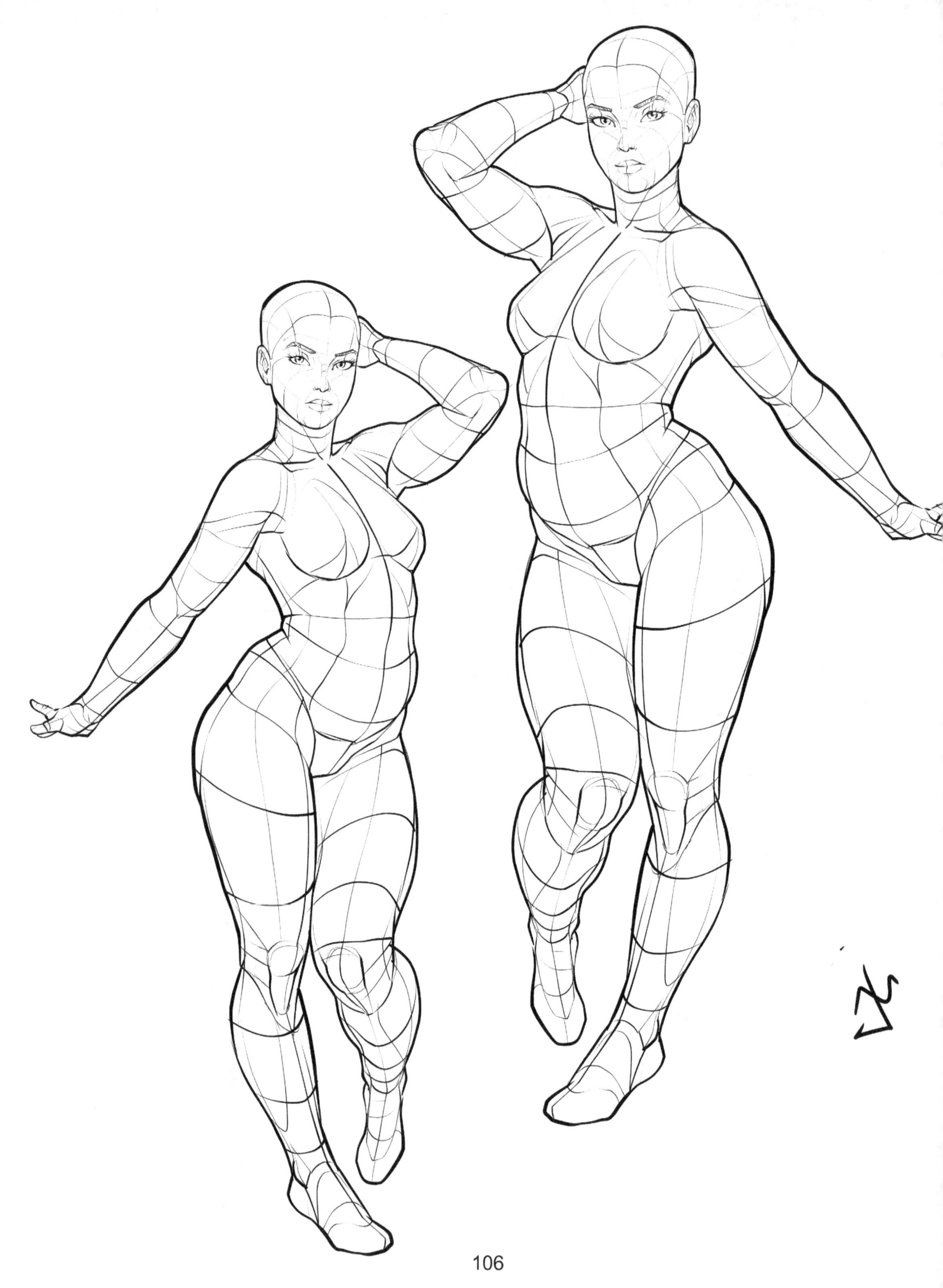

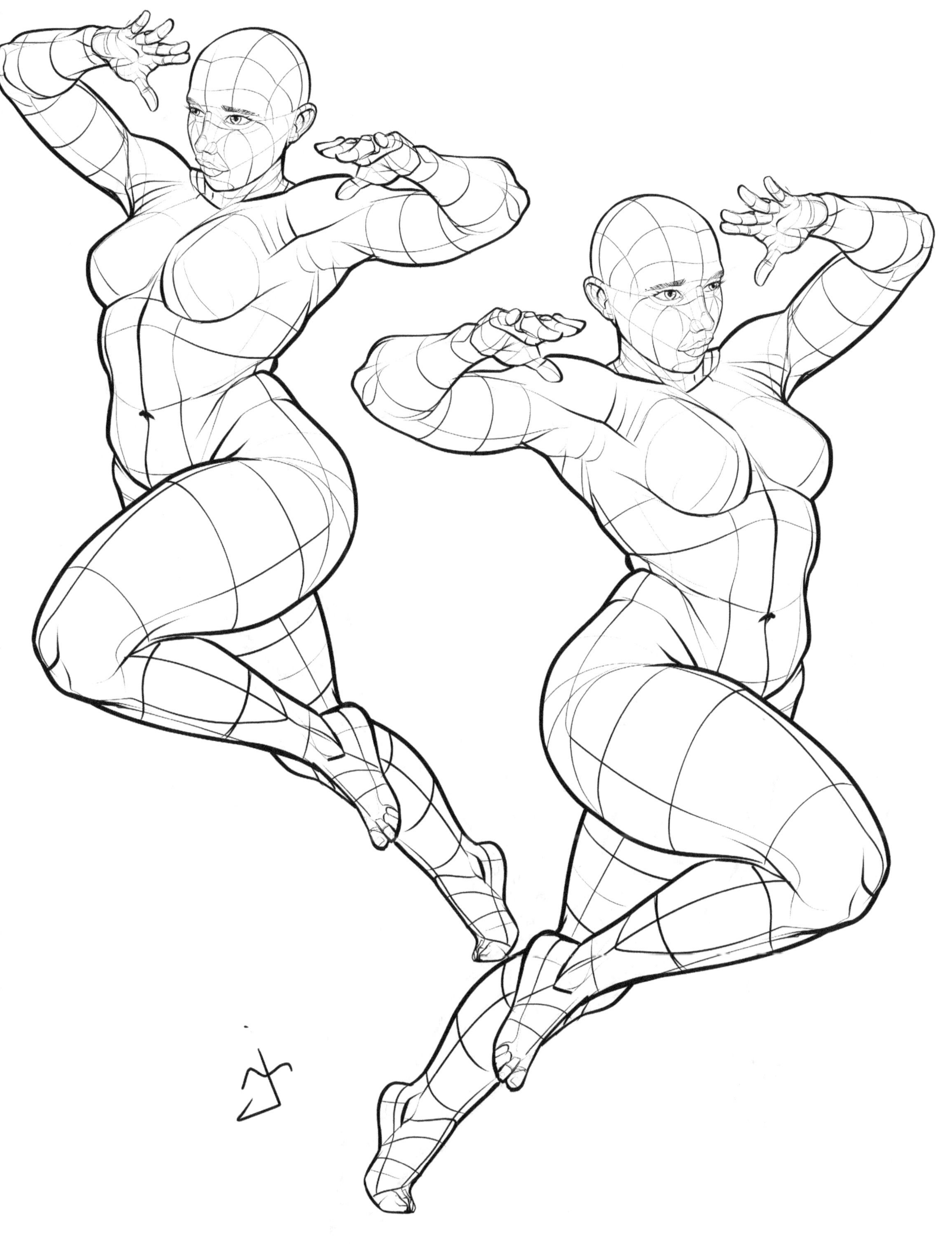

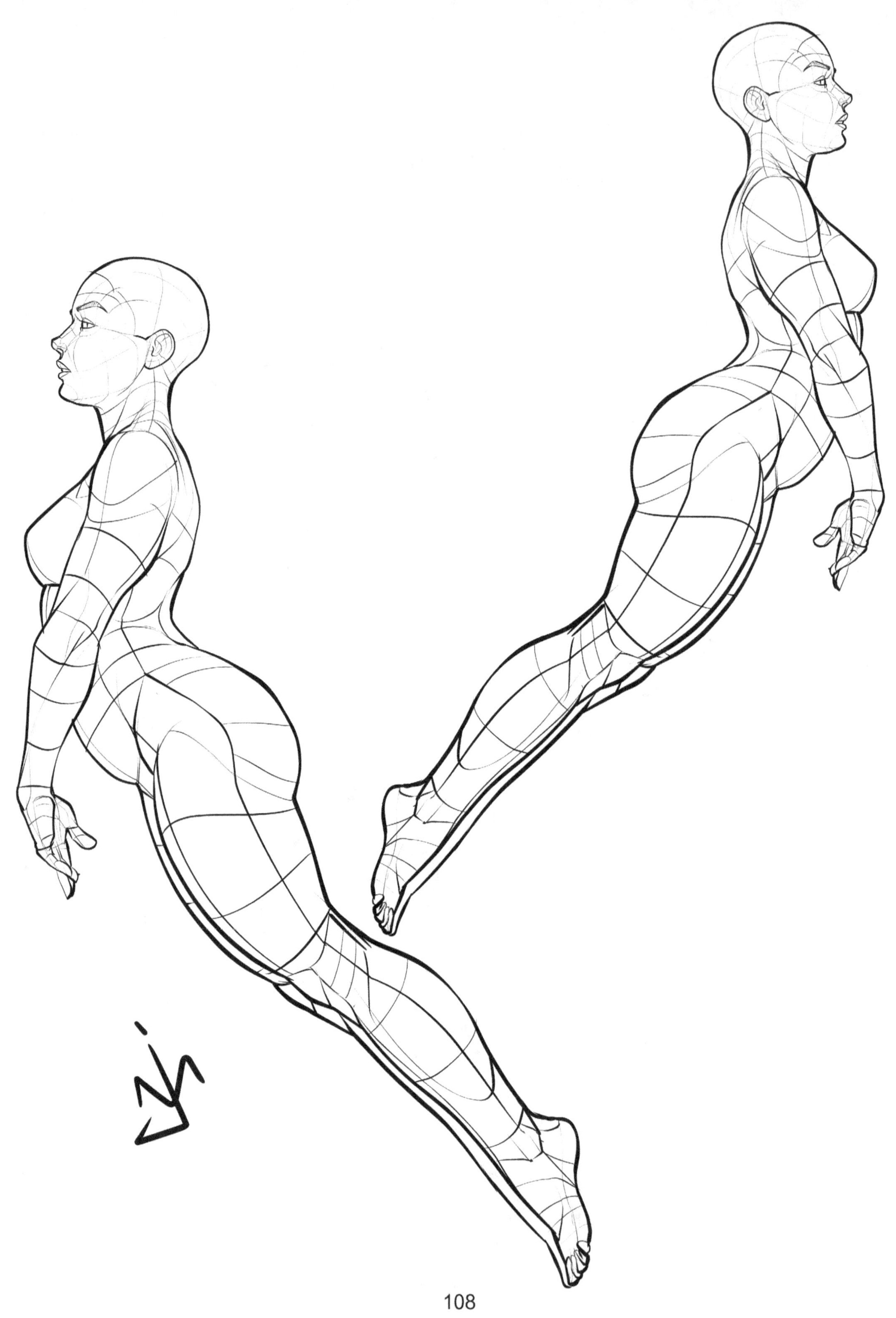

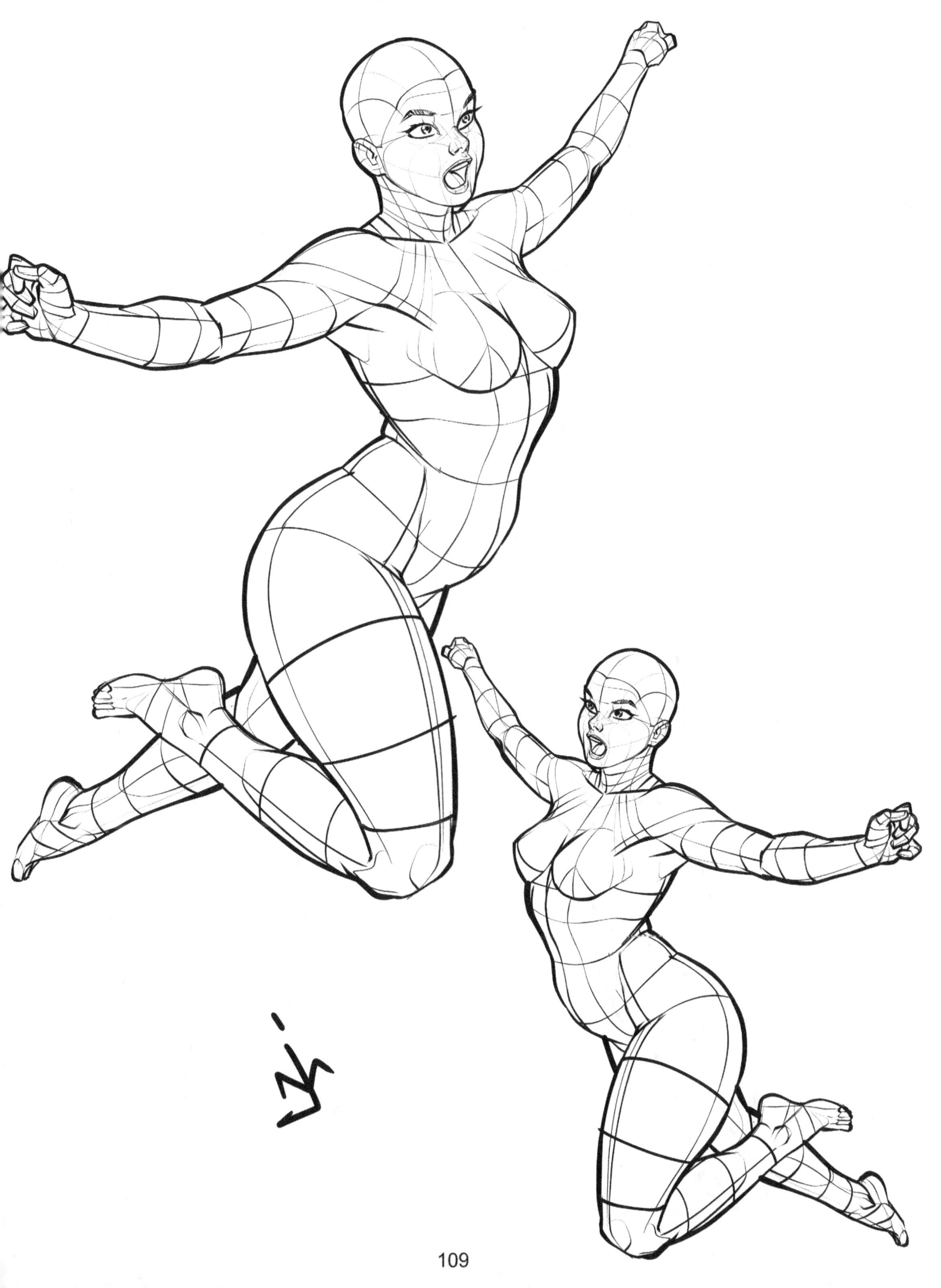

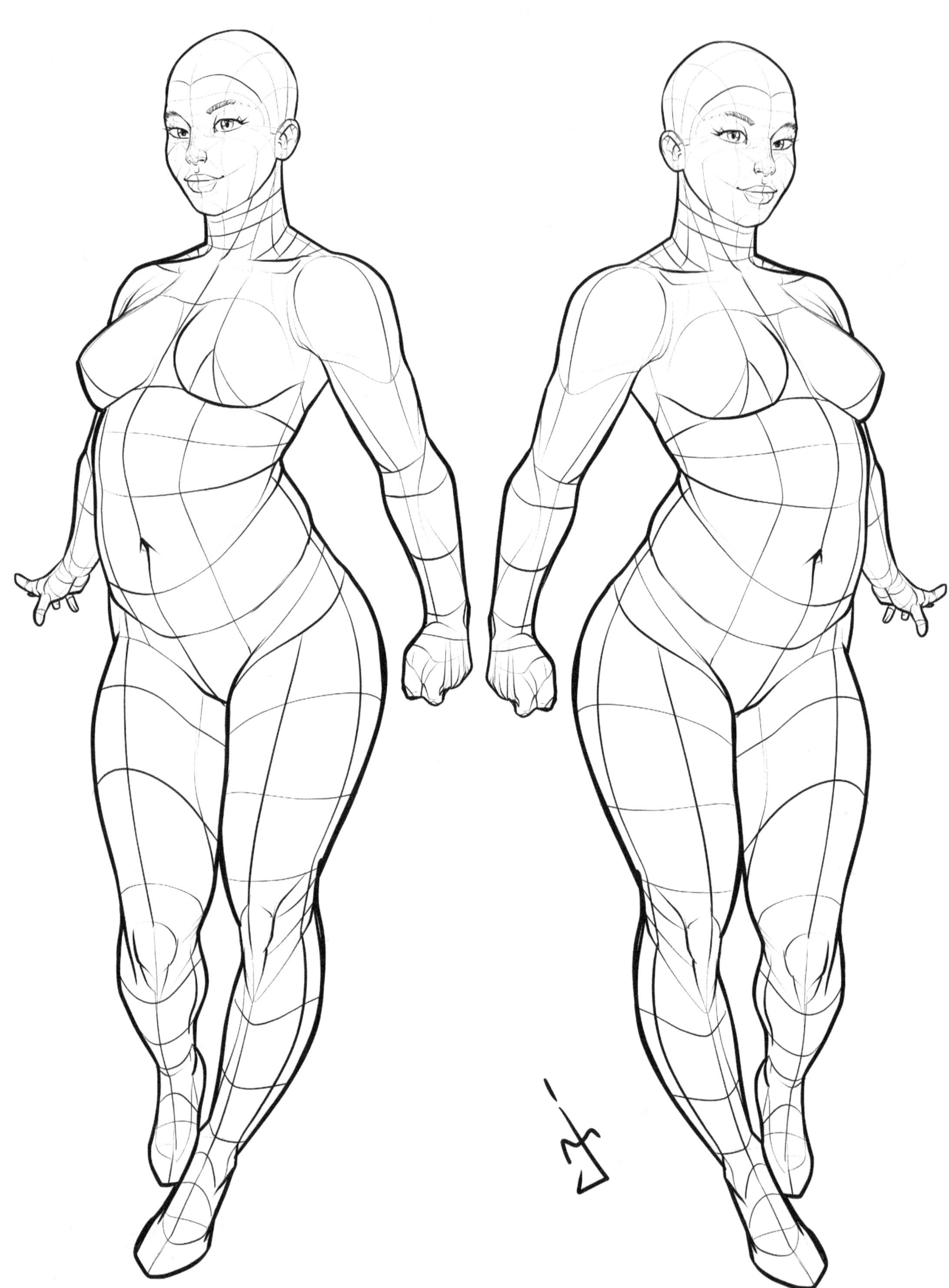

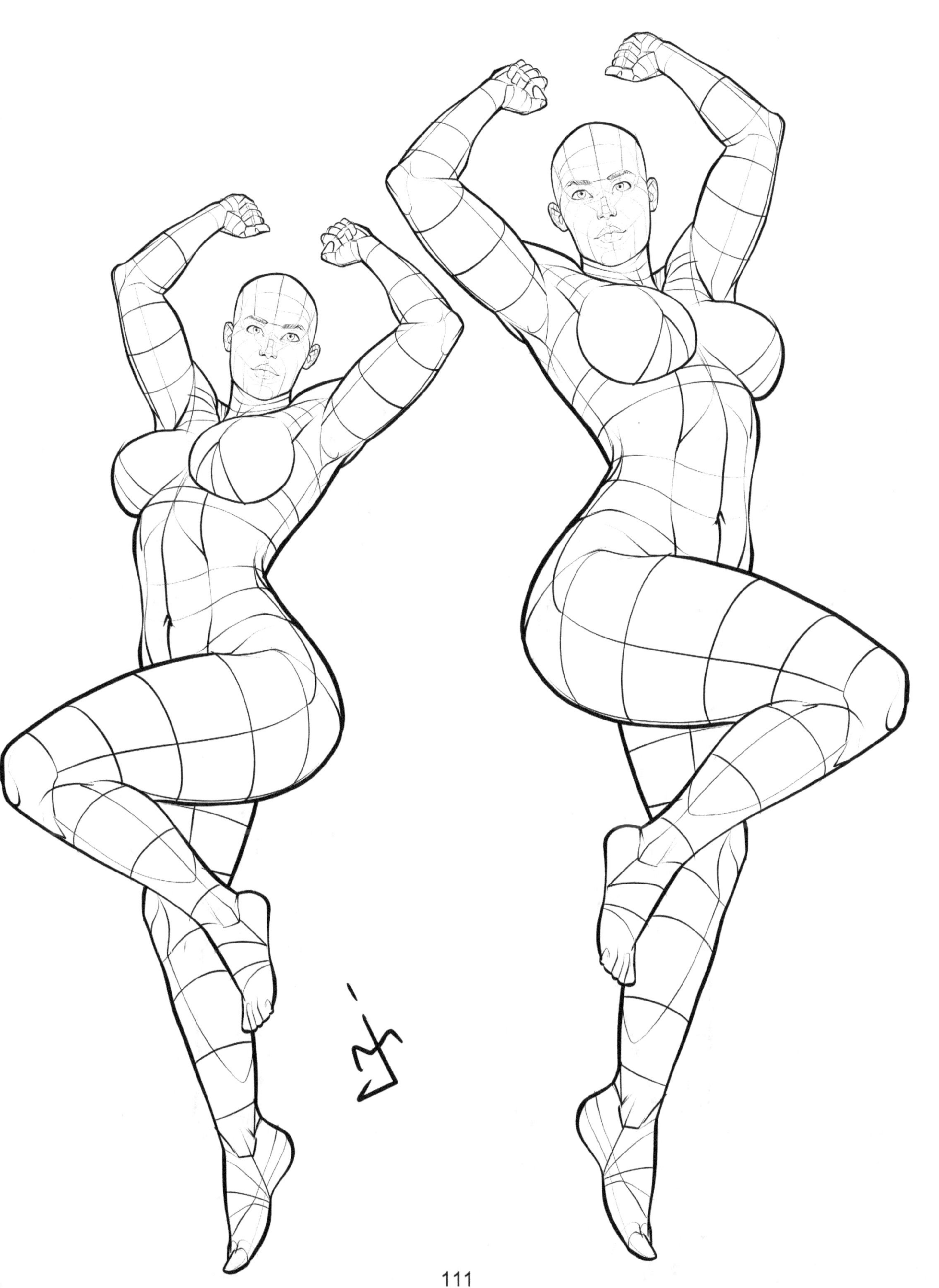

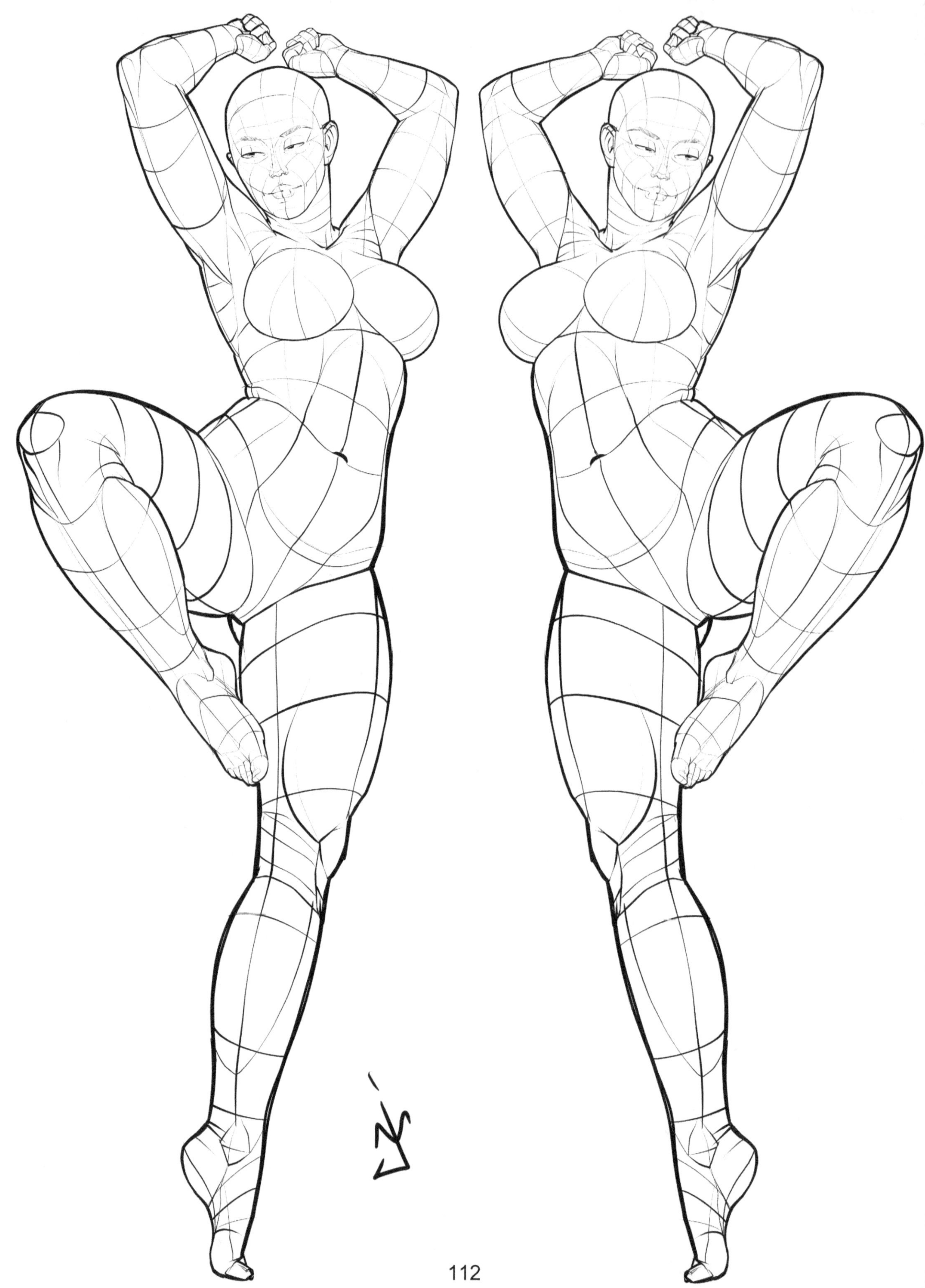

www.ingramcontent.com/pod-product-compliance
Lightning Source LLC
Chambersburg PA
CBHW081619250726
48657CB00009B/2637